Between Femininities

Between Femininities

Ambivalence, Identity, and the Education of Girls

MARNINA GONICK

State University of New York Press

Cover image: Thinkstock

Published by
State University of New York Press, Albany

For information, address State University of New York Press,
90 State Street, Suite 700, Albany, NY 12207

Production by Judith Block
Marketing by Jennifer Giovani

Library of Congress Cataloging-in-Publication Data

Gonick, Marnina.
  Between femininities : ambivalence, identity, and the education of girls /
Marnina Gonick.
    p. cm. — (SUNY series, second thoughts)
  Includes bibliographical references and index
  ISBN 0-7914-5829-6 (alk. paper) — ISBN 0-7914-5830-X (pbk. : alk. paper)
    1. Girls—Psychology.   2. Maturation (Psychology)   3. Feminist psychology.
I. Title.   II. Series.

HQ777 .G65 2003
305.23—dc21

                                                                    2002042634

10 9 8 7 6 5 4 3 2 1

To the girls, past and present

Contents

Acknowledgments

This book owes a great deal to both the place and the people who supported its first inception, as a doctoral dissertation. At the time I was a student there, The Ontario Institute for Studies in Education was a site of intense, exciting, and profound intellectual debate. And while hindsight may have furnished something of a rosy lens, my horizons were most definitely crucially expanded there. I continue to appreciate my committee members' practical and intellectual support. It was in Kari's Dehli's classes that I first heard about the research opportunity that became the thesis and then the book, first encountered many of the questions and theoretical works that underlay this project, and was first encouraged to think about how academic writing might be done differently. To Roger Simon, I remain deeply grateful, for the ways in which he pushed at the boundaries of the questions I knew how to ask and for very generously being there to help me think through them. The book (and I) are richer by far for his respectful, critically engaged reading. I am also grateful to Monica Heller, Tara Goldstein, and Michelle Fine.

Sincere thanks to Deborah Britzman for including *Between Femininities* in her series, Second Thoughts: New Theoretical Formations. Her particular combination of brilliance and generosity is all too rare, and I have benefitted hugely from both. My thanks also to State University of New York Press for all their assistance. I thank my colleagues at The Pennsylvania State University in the Language and Literacy Program in the College of Education and in the Women's Studies Program. The Social Sciences and Humanities Research Council of Canada funded this research, and I am very appreciative of the support.

Paul Rabinow speaks of friendship as a "primary site of thinking" and cites Aristotle's *Nicomachean Ethics* in affirming that friendship is essential to the good life, socially and intellectually. Ester Reiter, Paula Moser, Ellie Goldenberg, Janice Hladki, Linda Cullum, Liza McCoy, Holloway Sparks, Debra Freedman, and

Miryam Espinosa have all supported me and this work in important and immeasurable ways. For providing me with homes in Toronto while I was in the final stages of putting this manuscript together, I thank Ester Reiter, Leah Vosco and Gerald Kernelman, and Marilyn Learner.

I am grateful to my dad, Cy Gonick, and my mom, Fay Sasson, for the examples they set in infusing life with high standards, with passion for social justice, hope and tenacity of the spirit. I thank with much love my sister Rachel, my brothers Lev and Noam, and my nieces Sari, Mya, and Eve.

My deep gratitude to the girls for letting me into a part of their worlds and making this all possible. Back when I was meeting with them regularly, they impressed me with their courage and grace in facing life's challenges, with the depth of their perception, their visceral sense of justice, their sense of strength in togetherness, and with their warmth, wit and wisdom—all of which they continue to do.

Questions without answers must be asked very slowly.
—Anne Michaels, *Fugitive Pieces*

CHAPTER 1

Introduction

Well! What are you? said the Pigeon. I can see you're trying to invent something!

I—I'm a little girl, said Alice, rather doubtfully, as she remembered the number of changes she had gone through, that day.

A likely story indeed! said the Pigeon.

—Lewis Carroll, *Alice's Adventures in Wonderland*

To open this discussion on inventions of girls and girlhood, I invite you to the Blue Room. For in many ways, both my own entry into thinking about the discursive and social practises of femininity and the origins of the *About Us, By Us* video project that will orient our explorations of these practices can be traced to the Blue Room, otherwise known as the school staff room, and a meeting that took place there. The meeting in the Blue Room was convened to discuss a program funding proposal and the problem that precipitated its submission to the Toronto Board of Education's Youth Alienation Program. Joining us in the Blue Room are about fifteen other people: the school principal and vice-principle, two or three teachers, a parent who was also involved in the community group W.A.V.E. (Working Against Violence Everywhere), a few other W.A.V.E. members, two school board staff, and a staff member from the community recreation center. My presence at the meeting is due to the securing of only partial project funding from the board, which did not cover the request for hiring a program facilitator. Thus, in exchange for the opportunity to do some research, I volunteered.

The school is located in Toronto's west end and its population reflects the area's largely immigrant, refugee, and working-class residents. There are approximately five hundred students in grades Junior-Kindergarten through eight, with two hundred in grades five to eight. The ethnic makeup of the community is in constant flux but, at the time the program proposal was written, 40 percent of students had Portuguese backgrounds, 30 percent were Asian and Southeast Asian, 15 percent were Anglo-Saxon, and the reminder were from Latin America, the Caribbean, and Eastern Europe.

The proposal we are discussing had been written in April 1991 by the school's former vice-principal who had, by the time of the meeting, moved on to another school. The teachers present at the meeting had, however, also been involved in the proposal's development. While it does not lay out a specific plan for a video project, (I would initiate that some time later) the document does identify a number of areas of general concern, clustering around the themes of physical and psychological safety and participation in the school and larger community. The proposal anticipates that a project designed to address these areas of concern will benefit the entire school population, however; girls in grades five through eight are singled out as being in particular need of such a program. As one of the teachers involved explained, the project emerged out of a "concern expressed by teachers originally, who were concerned about the young women in this school population. . . . [W]hen they reached a certain age, they seemed to be silenced by the school environment. Because of the ethnicity of certain kids in the school, there was a parental thing which silenced them as young women as well" (teacher interview, July 1995).

For these teachers and the former vice-principal, who were "tremendously committed to the whole area of antiracist work and equity" (teacher interview, June 1995), the proposed programme was seen as a means to build on other school initiatives these individuals had organized under the exigence of the school board. For example, the school's grade seven and eight students had been among the participants of the board's citywide antiracist camp and there had also been one or two gender workshops within the school for some of its students. There was also an active student group facilitated by a teacher called M.C.Stars (Multicultural Students Against Racism and Sexism), which planned events for the annual March 21 International Anti-Racism Day, as well as events for holidays such as Chinese New Year.

WHAT IS THE "PROBLEM" WITH THESE GIRLS?
SCHOOL DISCOURSES OF TEENAGE FEMININITY

The proposal is impressive in its stated goals and procedures for achieving them. It addresses empowerment, building a strong and safe school community, and a collaborative process that would see the involvement of teachers, parents, community workers, and students. The proposal notes that although known to be a vulnerable age, girls aged ten through thirteen have few services and school resources devoted to them. Thus, this group of students would be the focus of the program. However, the program would not only be directed at them; it would also be largely defined by them.

While the themes of safety, community, and participation were rearticulated at the program committee meeting as the primary impetus for organizing an initiative, the discussion at this meeting also seemed to produce something of a shift in understanding about the identification and locus of the "problem."

"They're not joiners," the principal said by way of opening the discussion. "The only school program the girls are enthusiastic about participating in is cheerleading." "It's a senior school phenomenon," added the gym teacher. "The senior school starts off keen when it comes to teams but they have no long term commitment. The baseball team started out with thirty players and ended with six." "They're apathetic," rejoined the principal. "When some of them came to ask me if they could have a dance and I said no, there was no protest. They don't take control of a situation." "They're directed by their families. Some are tightly structured and others are hardly supervised. . . ." "They're not attached to community or anything. . . ." "They have a victim mentality, with girls at the very bottom. . . ."

It seems that for many of the participants in this discussion, rather than a perception of a problem in the relationships between the school, its teachers, its programs, the community it is offering, and the girls as students, the girls themselves are seen to somehow embody the problem. "The problem" was clearly seen to reside exclusively within the girls' purview, with some suggestion of their families as the source. Their attitude, their behavior, their outlook, their interests, and their demeanor somehow did not quite measure up, was not at all what was desired.

Overlapping, contradictory, and competing discourses also circulated around the room in accounting for "the problem" and how it should be addressed. "They have no voice." "They lack a feeling of control over their environment." "Their parents feel powerless." "They don't want to fail, so they opt out." "Their form of protest is to drop out." "It's second individuation process." "It's hormones." "It's a clash between the homeland culture and the downtown scene." Cutting across these explanations based in sociological, psychological, biological and feminist discourses—disciplines which have contributed to the constitution of girls as subjects, albeit with contested meanings (Hoogland 1993; Walkerdine 1990, 1993)—are discourses of gender, age, race, sexuality, class, culture, and nationality. While the girls embody the problem, it is the constellation of social positions that they occupy as adolescent, immigrant, working-class, and (some) nonwhite girls that seems to underline some of the concern.

It is possible to trace a long history linking participation in school-organized leisure activities to the kind of anxiety articulated by the committee about the production of proper subjects and citizens. For example, the early twentieth century saw increased school enrollment by working-class youth, whose future occupational identities schools were responsible for shaping, but what was also provided was the opening for schools to participate in the transmission of middle-class values through its organization of extracurricular activities of school clubs, school dances, student government, and recreational sports (Best 2000; Graebner 1990; Messner 1992). As Amy Best points out, the effects of the organization of these activities produced more than the stated intentions of extending democracy to the economically disadvantaged. It also created opportunities for the regulation and surveillance of working-class youth beyond the work settings they inhabited less and less, moving into their social spaces and leisure activities (2000, 6).

Middle-class youth have also not been immune from being the focus of adult anxiety. For example, following World War II, the emergence of a teen leisure market generated concerns about youth sexuality, delinquency, and complacency. A wealth of organized activity including high school proms, teen canteens, and sock hops sprang up to guard against these dangers, becoming the mainstay of middle-class cultural life and solidifying class and race divisions (Graebner 1990; Johnson 1993; Palladino 1996). The question we might pose therefore is, What kinds of new feminine subjects are being shaped in the current historical period through programs like the one the committee gathered to discuss? And secondly, what is being guarded against?[1]

In explaining the problem, the staff and administrators of this particular school are not inventing it. Rather, they are making use of discourses about girls and girlhood which are both very much rooted in a specific place and historical moment and currently in wide circulation. When the tensions of race, class, and gender rise dramatically, as they have in recent times, social anxieties converge and tend to be projected onto the bodies of adolescent women (Fine 1991; Griffin 1993).[2] However, such anxiety does not necessarily get conferred equally or in the same way on all girls. According to Kenway and Blackmore (1995, 16), implicit in much Australian school education and gender reform programs within schools is the notion of normal girls, who are usually seen to be Anglo, middle-class, and, I would add, white. Girls who are not positioned as normal are implicitly positioned as other than and as less than normal girls. They are seen as different from what is normal and preferable, as special or at risk. Their apparent lack is not seen to have anything to do with how they have been positioned by schools, but is rather attributed to some sort of dysfunction in their backgrounds. Kenway and Blackmore argue that this sleight of hand allows two things to happen. First, it allows schools to shift responsibility for any problems such girls may have at school to their home or "culture." And second, such girls are positioned by education structures and practices in such a way as to marginalize and dispossess them (Kenway and Blackmore 1995, 16).

Perhaps a few other things also happen within this dynamic. These discourses, I think, do more than just delineate the differences between girls. They also work to create girls. As Alison Jones has pointed out, girls become girls by participating within the available sets of social meanings and practices—the discourses which define them as girls (1993, 159). Here, this definition seems to emerge from within a medley of interlinked narratives of normal and its antithesis. Additionally, if making sense of oneself occurs through the construction of the other (Morrison 1992; Said 1993), then it is possible that in delineating the not-normal, the normal is able to know or recognize itself. I am suggesting that these narratives, on one level, make knowing what a "girl" is possible at all, and on a second level, make the normal girl imaginable, through the presence of the not-"normal" girl. Furthermore, in attributing this sense of lack to the (Asian, Portuguese, Afro-Caribbean, immigrant, refugee, and working-class) girls in the school, the largely white, middle-class Canadian committee (one of the teachers was a black male) may also reconfirm their sense of their own beliefs, values, ideals, and aspirations as the norm. In doing so the hegemony of this set of understandings is reinscribed and those who are seen as other are further marginalized.[3] The difference that couples the figures of the normal and problem girl, which are then projected onto real girls, seems to also serve as a site of contrastive identification for the members of the committee which works to affirm their own sense of themselves as adult and in control of their own identities, unlike the girls. The sense is that the committee views their role and by extension that of the school and the program we are planning as providing the conditions for the production of normal girls who will eventually become proper adults in control of their identities.

However, it is also possible that there was not as much homogeneity of opinion amongst committee members as I have presented thus far. Traces of what seemed to be a feminist, antiracist sentiment and the force behind the origins of the project remained. Among the quick scribblings of names, affiliations, and points of discussion that are my notes of the meeting, is a question: "Do the girls think there's a problem?" and a comment: "This project may even change the way the school treats its youth." The question was asked by a board staff member and the comment was made by a teacher (who had a hand in the writing of the original proposal); both suggest that there may have been committee members with divergent—maybe even dissenting—versions of the issues under debate.

What is important in our reading of the various versions is not whose truths are more correct or accurate. Nor is it to discover explanations and causes for how and why girls fall victim to overwhelming social problems, as has recently become the popular framework for engaging questions of girlhood. This book is not a developmental account of adolescent girls which forecasts the outcome of current socialization practices or psychologies. Rather, the interest here is in the interacting forces between discourses of femininity that make it (im)possible to know oneself and be known by others as a girl, and as a particular kind of girl. Girlhood, far from signifying a universal, biological grounded condition of female experience, emerges instead within particular sociohistorical, material, and discursive contexts (Inness 1998; Johnson 1993; Jones 1993; Lesko 1996; McRobbie and Nava 1984; Wald 1998; Walkerdine 1990). It is shaped and reshaped in complex ways through ongoing fantasized acts of relationality—with others, with idealized images, and with both conceptual categories and practices (Pitt 1996). Thus, the questions I want to ask in relation to "the problem" are: What is involved in making and claiming positions within femininity? What are the relationships between some of the very specific, material, discursive, and phantasmic practices which produce girls as beings with specificity? What are the contradictory and ambivalent (dis)identifications that both interpellate and repel those who might live this category?

Asking this set of questions, rather than those focussed on development or socialization, orients us away from essentialist notions of gendered identity and the humanist ideal of accomplishing an identity in control of itself and a self which is noncontradictory. Instead, it centers on an analysis of gender practices as potential "sites of critical agency," to use Judith Butler's term (1993), and towards using the fluidity and unpredictability of identity and difference as a resource for revealing, interrupting, and reconstructing meanings and power relations, thus casting the question of identity into the political arena.

I was standing in a crowded hallway talking to a girl I call Chantrea when a comment she made piqued my curiosity, provoking me to listen more carefully to the ways in which girls speak themselves through the conflicts, contradictions, and ambivalences of femininity. It is March 1, 1995, three months before the end of the school year which would also mark the end of two and half years I have spent in the school. The hall is full of boisterous students, just released from their desks by the ringing of the bell signalling the lunch break. The bench I am leaning against is my waiting place. Here, the girls that I have been working with on a video project assemble to ascend the two flights of stairs together, to our meeting room.

The school foyer is brightly painted in noninstitutional purples and blues and decorated with student artwork: paintings with seasonal themes, the award-winning posters in the schoolwide competition in celebration of Anti-Racism Day, and the elaborate cloth mural panels from some long ago project, hanging permanently from the ceiling.

Chantrea leans up against the bench beside me. She never seems to have a lunch of her own, but will often share in what the other girls in the group have brought from home or bought from the canteen. Today, as people pass by, she conducts a running commentary, punctuated with the nervous laugh that ends most of her sentences. "Mai," she remarks, as she spots her friend walking past us towards the school office. "She's becoming such a girl." No longer leaning, I give her my full attention. I scrutinize Mai for what could have elicited the comment. Hands in her front pockets giving her shoulders a slight hunched up look, long straight black hair worn loose down her back as usual, her jeans, large plaid shirt, and black boots don't look dissimilar from Chantrea's own. But then I see it. "You mean the lipstick?" I ask tentatively, as it is so faint as to almost not be there at all. "Well, duh!" Chantrea scoffs. "What is a girl?" I ask, laughing. "That's a girl," she replies emphatically. I turn in the direction she has indicated with a fast nod of her head. It's her classmate Julia, with long blond hair pulled up into a high pony tail that swings as she walks. Her bangs are twisted into curls that she repeatedly brushes away from her eyes. Though the weather is mild, she still wears her winter parka with its pink and pale blue patterned flowers. The fur on the edge of the hood was white when it was new. "So, how do you become a girl?" I ask. Chantrea groans. "Don't start with that, Marnina!" But then, tossing her hair over her shoulder before darting off to join her crowd that is noisily assembling a few feet away, she adds, "All I know is, I'm going to have a lot of trouble." She giggles and is gone. (FN 03/01/1995)

I recall this conversation in the hallway, setting it alongside the meeting in the Blue Room for what they suggest together about just how contradictory and complex the terms are through which girls can (or cannot) become knowable, recognizable, identifiable, and acknowledged as subjects within discourses of femininity. They both highlight, in compelling ways, the central themes of this book: the complications and ambivalence involved in creating and staking positions within femininity. Yet, situated where they are as the entry into this study, they may also be read as a series of ethnographic arrival scenes. Perhaps most expected they perform the task of introducing you, the reader, to the school, the girls, and myself and tell a fairly conventional story of gaining entrance to the research site. But the entry I am referring to here is not simply into the school per se, but an entry into a realm far more elusive: the imaginary terrain of the girls. As I will discuss in more detail in the chapters that follow, the space of the *About Us, By Us* video with its five fictional characters[4] and narrative storylines is a fantasy space creating points of contact with the imaginary object of femininity.

Using a realist narrative structure to tell the stories of the characters, the girls worked to develop a series of events that would convey the dilemmas faced by each character in a manner that they as writers considered plausible. However, as a negotiated process, not only did the girls not always agree on how this would be signified, but they also had contradictory ideas about the relationship between the fit of character and dilemma. Debating the issue from different angles and perspectives, the girls worked to make sense of the discursive conditions of social recognition that structure the formation of gendered subjects. Juggling their

knowledge of both hegemonic discourses of femininity and other, sometimes conflicting, discourses of femininity, the girls, in creating each of their characters,
shaped a series of experiences of gendered subjectivity that engaged with the social, economic, material, and cultural practices that produce girls. The positions
and relations created within the video's narratives both related to the girls' own
social struggles and provided fantasy spaces that a particular girl writing the story
or enacting it may identify with and thus want to inhabit, as well as ones she may
disidentify with and would probably not want to inhabit. Drawing on their own
experiences in their discussions of how to represent the characters and their
dilemmas, the girls' conversations often slipped into the personal; the exercise of
inventing characters was simultaneously one of inventing selves.

Moving in and out of the material and phantasmic worlds, the imaginative
work of the video presages possibilities of becoming other to ourselves and of the
social that we inhabit. Thus, naming the imaginary terrain of the girls as an ethnographic site offers a very different sense of what ethnographic entry is. As a stage
for the construction of ever changing subjects, scents of wishes, and wild desire,
the imaginary does not offer the ethnographer clear passage to securable selves
and social worlds. The terrain is marked instead by contingency, uncertainty, permeable boundaries between admitted and expressed knowledge and perceived
and expressed identities. Entering into such a site is to invite participation in
events that offer hints more often than firm resolutions. In creating the conditions for a record for thinking that is, of course, never fully known or repre-
sentable, such an ethnographic site reorders thought on the relation of writing to
knowledge, of writing experience to self and others, and of question to solution.
Simply put, it disorders them, drawing them together and then apart, creating
unexpected and sometimes troubling moments of contact and separation.

Thus, even as I mark these scenes as arrivals, I forewarn a synchronous backward movement (Was it Chantrea's scoffing, "Well duh!"?), a certain uncertainty
impeding a straightforward laying out of the spatial and temporal points on an in-
vestigatory map of this project. Contrary to the ethnographic arrival scenes that
Pratt (1986, 32) likens to those of travel writing, playing, she says, on the intensity
and sensuousness of personal experience to anchor authority in the text that ensues, there is something else stirring here. A stirring which, in recollecting the stuff
of ethnographic arrival scenes as déjà-vu, while also juxtaposing the real and the
imaginary, the familiar and the strange, threatens the authority of that experience.
It is both exposed to an already-been-there-seen-that familiarity and vulnerable to
its own failure to assert itself as originary, uninherited and in mastery of itself.
Moving backward and forward, arriving and returning, it is the dual mobilization
of the dynamics of social recognition in the negotiation of both collective and individual identities that is the subject of this book. On one level, I am interested in

the girls' articulation of the positions that define the discourse structures that make girls viable as a social category. On another level, I am interested in analyzing the relationships of identification or disidentification that specific girls in the group might express in relation to particular discursive positions. I ask: Through what regulatory norms is gendered experience materialized in the video's narratives so that a character becomes intelligible as a position that makes sense within available discourses of femininity? Once materialized, how does a given gender formation regulate identificatory practices such that certain fantasy positions are deemed desirable and others are disavowed? Within the matrix of gender relations, how do both desired and disavowed positions work together to produce and define the self? And within the array of identificatory sites that femininity might offer, what are the possibilities for disrupting normative femininity?

Thus, my purpose in insisting on a scene of arrival that reveals, interrupts, and reconstructs meanings and power relations is to link two intersecting themes: the fluidity, incoherence, and unpredictability of identities and an epistemological series of questions about writing that wonders how these identities might be represented in ethnographic texts. I elaborate below.

THE ITINERARY OF AN IDEA

What notion of girlhood can accommodate both the certainty that enables Chantrea to be able to respond to my question, "What is a girl?" as well as the ambivalence of her own becoming? For if this story of girlhood is, as I have already claimed, not a tale of a progressive perfecting of femininity nor one of a latent naturalness waiting to be uncovered, then the question of how one becomes a girl must be given considerably more attention than its apparent transparency would seem to require.

The itinerary I am proposing draws on theorizations from poststructural, psychoanalytic, and queer perspectives on and questions about subjectivity. In centralizing processes of identification as constitutive of the human subject, it is an itinerary replete with complicated detours through questions and problems of recognition and misrecognition. It is, in other words, a rerouting of an interest in asking "how one acts if one is this or that identity, to one that is about inquiring into how one becomes (and comes to be known as) this or that identity" (Sumera and Davis 1999, 195).

To begin the mapping of this framework and series of questions let us consider Stuart Hall's conceptualization of the term identity. He says "identity" is used to refer to "a meeting point, the point of suture, between on the one hand the discourses and practices which attempt to 'interpellate,' speak to us or hail us into place as the social subjects of particular discourses, and on the other hand, the processes which produce subjectivities, which construct us as subjects which can be 'spoken'" (1996, 5). Thus, this dynamic involves a double movement between a subject speaking/writing her way into existence by using the stories or discourses that are available and in the moment of doing so, also subjecting herself to the constitutive force and regulative norms of those discourses.

However, as Chantrea's sense of the likelihood of her own failure to correctly position herself within discourses of femininity suggests, people do not automatically internalize or live the discursive interpellation. Some enter into a process of struggle, resistance and negotiation. Others simply never do. Therefore, another mechanism is required for understanding the (in)effective suturing of the subject to a subject-position, the notion of an affective investment or a process of identification (Butler 1993; Davies 1993; Grossberg 1993; Hall 1996; Hollway 1984; Walkerdine 1990). Drawn from both the discursive and the psychoanalytic repertoire, the usefulness of the concept identification stems from the possibilities it opens up for theorizing the diverse, conflicting and disorderly ways in which individuals as subjects identify and/or do not identify with the "positions" to which they are summoned (Hall 1996, 14). With the possibility of multiple and contradictory identifications co-existing in the subject at the same time, "subjectivity" can be understood as precisely this struggle to negotiate a constantly changing field of ambivalent identifications (Fuss 1995, 34). More specifically, the concept is useful because while it offers a way to think about the relationship between how things are conceptually ordered and the deep investments invoked by such orderings, it also acknowledges that people may live rather untidily, outside neat social categories. In organizing a means of taking into account not only the ideas an individual might have about what it means to be recognized by others and recognize oneself as a person or a girl, the concept of identification also makes allowances for the variations within those categories and how people might invest in competing discourses simultaneously (Hollway 1984, 121). Finally, in arranging strategies for the realization of these multiple identities, while also confounding the possibility of ever doing so once and for all, it forces us to consider the likelihood that, as Britzman puts it, there is "always more to the story" (1998, 321).

We might say then that an "always more to the story" story of girlhood is a tale about the problematised making of the feminine body. A story about the repetitious making and remaking of bodies through and in relation to the prohibitions and imperatives of the impossibility of ever fully and finally inhabiting the feminine position (Pitt 1996, 38). It is a story, therefore, that acknowledges the play of specific modalities of power as productive of various subject positions, identificatory possibilities, and ideals of the normal body. For within every historical period and specific social and political contexts, differentially valued subject positions emerge along various axes of power. As Lawrence Grossberg states, "[A]lthough everyone exists within what we might call the 'strata' of subjectivity, they are also located at particular positions within the strata, each of which enables and constrains the possibilities of experience, but even more of representing and legitimating these representations" (1993, 99). Grossberg's assertion provokes and partially addresses Judith Butler's question, "[W]hich bodies come to matter—and why?" (1993, xii). An answer to this question, as we will discuss in more depth momentarily, is also succinctly explicated by Renée Himmel, fictional heroine of Rebecca Goldstein's 1983 novel, *The Mind-Body Problem*: "[W]ho matters is a function of what matters," she bluntly states (22). Aiding her in the process of meaning making is an imaginary "mattering map," with separate regions onto which what matters is projected, producing a range of shadings whose intensity depends on how many and various are the perceptions they contain. Noting that one and the same person can appear differently when viewed from different positions on the map, Renée wryly notes that "some of us do an awful lot of moving around from region to region" (22), returning us to the issue of the dynamic process of discursive interpellation of subjects to particular subject positions.

Far from random, access to subject positions is governed by both a proper "citation" of regulating norms (Butler 1993) and by a perception of sharing some "obviousnesses" with others belonging to the category, as that is understood within a particular time and place (Davies 1993). Linking the question of intelligibility to that of identification, the process of subjectification may be seen, therefore, to occur within a matrix of reflexive relations synchronized by discourse to produce and constrain identificatory possibilities, as well as the conditions by which one might recognize a self and have that self recognized by others.

The complicated dynamic of recognition and misrecognition that sets the process of (dis)identification into motion is critical to how a sense of identity is brought into being.[5] Using a psychoanalytic theory of intersubjectivity that develops Hegel's notion of domination and differentiation,[6] Jessica Benjamin (1988, 1995) argues that recognition is so central to human existence that its presence or absence is critical to consolidating or disrupting a sense of self. A similar argument is also made by Charles Taylor (1991, 1994), though he contextualizes the emergence of this relationship between identity and recognition within the development of Western liberal society and its particular ideology of individualism. Arguing that an understanding of an individual identity ("one that is particular to me, and that I discover in myself"), arises along with an "ideal of authenticity" ("there is a certain way of being human that is *my* way"), Taylor suggests that the development of an ideal of inwardly generated identity greatly increases the importance of recognition, as identity comes to crucially depend on dialogical relations with others (1994, 34).

For Benjamin, recognition is "that response from the other which makes meaningful the feelings, intentions and actions of the self. It allows the self to realize its agency and authorship in a tangible way" (1988, 12). Recognition is understood as including not only the other' s confirming response, but also how the self finds itself in that response: "We recognize ourselves in the other" (1988, 21). As Taylor points out, however, the importance of this response extends beyond that which is accorded by one individual to another. It also includes broader collectivities. He argues that a confining, demeaning, or contemptible image mirrored by one group of people to another can be a form of oppression resulting in a reduced mode of being (1994, 25).

The interface between recognition and identity has also been a rich site of inquiry in the work of Judith Butler. However, for her recognition is not conferred on a subject, as both Benjamin and Taylor partially suggest. Rather, recognition forms the subject. This critical difference in Butler' s formulation allows her to claim that the discursive condition of social recognition precedes and conditions the formation of the subject (1993, 226). Thus, in referring to the specific process of gendering she argues that it is the social and cultural category of gender, with its normative conditions and symbolic legitimacy, that articulates the intelligibility of the subject: "[S]ubjected to gender, but subjectivated by gender, the 'I' neither precedes nor follows the process of gendering, but emerges only within and as the matrix of gender relations themselves" (1993, 7).[7]

Figuring identity, like Butler suggests, as performances of relationality to both conceptual categories and practices invites certain forms of and particular sites for investigation. We might, for example, ask what the implications of this conceptualization might mean for theorizing the relationships between femininity, processes of identification, and ethical forms of relations between subjects. We might also wonder about the specificities of identity, the ways they come together, and the conditions of their emergence and circulation. And, once we have paused to consider those specificities, we might wonder further, as Alice Pitt does, how the stories we tell ourselves and others work to enhance our image of our identities as cohesive and coherent and the role that fantasy plays in this process (Pitt 1996).

Binding these queries together is an invitation to open up what seems natural about femininity and gendered identity to a consideration of other possibilities. Foucault formulates the task as follows: "We have to dig deeply to show how things have been historically contingent, for such and such reason intelligible but not necessary. We must make the intelligible appear against a background of emptiness and deny its necessity. We must think that what exists is far from filling all possible spaces. To make a truly unavoidable challenge of the question: What can be played?" (1981, 139–140).

Posing the question of "what can be played?" alongside that of "what bodies come to matter and why?" (Butler 1993) situates us at a central intersection of our "always more to the story" story of girlhood. They are suggestive not only of a complicated relationship between gender identity and normative femininity. They also implicate the dynamic process of discursive interpellation of subjects to particular subject positions in a process that is tied to the conditions for social recognition, the quest for visibility, the sense of being acknowledged, the profound desire for association, and the endeavor of endowing oneself with significance (West 1995, 20-21). In suggesting that gendered identity always preforms more than it intends, this already busy intersection is rendered a little bit busier by inviting a further question, as yet unasked, but central to the concerns of this book. That is, what is it to consider femininity as a question of identification?

As an oscillating movement between simultaneous and incompatible placements and consolidations, between subject positions and object positions, "me" and "not-me," identification is a process that renders subject formation as unstable and always incomplete. Thus, configuring femininity as a question of identification demands thinking of it not as a solitary quality or inherent characteristic of particular sexed bodies, but rather as an expression of certain kinds of relationality. Formed and reformed through ongoing remembered and fantasized acts, these expressions of relationality necessitate a consideration of how unclaimed or mistaken identities are just as critical to the conjugation of a feminine self as are perhaps more readily claimed and recognizable identities. As Alice Pitt (1996) puts it, if identity is secured, however provisionally, by the processes of assuming a sexed position, in doing so it bears as well an identificatory relation to its abject other. Linking the production of normative femininity to the constitution of "bodies that matter," we might say that both are secured through the mutually dependent production of a domain of the normative and a domain of abjection (Butler 1993; Fuss 1995; Hall 1996; Oliver 1993). Butler suggests, "[T]he zone of un-inhabitability constitutes the defining limit of the subject's domain; it will constitute that site of dreaded identification against which—and by virtue of which—the domain of the subject will circumscribe its own claim to autonomy and life" (1993, 3).

At the same time, it is the existence of both domains that also offers the possibility for expanding the horizon of these investments to embrace new forms of gendered subjectivity. Butler (1993) argues for example, that it is the ever present threat of the outside to expose the founding presuppositions of the inside that renders it a critical resource that can be used to rewrite the order of "insideness" and "outsideness," to rearticulate the very meanings, legitimacies, and uses of "insideness" and "outsideness," and to expand the meaning of what counts as a valued and valuable body.

I will show that it is precisely because identification is purchased via this set of constitutive and formative exclusions that subjectivity' s boundaries and in particular gendered subjectivity are constantly open to renegotiation. The play of difference and similitude in the formation of a subject means that recognition is from the beginning always a question of relation—of self to other, subject to object (Fuss 1995, 2). Conceived in terms of a slippery "elsewhereness" (Davies 1994, 36), the work of identification renders identity problematic at the same time as it is productive of it simply because such exclusions have consequences that cannot be fully controlled. The meaning or effect of a particular (dis)identification, as Fuss argues, "critically exceeds the limits of its social, historical and political determinations" (1995, 8). The impossibility of a full recognition, that is, of ever fully inhabiting the name by which one' s social identity is inaugurated and mobilized, implies the instability and incompleteness of subject formation (Butler 1993, 226).

The classifying acts of inclusion and exclusion producing the conditions for social recognition also engender what is for Bauman a product of the labor of all classification projects: ambivalence (1991, 3). Bauman links the naming and classifying compulsion, and thus ambivalence, to the enterprise of modernity, an interesting coupling, in view of the pivotal way in which ambivalence figures in psychoanalysis, a science born of the modern age. Using a Freudian perspective, Jane Flax defines ambivalence thus: "Ambivalence refers to affective states in which intrinsically contradictory or mutually exclusive desires or ideas are each invested with intense emotional energy. Although one cannot have both simultaneously, one cannot abandon either of them" (1990, 50). She goes on to note that such ambivalence is not necessarily a symptom of weakness or confusion but, on the contrary, "a strength to resist collapsing complex and contradictory material into an orderly whole" (1990, 50). In this sense, "ambivalence is an appropriate response to an inherently conflictual situation" (Flax 1990, 11).Grounded in fantasy, projection and idealization, identification in enacting such a conflictual situation is, as Freud writes, "ambivalent from the very start" (Freud, 1921/1991, 134).

My interest in the operation of ambivalence is twofold: at the structural level, in so far as it references the internal contradictions within discourses of femininity with their conflicting expectations and pressures, and at the subjective level, in the sense that there will be certain consequences for girls' struggle(s) for recognition in having to position themselves within discourses that have these structural characteristics.[8]

Analyzing femininity and its identificatory capacities through the lens of ambivalence resists collapsing complex and contradictory material into an orderly whole. For as Dorothy Smith argues, "[T]he notion of femininity does not define a determinate and unitary phenomenon" (1988, 37). And if its incoherence has led some feminists to insist on the impossibility of any singular understanding of gendered experience, then its indeterminacy is complicated even further by considering the ways in which discourses of femininity intersect with other dimensions of social difference, such as class, race, and sexuality (Bannerji 1991; Hill-Collins 1990; hooks 1981; Pratt 1984; Riley 1988; Spelman 1988). Focusing on the ambivalent structure of femininity and its consequences for girls' identificatory practices allows us, therefore, to locate the concept on and between its boundaries, to defy the distinction between fantasy and reality, and to map the inside and outside borders underlying its thresholds of meaning and nonsense, mattering and abjected bodies. Its very ineffectivity is perhaps also what presents the opportunity for the proliferation of identificatory possibilities and the expansion of stories for girls to turn life into.

Due to the fact that the concept of femininity is itself implicated in the social construction of the phenomena it appears to describe, Smith suggests that inquiry should begin with the ordinary and unanalyzed ways in which we know what we are talking about when we use the concept and can demonstrate that competence in how we can recover or cite particular instances (1988, 38). As will become clearer in the chapters that follow, my own investigation of femininity attempts such a recovery by assembling and organizing a series of "scenes of recognition" produced through the planning, development and filming of the *About Us, By Us* video with is fictional girl characters. Through the stories, the scenes of recognition delineate some of the discursive and social practices defining female sexuality, embodiment, relationship to self and others, material culture, use of social space, cultural-political agency, and power. I analyze the ways in which the scenes are at once the medium through which different racialized and classed femininities are rendered intelligible to self and others and the identificatory sites which reproduce the concept's negative capability.[9] Together, the multiple positions of femininity created in the video stories chart a discourse map of femininity which I will attempt to analyze in terms of the identificatory relations and investments mobilized in the negotiation of girls' gendered subjectivity. However, as chapter 2 will outline in full detail, the drawing of this map is accomplished as a result of a process that is neither neat nor linear. Rather, the transcripts through which this map is pieced together are a veritable cartographic nightmare. Fantasy mingles with reality, while fragments of rational thought, emotion, and lived bodily experience merge and separate. Threads of discussion spin in multiple directions: personal stories, commentary on group members, talk of different cultural texts. More often than not, numerous conversations occur simultaneously and rarely is one person able to finish a sentence before someone else begins.

The result is a map of bits and pieces, of paths begun and than abandoned, of enticing trails that lead nowhere and of completely contradictory coordinates. Rather than fighting to clean these up, to somehow weave them into a coherent story that may be read unobstructively, I include the interruptions, the inconsistencies, and the dead ends. What I am presenting is a map that reveals more than mere traces of its own construction and thus reveals more than what is usually considered polite in social scientific research. This is a textual strategy that is reflective of the ongoing and nonstatic nature of the conversation that structures practices of identification and as such it emphasizes that the stories of identification and this ethnographic telling of those stories are unfinished, multiple, and conflicting ones. And, as I will discuss presently, it is also a strategy that mirrors the messy methodology used and the context in which the girls' meaning making occurs.

While I am attempting an analysis that acknowledges the interlinking relations between gender, race, class, sexuality, and ethnicity in the production of identities, such an aspiration is not easy to accomplish textually. Among the challenges I encounter is how to theorize the sites and relations of difference mobilized by various girls without doing so by making them representative of their different racialized and ethnic categories. Thus, in this regard, as in others, the text is rife with gaps where some relations of difference may, at times, be foregrounded and at different moments, others.

The nature of the questions I am asking—questions about the social, psychic, and physical embeddedness of individuals and collectivities in the discursively constituted categories to which they are subjected—has forced something of a trespassing of disciplinary boundaries. Drawing on the analytical tools of discourse analysis developed by Foucault and widely used by a range of feminist critics and sociolinguists, while borrowing key concepts from psychoanalysis and philosophy, the questions about gendered subjectivity that I am asking arise in discussions most current within cultural and feminist studies informed by poststructural theory. This kind of cross-fertilization has proven productive for many interested in critically analyzing the discursive structures and signifying relations of gender, race, class, and sexuality, and the distinct cultural and social formations that result.[10]

Of course, because of its situatedness within the academy, a social institution that is an active participant in structuring ways of thinking, the act of writing is also highly implicated in the production and circulation of these very discourses and significations. As such, it participates in creating the social and cultural identities it purports to merely describe or analyze. I raise this issue now in anticipation of a more in-depth discussion in the chapter that follows, but also to signal the doubleness of my own project. For, since I am interested in analyzing identity as an effect of discursive practices, this book is part of the story it is trying to tell. In worrying the discursive practices of ethnographic writing, my goal is to attempt to

make the links between the processes of theorizing and analyzing identity and difference, the political and ethical dilemmas of representing the lives of others, and
the processes of "reconfiguring what will count as the world" (Butler 1993, 19).

ITINERANT WRITINGS/READINGS/PEDAGOGIES

Since subject position is everything in my analysis of gendered subjectivity, you
should know that as author of this text, I have multiple and contradictory functions, and this will very likely also have implications for you, the reader.

My various tasks of mapping discourses of femininity and analyzing the
identificatory practices they facilitate, while at the same time attempting to
destabilize ethnographic epistemologies and identificatory strategies have, like
the structure of the discourses of femininity I want to analyse, precipitated
something of a state of ambivalence. For, rather than synthesizing apparently
contradictory elements and claiming them as parts of some coherent whole, I
work to maintain them as sites of displacement, of inconsistency and complexity within my ethnographic text, mining them for what they might offer in the
way of new ground, across which systems of structural order and symbolic pattern might move, bend, and dissolve, opening up space for difference, struggle,
confusion, and emergence.

I acknowledge that certain challenges may be posed to the reader of such a
text: chapters that go on for too long, pieced together from bits of transcripts
whose fragments never add up to more than a partiality, and are made up of stories that, like Renée Himmel's, belong to mere fictional characters. But perhaps
what may prove most unsettling is the absence of what is usually commonplace
within social scientific texts: the provision of a classificatory introduction of the
girls whose writings, fantasies, and talking make up the practices I analyze.
Whose story then, am I asking you to consider?

Warning against the dangers of a defense against the anxiety induced by the
lack of coherence and irresolvable conflict, Flax advises that it is often better in
such a situation to analyze the sources of the ambivalence and one's inability to
tolerate it (Flax 1990, 11). Perhaps, as Crapanzano suggests, the uneasiness induced by maintaining contradictory stances within an academic text stems from
what it announces about the inconstancy of the self and the instability of vantage
point. One purpose of our rhetoric is, he writes, "to mark us as constant throughout our writing, to fix our perspective. We are taught to read accordingly—to per-
petuate an author's illusion of singularity, coherence and constancy, and in our
engagement with him our own illusions of singularity, coherence and constancy"
(1992, 9).

Rather than judging the absence of a single controlling voice in this text, therefore, as a problem of ethnographic lack, a failure in the contest of mastery over the unruliness that is the nature of data, I would suggest a shift in attention to text-reader relations and to ethnographic reading practices. By purposefully leaving a gap where one might expect to find an answer to the question, Who are the girls? I am attempting to enact a certain kind of pedagogy. It is a pedagogy that, as Patricia Williams says of her own writing, "forces the reader both to participate in the construction of meaning and to be conscious of that process"(1991, 7–8). Leaving gaps to be filled by readers, she states, compels them to participate self-consciously with her in historicized and contextualized meaning invention.[11]

In refusing you a passive reception of information already defined elsewhere, who the girls are, is precisely what I am rendering problematic in this text. For though it is a question I return to repeatedly in my analysis of the data transcripts, I am also suggesting that any version of the answer to the question also depends on who wants to know, the context in which the question is being asked, and for what purposes. The anxious writing/reading position that is created by ethnography as radical pedagogy is at least partially due to the dynamics of engagement created in a text which, in reminding us of the limits of our understanding, also demands that you read with an awareness of your own multiple and shifting positions, identificatory practices, and reading strategies.

My attempt to write in a way that encourages a certain consciousness of your responses to the workings of meanings of identity and difference in my text marks reading and writing as complex and closely entwined social transactions. As Bauman notes, every reader is a writer: the reader is a writer while s/he reads (1991, 192). "Reading like a writer," Morrison explains, carries certain demands. It means "being mindful of the places where imagination sabotages itself, locks its own gates, pollutes its vision. Writing and reading mean being aware of the . . . serene achievement of, or sweaty fight for, meaning and response ability" (1992, xi).

Traces of my own sweaty fights for meaning (and far fewer serene achievements of it), are accessible to you through the stories and transcripts that are not only included in the text but are also where my analysis is grounded. That is, rather than making knowledge claims from empirical evidence that you have no way of substantiating or contesting, my analysis emerges from these combined bits of story, always inviting further writing and rewriting. As Anna Tsing reminds us, "[E]thnographic insight emerges from stories told by one situated commentator to another" (1993, 225). Chantrea and the other girls' critical commentary makes mine possible and so in turn, does mine make yours.

Towards facilitating this engaged and mindful reading, this book is organized as follows. Chapter 2 is an in-depth introduction to the video project with an interwoven discussion of methodologies, the play of feminist desire in the goals of critical research agendas, and the ethical and political issues surrounding questions of representation and self-other relations inherent to an ethnographic inquiry. Situating my own study within some of the recent attempts to reconceptualize ethnographic practice, I review the critiques that have been made about traditional social scientific writing and outline my own strategies for producing an analysis of nonunitary gendered subjectivity and for writing in ways that attempt not to refix and resolidify difference and identity.

Chapters 3 and 4 are structured around three fictional characters whose stories serve as heuristic devices for mapping discourses of femininity and investigating femininity as an intersubjective negotiation. Using two of the genres most commonly associated with the stories of women' s lives—romance and transformation—the narratives explore the intersections of femininity, race, class, nationality, and sexuality with those of recognition, agency, and subjectivity. While each of the stories is built around different specific thematics, the two chapters are woven together by the motif of inside and outside, insiders and outsiders. Its various repetitions and reconfigurations signify forms of imaginary coherence in the ambivalent project of identity formation.

In chapter 5, I give further consideration to the question of ambivalence and the provocative possibilities it might offer for creating and supporting the conditions for feminist social change. I do so by returning to the characters' stories to draw out some of the merging and separate moments where the negotiation of femininity proves inherently conflictual. By looking closely at where different ambivalent responses are elicited, I hope to understand more about the discursive and social practices which legitimate and contest what it means to become a girl (and an academic) at the beginning of a new century.

CHAPTER 2

Points of Departure and Disrupted Arrivals: Negotiating the Research Terrain

S o, why do you want to know all this?" LeLy is once again asking for an explanation as to what it is I've been doing at her school for the past two years. She is trying to understand what it is my project is about. The question has come up before in a variety of forms. On numerous occasions she has wondered, "Why would an adult hang out with kids?"

At this most recent asking, I am at LeLy's invitation watching her at badminton practice in the school gym. Our discussion is accomplished in truncated pieces as she runs off to play sets with her partner against the other pairs of the school team and then tossing her racket aside, calling out to her friends, quickly checking the score charts hanging on the wall, she runs back to rejoin me on the bench by the sidelines. The team is currently practicing every day after school and is a contender for the championship in a citywide competition. LeLy is a strong player, and the pauses in our conversation are usually relatively brief as she and her partner make short order of most of the other pairs. She claims she was taught by professionals in the refugee camp in Vietnam where she and her family lived before they came to Canada when she was ten years old.

"I am hoping to understand a little bit about what your experience has been like," I answer.

"I don't mean to be racist," she responds, "but it's different. You can't understand. You were born here. It's different for us that just came here."

Questions of power, knowledge, and desire and the interplay of these forces in and through the research process, the relationship between researcher and researched, the production of knowledge, and epistemological frameworks structure this discussion. It raises important questions about notions of experience,

21

difference, representation, and understanding that underlie how and for what purposes ethnographic knowledge is produced. Thus, this brief exchange captures some of the central components of many current debates amongst critical ethnographers and other feminist researchers.

In outlining these concerns as an opening to a chapter ostensibly about the methodologies used in the making of the *About Us, By Us* video, I am emphasizing the complicated, multilayered interrelationships between the epistemological foundations of knowledge production, research ethics, and the hoped-for critical accomplishments of a feminist ethnographic project. I am suggesting that a discussion of research methods cannot be divorced from a discussion of the ways in which knowledge production is a set of social, political, economic, historical, and ideological processes (Bhavnani 1994, 27). In warning ethnographers against dematerializing their accounts so that the economic, cultural, and political conditions under which they labor evaporate from the final texts, Angela McRobbie (1982) argues such a dematerialization often leads to a mystification or obstruction of the complexities and messiness of field work. Although she does not explicitly identify the narrative strategies for accomplishing such a dematerialization, she stresses that the implications of not doing so include not only erasing the subjectivities of researchers but also maintaining the fiction that ethnographers' forays into the field are unmediated by the conditions under which they labor and by their own theoretical and political commitments. What seems to be required, therefore, is not only that researchers "become answerable for what we learn how to see" (Haraway 1988, 190), but also an interrogation of the theorist's "desire to know" (Walkerdine 1990, 201).

Taking up this dual charge will be a theme thread throughout the book, but I commence here with a number of different ways in which LeLy's question, "Why do you want to know all this?" might begin to be addressed. I will return to some of the specifics of my own project's history as well as some of the more general and historical understandings of the social scientific ethnographic enterprise. After this interruption, though not by calls to the net, points scored and lost, flying birdies, and swinging rackets (or perhaps just of another sort), I return to the conversation with which I started and to the issues of experience, difference, representation, and understanding it raised through a discussion of some of the new and emerging forms of ethnographic questioning and practice which inform my own project.

KNOWING "US" AND "THEM": ETHNOGRAPHIC
KNOWLEDGE AND THE END OF INNOCENCE

Any attempt to begin to fashion a suitable answer to LeLy's question needs to be broadly contextualized, since the history of this specific project is in no small measure bound up within the larger framework of the social scientific ethnographic enterprise. Embedded in her question is another series of inquiries that might be made as a means of offering some form of accountability for my presence at her school—a presence she is struggling to understand. What drives the ethnographic interest in others? What makes certain others of interest as subjects of research? What structures and authorizes this interest such that it is usually understood as distinct from what, in other social contexts, might be considered just plain nosiness—a distinction which, as was pointed out to me by some of the girls, was not always obvious to them.

LeLy:	It's Tevy's birthday.
Marnina:	Is she having a party?
Mai:	Yeah, she invite only me from the grade eights and I'm not going.
LeLy:	And Pearl?
Mai:	She's still mad at Pearl.
Marnina:	Why is she mad at Pearl?
LeLy:	Don't be that nosy, Marnina! (04/05/95)

In tracing some of the "desires to know" within what have been the agendas of (different) ethnographic traditions, the themes of regulation, normalization, seeking the self through constructions of the other, and hopes of emancipation reoccur. These desires, like those outlined above, are also fraught with tensions between them and boundaries that are at times difficult to differentiate. They get played out both at the sites of the research process and in the texts that ensue. Thus, not only researcher and researched, but also readers become bound up in the imbrication of power, knowledge, and desire.

Walkerdine's description of the research process as surveillant voyeurism captures this complex dynamic. The term raises important questions about linkages between research methodology and the uses to which research is put. It also underscores the importance of examining the researcher-researched relationship as a critical element towards understanding how it is that knowledge is produced. For Walkerdine, the quest for knowledge of the other or the "will for truth" is about desires "for power, for control and for vicarious joining in as well as a desperate fear of the Other" (1990, 174). The truths that are produced within the space of observation feed into the discursive practices that regulate those observed (Walkerdine 1990, 195). The professional knowledge of sociology, as well as that of other disciplines are, as Dorothy Smith (214) states, "articulated to the ruling apparatus" (1990, 214). Through providing specialized knowledge about the individual—within and between the various "apparatuses of ruling"—the disciplines are complicit in the processes of surveillance and monitoring of the population.

The form and content this surveillance and monitoring may take are various and are undoubtedly specific to particular historical, social, and political contexts. However, the form that this specialized knowledge engenders that seems most relevant to a research project located within the site of a school, an institution concerned with producing norms and normative identities, is, as Said describes, the power of rule which takes on the sense of a measure or standard (Said 1979). These, he argues, work discursively over the cultural universe of identifications, meanings, and stipulations of truth. The cultural representations that result help form the images some have of others. If assimilated by those others, they help form the images they have of themselves as well, and they become embodied in institutions and inform policies and practices (McCarthy 1992, 641). According to Said, professional intellectuals and the disciplines they work within play a critical role in generating and circulating the hegemonic aesthetic- veridical discourses on the characteristics and relations of the social and geographical world. The target of discursive power, he argues, is a population whose subordinate identity is being textually etched out as a counter to and foil for the "fundamental group."[1] The power that is wielded by the fundamental group through the proxy of its professional intellectuals is one of the ways in which both groups are defined. That is, the discourses that intellectuals maintain and extend author themselves as thoroughly as they author others. The research process can be seen, as Walkerdine suggests, as one of the regulative practices which produces the subjectivities of both researcher and researched (Walkerdine 1990, 199).

Trinh T. Minh-ha also addresses the interstices of power, knowledge, identity, and desire within the research process. She writes, "In writing close to the other of the other, I can only choose to maintain a self-reflexively critical relationship toward the material, a relationship that defines both the subject written and the writing subject, undoing the I while asking "what do I want wanting to know you or me?" (1989,76).

Trinh seems to be suggesting that much of what drives the research process is a search for the self in the other. That which is other in traditional ethnography is usually non-Western, or if Western, a group which is in some way defined as marginal or subcultural. Thus, the project I described in chapter 1 of the identification of the not-normal girl as a means of constituting the normal one can be seen in some ways as accommodating a very traditional ethnographic convention. According to Comaroff and Comaroff, the ethnographic encounter is one in which "the West sets up a mirror in which it might find a tangible, if inverted, self image" (1992, 1). The Comaroffs suggest that as a Western discourse, ethnography "tell[s] of the unfamiliar . . . to confront the limits of our own epistemology, our own visions of personhood, agency and history" (1992, 1). In doing so, "the ethnographer," writes Vincent Crapanzano, "also marks a boundary: his ethnography declares the limits of his and his readers' culture" (1986, 52).

However, the project of identifying discourses of girlhood can also be accommodated within some of the new and emerging forms of ethnographic inquiry that have been legitimated by the critique I have begun to outline above. The focus of intellectual debate among anthropologists and cultural critics more widely, this revision of ethnography changes the understanding of the general character of what ethnography is about and the kinds of stories that can be told. Rather than drawing boundaries of self against other, us against them, it attempts to open a discussion into how subjects are constituted by the very discourses that incite them. Suggesting the necessity of facilitating new forms of relationships between researcher and researched, writer and reader, a central tenet of this work is the questioning of the tropes of representation, even as it practices representation as a way to intervene critically in the constitutive constraints of discourses.[2]

This experimentation with new objects and styles of research and with new writing has taken place across disciplinary boundaries. It does however, have some specific significance for feminist agendas. Feminist researchers have struggled within multiple research paradigms to foreground the contestability of modernism's truth claims about women (Lather 1991). The reworking and reconception of traditional research epistemologies and methods have been seen as both a challenge to some of the more exploitative elements of traditional research models, as well as a means of understanding and transforming the social reality in which women live their lives.[3] Thus, the insertion of "woman" as a subject of research is both integrally connected with alternative research strategies and linked to a feminist political project.

Patti Lather traces this feminist preoccupation to Audre Lorde's (1984) call for tools of knowledge production based on subaltern ways of knowing which had previously been excluded from discussions. Feminist researchers have sought these counterpractices of knowing in personal voice, archival resources such as diaries and journals, dialogic and interactive interview formats, reflexivity regarding interpretive imposition, and practices such as cowriting, among others (Lather 1996, 2). Set up in opposition to the knowledge projects of positivist science, these researchers forgo objectivity thought to be achieved through detachment and a strict separation of subject and object, knower and known, in favor of egalitarian relations that require authenticity, reciprocity, and mutual respect between the researcher and subjects of research (Stacey 1988). They reject the idea of speaking "for" and supplant it with the notion of voices in the text, or ways of writing that are dialogical or polyphonic. As Clifford writes, it is an attempt to develop a "cultural poetics that is an interplay of voices, of positioned utterances" (1986, 12). These new and questionably better methods and texts were viewed not only as a means of accomplishing feminist political agendas of recovering voices previously ignored, but also as a means of empowering research subjects through the research process.

However, while this desire to know and to empower may stem from a progressive political agenda, feminist attempts to find a less exploitative, more innocent way of proceeding do not take into account the full weight of research as surveillance and normalization (Lather 1996, 2). Nor do they fully acknowledge, as I will discuss in more detail in the next section of this chapter, the ethnographic real as a contested territory (Britzman 1995, 231).

Despite the emancipatory intentions of those who use the discourses of empowerment and voice and the critical concern of those who raise questions about the discursive relations of the ethnographic encounter, these discourses and practices have embedded within them their own normalizing, repressive tendencies (Game 1991; Gore 1992; Mascia-Lees and Sharpe 1994; Orner 1992). While discussions about the problematic constructions of feminist emancipatory discourses have been mainly directed at feminist and critical pedagogy, it might also be useful to consider them in the context of feminist research. The silencing and disenfranchizing of those marginalized by the culture at large is not in question. As has already been pointed out, the discourses academics produce, maintain, and circulate play a role in this process. What is in question is the positioning within these discourses and texts of the student or researched in relation to the pedagogue or researcher in "the university rescue mission in search of the voiceless" (Viswasnaran 1994, 69).

Drawing on Foucault's notion of "regime of truth," Gore suggests that the conceptualization of power, empowerment, and knowledge internal to critical and feminist discourses is problematic. She suggests that the "what we can do for you" paradigm of empowerment rests on an assumption of an agent who empowers and who is herself already empowered (1992, 61). The presumption is that the individual doing the empowering—the usually white, Western, middle-class teacher/researcher—has already dealt conclusively with her own inscription and involvement in oppressive power dynamics and is now in a position to pass that power on to an oppressed other.[4] As McRobbie points out with respect to research projects based on/for girls, this may be an immensely patronizing stance. She asks, "[H]ow can *we* assume *they* need anything done for them in the first place? And conversely that we have anything real to offer them?" (1982, 52). Perhaps along with interrogating the researcher's desire to know there is also room, as Walkerdine suggests, for asking, what is the feminist investment in "making them see?" (Walkerdine 1990, 200).

Empowerment has also been articulated as the ultimate goal of some experiments with ethnographic writing. Embedded within a critical discussion about authorship (Strathern 1990), this concern for empowering the voice of informants through the production of texts that are dialogic and multivocal is closely tied to a desire to fundamentally alter the power relations inherent in the anthropological endeavor (Mascia-Lees and Sharpe 1994). However, questions have been raised not only about the possibility that the singular voice of the ethnographer has been too easily denied in claims about multiple voices (Probyn 1993; Strathern 1990; Wolf 1992), but also that the empowering dialogic text may challenge the category of the "primitive" even as it reinscribes it. Mascia-Lees and Sharpe point out that both ethnographer and informant know the text contains exclusions and distortions, yet it is represented as somehow less exploitative, more authentic, and a better translation (1994, 652). As Ann Game (quoting Foucault 1984) questions, "Does the concern with the discursive relation of the ethnographic encounter end up reinventing the question 'Who really spoke? With what authority or originality?'" (Game 1991, 32).

The call for voice is problematic, as Orner suggests, because it seems to presume voices and identities to be singular, unchanging, and unaffected by the context in which the speaking occurs. These discourses do not adequately recognize that one's social position, one's voice, can "at best be tentative and temporary given the changing, often contradictory relations of power at multiple levels of social life" (1992,79). Moreover, there is a sense in which the mediation involved in this "bringing to voice" is ignored. This question remains unaddressed: "Under what institutional and historical constraints" is this speaking, writing taking place? (Game 1991, 31). The construction of the teacher/researcher as the singular enabler or provider of voice, therefore, does little to shift power relations. At the same time it erases the many multifaceted contexts, meanings, and ways in which voicings and refusals of voicings may occur and may be interpreted by not only the researched, but also those who will eventually have access to these voices via the texts produced.[5]

There is for Ruth Behar something ironic about this state of affairs. She observes that in seeking out and telling the stories of other women (usually less privileged than themselves), feminist ethnographers are now in the strange position of being able to mime the role of the doctor-husband portrayed in Charlotte Perkins Gilman's parabolic "The Yellow Wallpaper" (1892). Presuming to know what was best for his wife, he confined her to a room with yellow wallpaper where she was not to tire herself by doing any kind of thinking or writing. Behar suggests that the stories feminist ethnographers collect "need interpretive homes that will not turn out to be prisonhouses with yellow wall paper" (1993, 272). And this is, of course, both impossible and still not enough. Words once fixed on paper become common property to the extent that one cannot control where they might travel, and in whose hands they may be twisted and used (Ternar 1994, 152). Furthermore, the underlying assumption behind requiring safe places, like the hope that better-intentioned research could overcome the power imbalances of inquiry situations,[6] seems to be that a noncomplicitous place of knowing and desire to know can be found.

These assumptions are now in doubt, as feminist researchers confront what has been variously termed the loss or end of innocence (Flax 1992; Rosaldo 1989; Van Maanen 1995; Viswasnaran 1994). This loss has, in part, been precipitated by two related crises: of representation and epistemology. It is to a further discussion of these crises and the implications they have for ethnographic research that I now turn.

RESEARCHING EXPERIENCE/EXPERIENCING RESEARCH:
CRISIS IN RESEARCH EPISTEMOLOGY AND
REPRESENTATION

As LeLy rushes off the bench to play another round in the practice badminton tournament, I wonder again how it is that our best conversations seem to happen when the tape recorder is buried deep within my knapsack. "When is data?" Patti Lather recently asked while at the Ontario Institute for Studies in Education for a presentation of her research on HIV-positive women. "Data is," she said, answering her own question, "when the tape recorder is on."

Absent tape recorders, the failure of the taken-for-grantedness of feminist intentions, and the constructed nature of data and the research encounter, as implied in Lather's comment, suggest that an opening up of questions about the foundations on which knowledge production have rested apparently comfortably and securely needs to be further considered. This is not, however, simply a question of methodology. As I have already discussed, better methods alone seem to have failed to extricate feminist research from the quandary in which it appears to be mired. But, perhaps as LeLy's response to my answer to her question, "Why do you want to know all this?"—that is, the impossibility of realizing my feminist desire to understand her experience—suggests, rather than a methodological matter this is a question of the more fundamental issue of epistemology.

LeLy's response gestures towards a number of problematic assumptions about the way in which experience and its understanding and representation form the basis for various kinds of knowledge claims within traditional and feminist ethnographic practice. These problems include both the way the experience of the researcher is deployed as an epistemic category and, relatedly, the way the experience of the researched is assumed to be an object of discovery and understanding.

One of the underlying beliefs behind the accomplishment of ethnographic knowledge production has been that the ethnographer is capable of producing truth from the experience of being in the field. An insider's view is assumed to result from an extended period of time participating and observing another social group. Using a series of rhetorical strategies to convince readers of the authenticity and thus authority of the descriptive account, the ethnographer conveys the successful attainment of this view within the texts that are produced following the fieldwork experience. Access to the cultural knowledge found in the field is, in turn, promised to any future readers of these texts. The goal of understanding is therefore assumed to be within the reach of both ethnographers and their readers (Britzman 1995).

The linking together of understanding as accomplishable by way of the ethnographic experience is often established through introductory descriptive passages that function to set the scene for the entire work. These passages are responsible for setting up the initial positionings of the subjects of the ethnographic text: the ethnographer, the informants, and the reader (Pratt 1986, 32). They lay out the spatial and temporal maps of those investigated and set the stage for the ethnographer's gradual transformation from stranger into fully immersed participant-observer and quasi member of the group under study (Roman 1993, 283). In furnishing the guarantee of an eyewitness report, by an outsider turned insider, these scenes establish a contract between writer and reader that not only helps to create a shared understanding of the real as represented in the text (Atkinson 1990, 70), but also work to persuade readers that "you are there, because I was there" (Clifford 1983, 118). Readers are therefore positioned as vicarious insiders and as such are also in possession of the group's cultural knowledge (Britzman 1995, 230).

However, researchers working within poststructuralist, feminist, and postcolonial frameworks have suggested that such understandings need to be reexamined. Rather than viewing experience as a concrete reality with a fixed essence that can be simply reflected by language, Chris Weedon argues that experience is itself constituted by and in language (1987, 85). If experience is largely understood through language, and language shapes how we see and act with and on the world, then the writing of ethnography cannot be seen as the mere translation of an experienced reality. Rather, ethnographic writing constructs the very materiality it attempts to represent (Britzman 1995, 231). By retrospectively ordering the past, writing, suggests Kondo, is a quest in which the ethnographer attempts to find meaning in the chaos of lived experience and in events whose significance was elusive while they were being lived (Kondo 1986, 82). In searching for structure to impose on experience it is all too tempting to reduce the complex to the readily apprehensible, assuming authority and control over one's own motives and omitting states of serious confusion, violent feelings or acts, censorships, important failures, changes of course, and excessive pleasures (Clifford 1986, 13). Writing may thus also be seen as a way of freezing the disturbing flux, encapsulating experience in order to control it.

This questioning of the researcher's experience and its textual representation extends as well to the other side of the researcher/researched divide. That is, the experience of others as the objects of discovery and understanding of the ethnographic inquiry and the way it has been represented has also been challenged. Among the sites where this sense has emerged are both the critique by women of color of the women's movement and also the analysis by feminists of various standpoint epistemologies (Lamphere 1994, 222). Based in the notion that one constructs knowledge from a particular social location or standpoint shaped by race, class, and gender,[7] this analysis contests both the epistemological possibility of understanding the experience of others, as well as the political legitimacy of representing it. It suggests, as LeLy did (by pointing out the differences between us as an insurmountable barrier for the achievement of my feminist desire to understand her experience), that the difference of others may not be fully consumed, assimilated to theory and description by cracking codes of structure and through better translation, as has previously been the assumption of ethnographers and other social scientists (Marcus 1994, 566).

Since the work of researchers always stands in some relation to othering, questions about the political aspects of the crisis in representation must include the ways in which representations of the experience of others have reproduced this relation. While some of the ideologies and contexts in which this occurs were previously discussed, it is also important to examine the actual practices or what Fine, following de Lauretis (1987), calls the "technologies of othering" (Fine 1994, 78).

Such practices are found within social scientific efforts to produce general descriptions of people's experience by abstraction and reification. As Dorothy Smith writes, "The complex organization of activities of actual individuals and their actual relations is entered into the discourse through concepts such as class, modernization, formal organization. A realm of theoretically constituted objects is created, freeing the discursive realm from its ground in the lives and work of actual individuals and liberating sociological inquiry to graze on a field of conceptual entities," (Smith 1987, 130). Writing of conceptual entities rather than actual people results in representations that tend to flatten out differences. Contradictions, conflicts of interest, doubts, and arguments, not to mention changing motivations and circumstances, are smoothed over in the interests of homogeneity, coherence, and timelessness (Abu-Lughod 1991, 152). Pratt characterizes this move as a widespread and stable form of othering. She writes, "The people to be othered are homogenized into a collective 'they,' which is distilled even further into an iconic 'he' (the standard adult male specimen). This abstracted 'he'/'they' is the subject of verbs in a timeless present tense, which characterizes anything 'he' is or does not as a particular historical event but as an instance of pregiven custom or trait" (Pratt 1986, 139). The appearance of a lack of internal differentiation, suggests Abu-Lughod, makes it easier "to conceive of groups of people as discrete, bounded entities—populated by generic cultural beings who do this or that and believe such and such." It is the erasure of time and conflict, she argues, that makes what is inside the boundary set up by homogenization something essential and fixed (1991, 153).

Joan Scott (1992) suggests that the ramifications of such practices are that stories of individuals are read as if their experiences were transparent concomitants of the social category stressed in the account, thus reconfirming unselfconscious assumptions about those categories, instead of leading to a consideration of how they were constructed. Furthermore, if these stories are read as representing the authentic voice of a particular category of people, they can become further exclusionary devices that marginalize all those who speak outside an imagined authenticity (Martin and Mohanty 1986; Tsing 1993).

Any talk of understanding the experience of girls, or even of a particular girl, must therefore be seen as problematic. Not only are there shifting meanings of what a girl is, but these meanings shift in contradictory ways. There is therefore no way, as Jones argues, in which girls as a group, or as individuals, can be fixed in our understanding (1993, 159).

Underlying this questioning of the ethnographic enterprise is an ethical concern regarding how the messy, contradictory, and unstable fieldwork experience is reworked into coherent fact. James Clifford offers us this very interesting formulation of the issue. He asks, "If ethnography produces cultural interpretations through intense research experiences, how is unruly experience transformed into an authoritative account? How precisely, is a garrulous, overdetermined cross-cultural encounter shot through with power relations and personal cross-purposes circumscribed as an adequate version of a more or less discrete 'other world' composed by an individual author?" (1988, 25). It is the recognition of the constructedness of the research process that suggests the necessity of questioning not only the epistemological foundations of ethnographic authority, but also the authority that is assumed through this experience to represent the experience of others. For as I have already discussed, being watched may have implications for the observed, but the act of watching also does something to and for the observer. It positions the social scientist as an expert, as one who knows and one who is therefore allowed to speak for or represent those described.

And yet, it is important to point out, as Ruth Behar does, that much of the discussion of ethnographic writing (Geertz's "burden of authorship" [1989] or Clifford's "ethnographic authority" [1988]) seems to ignore that authorship is also a privilege constituted through the gender, race, sociohistorical background, class origins, or class diasporas of the ethnographer doing the writing. All who come to the writing of ethnography do not arrive by means of the same pathways.[8] Behar writes: "We all bring different burdens of memory, different sanctioned ignorances, to the task of writing ethnography. And there is a special burden that authorship carries if you have ever occupied a borderland place in the dominant culture, especially if you were told at some point in your life that you didn't have what it takes to be an authority on, an author of, anything. It means writing without entitlement, without permission" (1993, 340).

The contestation that has led to the crisis in representation is not only about the inequalities of social power arrangements, but also about the implicit authority and privilege that have historically accrued to certain social subjects. The possibility of reproducing colonial, class, and gender domination in academic writing has led to widespread doubts, especially among feminists, about the legitimacy and advisability of women in dominant social positions (for example, white, middle-class, Canadian) researching, representing or writing about women in other, presumably subordinate social positions (Asian, working-class, Black, immigrant).[9] As Aihwa Ong states, much as feminists may try to make the writer-informant relationship more equitable, in using the stories of women less privileged than themselves, feminists will probably gain more from the encounter in terms of their careers and the extension of their academic authority than will informants (1995, 353). Negotiating the political dimensions of the crisis in representation, therefore, forces a recognition of the power differentials between researcher and researched that taunts even the best-intentioned research. It compels those who attempt to write of the experiences of others to ask, as Yezierska did about her own writing in quite a different time and context, "[W]hat is the difference between a potbellied boss who exploits the labor of helpless workers and an author who grows rich writing of the poor?" (1950, 133). And can there be, after all, an adequate response, when an informant says, as Mai said to me as we walked through the library thesis stacks of the Ontario Institute for Studies in Education, in yet another of my only semisuccessful attempts to provide a tangible answer to Lely's question "[W]hy do you want to know all this?": "Well, when you become a Dr. and get rich, you'll forget all about us" (FN 06/29/95).

RESEARCH GEOGRAPHIES

How do I begin to draw the map of a research project built on the precarious terrain of a femininity in constant danger of failure and an ethnography that is not in mastery of itself? Where do I find words that, however, imperfectly, begin to recount my travels through research territories and landscapes of thought that are impossible to fully know or represent? While calls for accountability in knowledge production demand a critical mapping out of the space in which the ethnographic experience unfolds, to narrate such a story usually requires imposing a structure, a vision that not only was not always perceivable by me while doing the project itself but continues to slip and slide within and between the cracks and crevices of the ethnographic enterprise, critical feminist agendas, and issues of authority, representation, regulation, and normativity. The pathways through this project—my own and those used by the girls who participated—are as a result impossible to retrace.

While I will return to these issues in the final section of this chapter, here I attempt such a retracing, even while recognizing the impossibility of doing so. Reconstructing the history and ecology of the ethnographic space in which this project unfolded seems particularly consequential since, as Frazer points out (1992, 104), the process of experiencing, understanding, and talking about femininity continues in and is shaped by the research process, just as it is shaped by school, family, and all the other social contexts of girls' lives. Thus, I begin again at the beginning with the school-community committee, the problem, the program that provided the grounds for an ethnographic encounter, and a story of the girls on whose experience this book rests.

Rather than generating yet another program that would not attract participants, the school-community planning committee settled on a two-phase approach to the problem. Students would be consulted through a series of focus groups and the outcomes from these groups would, in turn, be used to develop a program. In order to familiarize students and researcher with each other and the researcher with the school environment, classroom observations were also suggested. As a result, for the first six months of the program I found myself, notebook in hand, in Mr. White's grade five/six classroom on every Wednesday afternoon, working at establishing relationships with the girls in this class.

In clusters of three, four, or five I occasionally took a group of girls to the Blue Room to discuss the school project, how it might be organized, when it should take place, and who should be involved and to elicit their ideas for a program they might be interested in working on together. Some suggested that the program should be for girls only, and others that it should be for both boys and girls, that it should be for the students in their class alone and that it should involve the whole school, and that it should start immediately rather than waiting for September. There were suggestions that we could do a play about stopping violence and that we could present it at the school's annual spring concert; a series of posters with pictures and messages against taking drugs, smoking, and drinking; a television commercial with a song about racism or making fun of people; a telephone peer support line; a club with matching T-shirts and other club insignia. There were even fundraising ideas for the purchasing of the T-shirts: a bake sale, a raffle, or a car wash. "We have lots of good ideas," said a girl whom I will call Julia as we walked back together to her classroom (FN 03/31/93).

Contrary to the warnings I had received from the school staff about the difficulties I would have in engaging the girls in discussion, I found most of them quite willing and even eager to talk. Undoubtedly this was partially due to the opportunity it afforded them to get out of lesson time to meet with me. But, from my first day in their classroom there were also invitations to me by some of the girls to sit beside them in classes (FN 02/24/93). When permitted they would also move from their regular seats to sit with me at the table I occupied at the back of the class. In March, I had the dubious honor of having a character in the story one girl was writing, a shooting victim, named after me (FN 04/10/93). After a while some of the girls also invited me to join them in their after school activities—by May I was getting more invitations than I could possibly take up.

> As the second bell rang and the class started filing in from lunch break, Lan, Tammy, Jani, Pearl, and Julia each made a point of passing by my chair on the way to their desks to pass on various bits of information and news. Tammy and Julia asked me to stay after school to watch their baseball practices; Lan asked me to watch and/or play a game during afternoon recess and Jani wanted me to watch her baseball practice also during afternoon recess. (FN 05/05/1993)

While here it seems that the desire of the researched to be watched was at least as great as (if not greater than) the ethnographer's desire to watch, not all the girls in that class were as interested in me or my project. Some completely ignored me, and neither before nor after the specific focus group time I arranged to have with them seemed interested in any further interactions with me.

By the following September, some changes had taken place at both the school and the school board. There was a new school principal and a change of staff at the central board office. Funding from the board for phase 2 of the project had been denied. There were more than mere hints of tensions over the project between the remaining initiating teacher and the new principal, which the teacher did not hesitate to make apparent to me, stating that the new administration lacked commitment to the program (FN 10/15/93). The new principal did, however, declare her support for its continuation, thus safeguarding my developing research project, if not the original scope of the program. From that point on the school and board took on a stance that might best be described as one of benign negligence. I was, for the most part, left to my own devices, with the exception of the occasional need to request permission, equipment, or information on school procedures.

The focus groups of the previous school year had furnished me with an idea for a program. That first September this consisted in producing a school magazine. It seemed to me that a magazine not only had the potential of addressing the planning committee's various concerns and my own emergent research interests, but might also be a means of engaging with the many suggestions and issues that the girls had raised in the focus group sessions. Furthermore, although I had not found the apathetic girls that the committee had described, it seemed possible that there was some common ground between the expressed interests of the committee and those of the girls. Might the girls' talk of clubs and shared symbols perhaps be an expression of desire for belonging, for community, and for sites of visibility and recognition? Was this perhaps what was at play in their desire to be watched? Could this be interpreted as an articulation of the requisite conditions for participation in school programs? I saw the magazine as a potential vehicle through which the girls and I might explore these issues and the relationships between themselves, the school, their families, communities, and place in the world.

The first meeting of what was to become known unofficially as the Magazine Group was set for Monday, October 18. Prior to that date all the grade six, seven and eight classes in the school were visited to announce the new program and fly-ers inviting those who were interested in participating were distributed. On the morning of the eighteenth a reminder about the meeting was included among that day's morning announcements over the school's public address system. Among the twenty-one students who showed up at that first meeting were some of the girls I had spent the most time with from Mr. White's class, Mai, her younger sister Tammy, Lan, Tevy, Chantrea, and Karyn. Along with LeLy, who was a new arrival to the school that year, and Trinh, Tammy's best friend, these girls eventually came to form a core of regular participants. However, the group always had something of a permeable border. Participation was voluntary and the group cyclically swelled and shrank in size. At times it was all but abandoned by the girls. Over the two-and-a-half-year period some forty girls peopled the notebooks in which I wrote up my fieldnotes to differing extents.

The magazine project was followed by the production of a video in the sec-ond year of the program. While the magazine had been my idea, the suggestion of making a video came from the girls. Mai, LeLy, and Lan were once again regular participants, as were their classmates Fanny and Kenisha. They were also joined by Maria, a sometime participant from the previous year and from another grade seven/eight class. Thus, while the first year's most frequent members were pri-marily of Asian backgrounds (Chinese, Vietnamese, and Cambodian), the second year saw a more racially diverse group that included girls of Portuguese, Afro-Caribbean, and Anglo backgrounds. Interestingly, in the first year the group was dominated by a loose friendship network of Asian students (all immigrants or refugees to Canada), that did not seem impeded by the differences in ages, grades, or their varied backgrounds, which, due to old national rivalries, have often been found to strain intra-Asian relations within diasporic communities (Espiritu 1992). Some seemed mainly school friends but others also spent considerable time outside school with each other, although the Vietnamese girls sometimes spoke of their parents' warnings against visiting the homes of their Cambodian classmates. But in the second year, grade classification became a very salient issue, with both the grade seven and eight students forming tighter boundaries around themselves, at least for socializing within the school. Significantly, the group of core participants in the second year were mainly from the eighth grade.

In both years many of those who participated in the program considered themselves inhabitors of the margins of the school's social life and at the bottom of its social hierarchy. As often happens in an ethnographic encounter, I established an especially strong and gratifying relationship with a particular individual (Myerhoff 1978, 29). And as also often happens, in addition to being particularly articulate and insightful on the workings of social life within and outside the school, LeLy frequently considered herself something of an outsider, even among this group of outsiders. Their marginalized status in the school is, I think, not an inconsequential detail in accounting for not only how and why these girls came to be participants in this group and in my research project, but also for what the group may have afforded them. As I will substantiate in chapter 4 through a discussion of the social, political, and cultural particularities of school life, opportunities for visibility and recognition were both intensely desired and not necessarily easily come by. What will become clearer in my analysis of the data chapters that follow are the various registers of recognition as a mediating feature of the ecological space of the group.

I met weekly with the girls, increasing to biweekly and daily meetings when at one point the group got too large and divided into two (grade seven and grade eight), or when we were working intensely on a particular activity and rushing to make deadlines. We usually met over their lunch break, which was another contributing factor in the constituency of the group, as some other students went home for lunch and returned only in time for afternoon classes.

Gathering in front of the school office after the bell signalling the break had rung and the girls had collected and distributed lunches from home to younger siblings, or bought sandwiches and pizza from the school canteen, we would make our way up the stairs to the room that had been assigned to us. With the contents of our lunches spread out over a table, we chatted noisily about what was going on in their lives, school and classroom events, social activity, who was going out with whom, family outings, and aggravations.

Then, clearing away the lunch debris, we would pick up from where we had left off on the various projects that eventually would become elements of the magazine and video. Depending on the kind of task and the vagaries of group politics, at times we worked altogether and at others in small groups that often consisted of best friend dyads. I tape recorded many of our lunchtime exchanges and various large and small group discussions, accumulating, I realized only when I began the arduous task of transcription, far more data than was reasonable. This compulsion to capture on tape is, however, attributable to more than the inexperience of an over-zealous ethnographer. As previously suggested, I did not enter into this project in search of data to answer a particular question or to support or oppose a particular theory, hypothesis, or body of literature. Rather, my own thinking about how to study these girls took something of an unconventional form. I simply became curious. And with the magazine and video serving as the vehicle of inquiry, I followed this curiousity through the pathways opened by the issues and concerns raised by the girls. Thus, part of the amassing of data had to do with the indefinition of a research question. When a series of discontinuous epiphanous moments struck, which I will begin to outline momentarily, they determined not which conversations would be recorded—for by then it was too late—but resolved which of the remaining tapes would be transcribed. These primarily included those discussions relating specifically to the five video characters and group conversations that related to the thematics of the characters' stories.

In addition to the group meetings my initial six months of classroom observations in Mr. White's room were followed up by periodic visits throughout the following two years to the various classrooms and activities where participants spent their school days. In the second year of the program most of these classroom observations were spent in Mr. Burns's grade seven/eight class, this being the homeroom for the majority of group members.

While most of our time spent together was at their school, eventually we also spent time outside it. A corner donut shop became a regular after school hangout spot for the group—to continue discussions begun at lunch or to chew over a specific event, like a school dance or a classroom incident that might have taken place that afternoon. Other activities included excursions to the mall for shopping and movies; birthday parties in their homes and trips to Chinatown for celebratory meals in restaurants; the Metro Toronto Reference Library for help with homework assignments; visits to my place and to the university; and winter Saturday afternoons skating at City Hall.

Although such an ethnographic experience is not shaped on equal terms, in characterizing the creation of the space in which this ethnographic study took place I have attempted to depict a process whereby the girls, like the ethnographer, were also actors and agents. As Kondo suggests, "[I]nformants are not simply inert objects for the free play of the ethnographer's desire" (1986, 80). Rather, the negotiation of reality that takes place in the doing of ethnography involves complex and shifting relations of power, in which the ethnographer acts but is also acted upon. Understanding is multiple, plurivocal, and pervaded by relations of power on the part of both researcher and researched. Not only did the ethnographic space we inhabited emerge through various negotiatings and maneuverings within these relations, my research questions did as well.

Epiphany

In hindsight, the significance of processes of identification and disidentification with the discursive and social practices of femininity surfaced as an issue to be reckoned with almost from the outset of the project. This is not to say that it was at this same time that I recognized it as the frame around which this book would be written. That would not happen until much later.

The magazine, as I have already outlined, was originally conceived as a mechanism by which I, as project facilitator, might attempt to combine my own goals, those of the program planning committee, and the expressed interest of the girls. This juggling act, as I discovered early on in the discussions with the girls about the kind of magazine we would produce, was not one that would be easy to balance.

For the planning committee, the key to the program's success was premised on the students' participation in identifying their own needs, designing and implementing a plan of action, and being largely in control of the final product. "Empowerment," "having a voice," and developing a sense of "can do," were all catch phrases that went around the room when the planning committee outlined its goals. My own desires for the magazine included creating a forum in which we might explore possibilities for girls' lives that would go beyond the established "getting and keeping a man" of dominant ideologies of feminine subjectivity found within teen magazines and other cultural products directed at girls (Kearney 1998; McRobbie 1991; Scanlon 1998). However, it became clear that my own agenda of producing a magazine that would be both feminist and critical in outlook clashed with the interests of the girls at our very first meeting.

When asked what kinds of things they wanted to work on, they responded with what they were familiar with in the teen magazines they read, fashion, makeup tips, entertainment, surveys, and so forth. Having anticipated this response I had come prepared with some copies of *New Moon*, an American noncommercial magazine published as a feminist alternative to teen magazines. Many of the articles were written by girls of about their own age. What I had not anticipated was the girls' complete and immediate dismissal and disinterest in even looking at *New Moon*, never mind considering using it as a model of what could be produced by our group.

If I was to adhere to the premises laid out by the planning committee that the program must be student initiated and controlled, then my feminist, critical project was in danger of being subsumed by the girls' desire to reproduce media forms that reinforce power relationships, stereotypes, and the objectification of women. Yet, the mere reproduction of these media forms (assuming we could even come close to achieving the look of a teen magazine) would surely be counter to the goal of empowerment that was the impetus for the program in the first place.

Attempting to salvage my project, I asked the girls to bring in copies of the magazines they do read and arranged a few extra sessions with them, so that together we might look through these and some other feminist teen magazines I found that more closely resembled the style and format of the commercial products they were familiar with. I analyze these discussions in depth elsewhere (Gonick 1997). What is important to highlight here is that it was through this exercise, where the girls once again rejected the feminist magazines in favor of those that presented a more hegemonic femininity, that I began to focus my investigative attention on how it is that girls as female/feminine subjects "are gradually, progressively, really and materially constituted through a multiplicity of organisms, forces, energies, materials, desires, thoughts etc" (Foucault 1972, 97). It inspired me to ask, as Foucault suggests, how things work at the level of ongoing subjugation, at the level of those continuous and uninterrupted processes which subject our bodies, govern our gestures, and dictate our behaviors. For as we talked about the different features of the various magazines, it seemed that the girls' stated likes and dislikes were organized by the meanings they made of the different images of femininity presented. Their reading practices were partially structured around wanting to be or not wanting to be like the kinds of girls they understood the magazines' pictures and texts to portray. Thus, the shifting relations of power between researcher and researched necessitated a renegotiation of the sort of magazine we would produce, shaping the discursive history of the group to focus on a concern with the varying discourse structures of femininity.

Moreover, these shifting relations also figured in the developing ecology of the ethnographic space. Since participating was always a voluntary endeavor, it was clear to me that my success at attracting and holding onto "my" research participants would depend, in no small measure, on a shared negotiation of how this space would be organized. While we undoubtedly had different uses for the group and different pleasures and investments in it, their involvement in defining what purposes it might serve them, how they themselves would operate while in it, what we would produce there, as well as who should occupy it rendered the ecology of this space as somewhat unique within the school structure.

Here they are working on one such definition:

1 Tammy: When we're sad we come here and we always laugh.
2 LeLy: I know.
3 Tammy: No, when we're mad or sad or anything we could come
             here.

4	Trinh:	And when we're tired—
5	Mai:	Or we have a bad day.
6	LeLy:	Like last time, right? Miss Kirk call us a bum and we really wanted to come here and have fun, like scream everything out—
7	Trinh:	let our anger come out.
8	LeLy:	Yeah, like you have a knot inside that you have to untie or something.
9	Marnina:	It's important to let it out.
10	LeLy:	Umm, that's why we like to come here. (Trans. 05/21/94)

Conjuring it up as they go along, they are clearly in the process of inventing a specific kind of space for themselves. Their desire appears to be seasoned with both a certain longing and insistence. While the physical "here" they are referring to in the transcript is my apartment, where we met on a few occasions to work on our project, the claims they are making might be construed as one of their terms for the ethnographic space and the forms of relations between us. It is a place that is explicitly distinguished from the rational space of the classroom, as one of and for expression—expression of their emotions—a place for sadness, anger and laughter (1, 3, 4, 6, 7). The issue of space is a complicated one in the lives of women, as Kathleen Rockhill states: "The issue of space—the lack of space . . . is [complex] because our lives are not allowed to take up space. That is to say, we have no space in part because we are seen and see ourselves as having no right to take up space" (1987, 319).

This sense of lack of space has both material and metaphysical dimensions and in the context of the girls' discussion, both may have been factors in their invention. They often complained of a general lack of physical space—home was regularly described as cramped, where adult demands for order and quiet took precedence. At school, the general lack of provisions made for girls was cited on numerous occasions as our efforts to secure a room for exclusive group use, as well as for occasional access to a computer and video equipment, were frustrated over and over.[10] Certainly within the organization of official classroom time and activity little latitude exists for the kinds of unbounded expression that they are claiming here. Nor does it seem a possibility even within the semisocial spaces organized within the school, like the group M.C. Stars. At one meeting I attended the group was in the process of organizing a student design contest for the badges that would be sold as entrance tickets to a dance they were planning for Anti-Racism day. Miss Wright, who was facilitating the meeting, spoke at length and students participated after they had put their hands up and been acknowledged by her, directing their comments at her, much like in a classroom. I marvelled at the contrast in group process. Here they worked efficiently through the lunch hour, everyone arriving on time, sitting in their seats throughout the meeting, the discussion never wavering off the official agenda. But the difference between the ecology of this group and that of the magazine group struck me most forcefully as I watched Tammy, who was sitting next to me, delicately taking the wrapping off her sandwich so as not to make any noise, grimacing guiltily when the wax paper unavoidably rustled momentarily (FN 10/05/94).

Lack of physical space seems to be coupled with a related shortage of what, for want of a better term, I am calling metaphysical space. That is space in which one's expressions of what Foucault (1984) terms "technologies of self," or the instrumental means and practices of self-action, as understood historically, are recognized by others. Here, in the girls' terms of reference, perhaps the expression of emotion is one such technology of self. However, to be actualized as such requires recognition from another and when this is denied, these expressions are not allowed to take up space. It is also possible that it is due to a lack of space within the discourses of normative femininity that the expression of these "technologies of self" are stifled.

From my perspective, it often seemed that the girls used the space as a means of practicing ways of being female in public discourse and as an opportunity to find out how others would react, through conversation, loud disagreements, lewd talk, vicious insults, and providing support for each others' creative ideas, in short, what Macpherson and Fine (1995) call ways to "try on" varied ways of being women.

While the space would not have existed were it not for my project, in the context of the group discussions, I was not the only audience for their words, stories, and performance of selves. The space seemed to provide them with an opportunity to ask each other questions about their experiences, to explore samenesses and differences, as well as to check, compare, share, and make meaning together of this experience. The circuits of recognition operating in the group were used to position themselves as certain kinds of girls within and beyond the group setting, not only in relation to me, but also in relation to each other. There were times when I was clearly not the principal addressee of their talk at all. As Kenisha once indicated, when I asked her to wait to have her say, since I wanted to be able to hear everyone and the group discussion had become completely chaotic, "I'm talking to Fanny, I'm not talking to you" (Trans. 05/30/95).

In the following conversation Samantha and Elsa use the group discussion we are having about the music video "WHATAMAN" by Salt-N-Pepa, which we had viewed together and the girls had interpreted to be about how men treat women, to launch into a collaborative working through of this issue in their own experiences.

| Samantha: | . . . okay, agree with me if this is true okay? If they're fighting, right? My dad will say, "I don't want to fight with you" and he'll start walking away and then as soon as my mom lets it rest, he'll come back to her, and he'll go, "Well the nerve!" like he just thought of something to say to get her mad. And they'll start fighting again. |
| Elsa: | [laughs] Yeah! My dad comes home drunk, right? And than he starts arguing with my mom, he goes [in a deep voice] "How come you didn't put my tea on?" and he didn't even say anything to my mom. Then he starts fighting. (Trans. 02/07/95) |

Seeking consensus between themselves on how difficult men can be, they negotiate meaning about what might well be the very confusing behavior of and interactions between mothers and fathers—men and women. Agreeing on the irrationality of their fathers' conduct—an irrationality that for them both verges on the frustratingly ridiculous and seems to elicit a tinge of fear—they appear to mobilize a sense of themselves as women.

While the space in which our ethnographic encounter unfolded was indeed shared and shaped by both researcher and researched, it was not an uncontested one. Differences of opinion surfaced not only about what kind of product the group should produce, but also about who were and were not legitimate group members. This became something of an explosive issue as the group planned our first public event, a photo shoot of models for the fashion section of the magazine. Beyond the significance the event held for the success of our work together, it was also seen as a potential site in which to secure some visibility for themselves within the school. Perhaps even more importantly it promised a means of winning the attention of the popular crowd, who the girls hoped would be drawn by the prospect of modelling.

At that time, a very regular and reliable core group had formed, Mai, LeLy, Tammy, and Trinh, all of Asian backgrounds. More recently two Anglo girls, Lizzie and Sarah, had begun to take an interest in the group's activities and had begun to attend regularly. Their involvement gave Julia, who was Portuguese and a sometime participant, more access to the group. I was initially pleased with the newcomers. Lizzie in particular had excellent writing skills and a wild imagination, both assets for the production of a magazine (and a research subject). I had also had ongoing concerns about the small size of the group, both in terms of how the program would be evaluated by the school's administration, as well as in terms of the numbers of research subjects it provided me. The three newcomers would almost double the size of the group. Mai, LeLy, Tammy, and Trinh, however, were less than enthusiastic about their presence. Not only were there social divisions within the school between the Asian students on the one side, and the Portuguese and Anglo students on the other, but it seemed a history of tensions existed as well, between particular individuals. As we spent intensive time together, meeting every day in the time leading up to the shoot, these tensions started to smoulder and then erupt.

Although there had been many disagreements and rowdy arguments, we had managed to complete most of the elaborate preparations for the event. On the day before the shoot was to take place, we spent our time together decorating backdrops for three photo scenes they had planned. Before the work could be completed, however, the bell rang and as they dispersed to their various classrooms, the girls decided they would return to finish the work after school. I left to attend my own classes that afternoon, uncertain about how successful the next day's event would be but fairly confident that everything would be ready, only to discover when I got home much later that night a series of three or four messages on my answering machine indicating all had not gone well. Left at intervals throughout the evening by the group of four, the messages were elaborate pronouncements about not only the disasters that had occurred that afternoon, but also threats that I was in danger of losing my only reliable participants. Each succeeding message was a variation of the first, although with some diminishing intensity. Here, in part, is the first one, a call the girls made on their way home from school from a pay phone at the local laundromat, before retreating together to Tammy and Mai's house to await my return call.

Tammy: Marnina? If Lizzie's gonna stay, then me, Trinh, LeLy, and Mai is not going to be there. We're gonna quit, because she has a bad attitude—she messed the stuff, everything fell down.
Trinh: [in the background] We're mad!
Tammy: And we're mad! If she's going to be in it, we're going to quit! . . . And about Julia—she can't join because she didn't even plan anything. We're the ones that did the hard work and now she's joining and we don't want her to join. And now if Lizzie's going to stay then we'll quit! Can you phone? Okay, bye.

This ultimatum begins to capture the intense intricacies of loyalty, territory, debt, and dependence that inform the layered interactions of researcher and researched, structuring our ongoing choosings of each other, and shaping the developing ecology of the ethnographic space. Within the school's social and racial divisions and hierarchical systems, one that is not separate from those in the larger Canadian context, the girls are laying claim to what they considered their territory, earned by their hard work and long-term commitment to the project. They had demonstrated a certain loyalty to me and the project and, when coexistence became untenable, were demanding a return of this loyalty to them on my part by insisting that I choose between them and the newcomers.

This episode also points to some of the possible consequences of organizing a school research project around group work. While I was an observer in Mr. White's class, a number of individuals, including some boys, actively sought me out. Once I became affiliated with a particular group of students through the program this kind of seeking out almost totally ceased. As a result, my access to potential research subjects was limited due to the ways in which social divisions and hierarchies were organized within the school.

Beyond the numerous kinds of debts and dependencies incurred on both sides of the researcher/researched divide, there is something more than my need for their participation and their willingness to participate, to share their stories, and their remarkable reliability that this test of mutual commitment bespeaks about the complex and changing forms of relations, discourse, and conduct this space engendered. It also underscores the ways in which the space evolved into one that did not perform a unidirectional empowering of researched by researcher, but rather, into one in which shifting relations of power generated multiple layers of reciprocal returns.

When we met as a group for the last time, after the video had been completed and the school year marking their graduation from middle school was coming to an end, we improvised a small ceremony to also acknowledge the end of our work together. Sitting around a table, not at the school but on Centre Island amidst the remains of our picnic lunch, we took turns speaking about the meanings the group carried and the ecology of the space in our lives.

LeLy: I learned a lot from this group. A lot. I don't mean in
                   school work or anything, but in personal life. . . .
Mai: Okay me. Last year we had too much people, right? And
                   we're not really close to them. So this year, we talked a
                   lot more about how we feel and school work and guys
                   and stuff like that and you're a good friend, cause you're
                   listening to us talk and understand us—
LeLy: when Mai mentioned the word "friend," like I don't re-
                   ally, I don't really understand how the way our rela-
                   tions work, right? Was it like, you're like, you told me
                   last time that you were coming here for doing research
                   and stuff. You're more like, we're a book. Like a book
                   to you. Is it?

Marnina:	Hmmm. Well, I guess the thing is it's not that easy to separate. It's both; it's not just my research but it's not just friends either.
LeLy:	Yeah, cause I was getting sort of confused—
Marnina:	it is confusing-
LeLy:	cause you know sometimes like you're coming here to do research and than it feels like we're the book and you're researching from the book. But sometimes, I was wondering like if we're the book to you, why would you go places with us, like movies and stuff, you know? It's sort of confused in my mind. Go Maria. I talk too much. I should shut up.
Maria:	[speaking slowly] All I can say is that [sighs] it has been friends. There were times when it was important, like some of the things we discussed are really important to me. And there were other times when we had lots of fun and I really enjoyed being here, with everyone. Now I know I have some really good friends. And I have and [pauses] I enjoyed talking to you, you listening to us and—

. . .

Kenisha:	I just came to the school. I don't know any people and it was fun. I learned some things and some things was very important. I think I was pretty interested and I had a lot of fun with you guys and with you.
Mai:	We would never have known each other if it wasn't for you, right? We wouldn't be that close to each other—
LeLy:	yeah, we wouldn't know each other.
Mai:	But we have to grow up, find new people.
Marnina:	Things are going to change. But I think what Maria said was really important too. You have good friends here and even though you might be at different schools next year there are ways to stay in touch. [Maria begins to cry.]
Mai:	Maria, don't worry, just cry, just cry and let everything [inaudible] . . . like those good time, lots of good times. We'll see each other, you know like over the summer, don't worry. Think.
Maria:	[sobbing] It will never be like before. It will be different.

. . .

Mai:	We don't live far from each other, you know. Right, Maria? It's not just Marnina. Probably we're never going to have a group like this.
LeLy:	If you want a group you can make one, you know.
Maria:	[still crying] Not the same. It'll never be the same.

Marnina: No, not the same, but it could still be good. Maybe you
                  could think again about starting groups in your new
                  schools. I mean, I know we talked about this already and
                  you didn't think it would work, but maybe there is a way
                  we can come up with some ideas together to make it
                  happen. (Trans. 06/30/95)

Passionate and ambivalent, these renderings of the group's varied meanings
evoke a sense of the unique ecological space it held in the lives of those of us who
inhabited it. Its constituent features are, however, not easily reconcilable, learning, feelings, understanding, talking, listening, fun, and friendship on the one
hand and research on the other. While the initial responses of LeLy, Mai, Kenisha, and Maria are structured as definitions of the individual returns they
gleaned from the time spent together, LeLy also problematizes the feasibility of
harmonizing the various constituent elements, upsetting any taken-for- granted-
ness of innocence in my presence in their lives. Her intervention suggests that the
question of returns must be mediated by the terms of the researcher-researched relationship. This, however, proves difficult to pin down, precisely because the role
of the researcher is an ambiguous one.

Rather than a distinct role, "researcher" draws on other cultural roles, like
that of friend, teacher, expert (Frazer 1992, 103). In the context of this project my
role as researcher was, perhaps, even further muddied by my function as group facilitator, keeping me juggling competing definitions of appropriate behavior and at
times confusing both the girls and myself.

Paradoxically, it was also this very ambiguity that permitted a certain manifestation of returns for both researcher and researched. They initiated activities
and generously included me in their plans and also thoughtfully extended invitations to school functions they thought might be of interest to me. This made my
work easier and helped to ease my conscience around the intrusions that seem an
inherent aspect of research. They also, no doubt, had their own purposes in mind.
The enlisting of my presence for outings meant use of free movie passes with the
accompaniment of a (paying) adult, access to my driver's license as ID for skate
rentals, the pretence of a school outing (since a "teacher" would be present), and
thus permission from parents to go out with friends.

The various ways in which the friends/researcher formulation is opera-
tionalized in the discussion above also highlights something further about the
ecology of the space and returns that go beyond the individualized. Not merely an
observer of a prior existing space, it was my presence as group facilitator that produced it. This orchestrated effort created opportunities for friendships which, as
both LeLy and Mai suggest, were unlikely to have existed otherwise: "We would
never have known each other if it wasn't for you." However, it is not quite accurate

to say they would not have known each other were it not for the group. With the exception of Maria, they shared a homeroom, and had even been assigned adjoining seats in the same cluster of desks there. Both grade eight classes were brought together every day for classes in French, geography, music or family studies, so Maria and the other girls would have been familiar with each other on this basis. Within the context of this school, however, it was not common for girls whose backgrounds were Asian, Afro-Caribbean, Portuguese, and Anglo to associate with each other, and certainly not in this profoundly intimate way. What marks this space as unique is, therefore, in part the opportunity for conversation across racial difference that actually engages with this difference.

With the prospect of the group's approaching disbandment, the issue shifts from the dependence of the space for its existence on my presence to the loss of the group as a collective entity: "It's not just Marnina," Mai attempts to comfort Maria. "Probably we're never going to have a group like this." It is a recognizing of the uniqueness of the space in their lives and the value it held. For through the work we did there together the girls seemed to forge a sense of belonging with which they were able to negotiate and contest their positions in the margins as women, as outsiders in the social world of the school, and as immigrants in Canadian society. Within the confines of the group, perceived injustices suffered at the hands of teachers, parents, other family members, friends, and enemies were a regular feature of the discussion.

In some sense these conversations can be viewed as being about a forging of a certain kind of belonging for me as well. I was aware (and often overwhelmed at the thought) that these conversations would travel beyond the confines of the school classrooms, donut shops, and playgrounds where they occurred and into the texts that I would eventually produce. For me, it was a space in which to explore feminist questions about femininity, power, the relationships between them, and social change. I also attempted to use this space to interrogate the research processes with which I was involved and was often prompted to do so by some of the girls, particularly LeLy. As her questions, "Why do you want to know all this?" and "What are we to you?" demonstrate, she was also engaged in actively interpreting and trying to make meaning of me, the ethnographer. The questions created an ethnographic space in which I was pushed to examine and explain my own practices and she could similarly both teach and learn. There were, in fact, many such moments between us—moments in which her question resignified my position, as well as her own. In hindsight, the space I attempted to create might be described as one in which I could, as a reader of what others did, question how that experience was structured, how it performed certain repetitions, certain problems, certain desires, and how what was constituted as experience was reminiscent of the available and normative discourses of femininity.

The geographies of research in which ethnographic stories unfold are territories that are always overdetermined by the relations of power that exist within a given social sphere, but they are also negotiated, invented, fought over, shaped, and shared by both researcher and researched. Relatedly, the particular process through which knowledge is produced might also be considered one that occurs and is determined within a similar dynamic. I turn now to a discussion of the specifics of my research methodology and a consideration of some of the ways in which knowledge may be seen to be constructed and coproduced by researcher and researched.

TEXT, TALK, AND VIDEOTAPE: RESEARCH METHODOLOGY AS FEMINIST PEDAGOGY

My inquiry into the discourse structures of femininity stems from a feminist interest in social change with an agenda for multiplying, diversifying, and transforming the possibilities for girls' and women's lives. For like Daisy Goodwill, the heroine of Carol Shield's award-winning 1993 novel, *The Stone Diaries*, I have also noticed that of the stories available for living life as a girl/woman, most seem to restrict rather than expand the realization of human capacity. She says, "Men it seemed to me in those days, were uniquely honoured by the stories that erupted in their lives, whereas women were more likely to be smothered by theirs. Why? Why should this be? Why should men be allowed to strut under the privilege of their life adventures, wearing them like a breastful of medals, while women went all grey and silent beneath the weight of theirs?" (121).

It is not, as I have already suggested, the "why" part of Daisy's question that I am interested in here. Feminists have spent the last several decades answering precisely that. Rather, like Jane Clifford of Gail Godwin's *The Odd Woman*, who "ransacks novels for answers to life," "only to find that survival depends on eluding already-written stories" (50), it is the related question of the linkage between stories and lives that I am curious about. What are the kinds of stories that girls turn life into, the kinds of lives that girls turn stories into? How do these stories interface with possible formations of gendered subjectivity? What are the ways in which this greyness, this smothering and diminishment might be recast so as to bring about the conditions under which new story lines will successfully invert and break the bounds of the old (Davies 1992, 58), creating the possibility for "something else to be" (Morrison 1973, 52)?

Definitions of what it is to be successfully female develop in particular historical and cultural contexts. However, rather than being seen as discursively constituted, gendered subjectivity is generally seen, according to Davies, "as belonging to, coming from and signifying one's essential self" (1993, 74). Since they are usually understood as the transparent medium through which real worlds may be seen and represented, discourses and their attendant storylines are taken up as one's own in ways that are not usually visible. On one level the methodological challenge of this project is, therefore, how to make visible the identificatory practices which girls use in their ongoing construction of stories about themselves as Woman (a cultural and social object), those identifications which are made but then rejected or denied, and the means through which alternative, resistant, constructions of self, woman, and knowledge might be engaged. The challenge, on another level, is to do so while juggling the libratory intentions of a critical feminist agenda, regulative disciplinary conventions, the limitations of an epistemology of experience, and the struggle for a noninnocent stance.

While the latter set of concerns will be revisited in the next section of this chapter, I concentrate here on the former, which consists of two related issues, how the reading of identificatory practices might be accomplished, and a consideration of what kinds of interventions a critical feminist interest in social change might employ.

As I have previously mentioned, the group's production of the magazine and video served the dual function of both providing a forum in which the girls could explore issues that were of importance to them and consequently also the means by which the questions that are raised in this book were generated. However, through an often chaotic process of group discussion, reading of other cultural texts, and writing, the creation of the magazine and video also served as the methodological tools used to address both concerns mentioned above. Thus, what I am suggesting is that the ethnographic space, where what was being practised were various ways of being women, also became the very space for both the production of the research problem and an opportunity for the method. Demonstrating as Simon and Dippo argue that since "all methods are ways of asking questions which presume an underlying set of assumptions, a structure of relevance, and a form of rationality" (1986, 195), every form of methodology embeds some conception of the research problem and vice-versa.

Writing, suggests Gilbert and Taylor, is not a natural and personal response of the self, but is rather a learned social discursive practice of a gendered subject (1991, 42). Writing is thus acknowledged to be about taking up a particular speaking position in a discourse, and then bringing certain subject positions into existence: "It is a way of making theory in gender, of making a politics of everyday life, thereby re-writing the ethnic female subject as a site of difference" (Trinh 1989, 44). Similarly, writing the stories of the five female video characters and the dramatization of each of their specific dilemmas or issues made this bringing of certain subject positions into existence particularly clear. I use the characters' stories and the process by which they were created as a means to uncover the complex, contradictory, and textured structure of the discourses available to girls through which to negotiate their identities. These discourses—of gender, sexuality, race, nationality, ethnicity, class, and age—find expression in the unfolding of the problems or issues that are the focus for the events in the characters' stories. Each of the characters, then, may be seen to represent the articulation of a position or series of positions within the various narratives currently in circulation that constitute girls as beings with specificity. Taken together, the video characters' stories may be read as a discourse map of femininity which lays out multiple positions that are charted through the characters' distinct qualities. Thus, a certain kind of intelligibility emerges about the different identificatory possibilities offered by these narratives through the ways in which characters may be seen to occupy these various positions.

To compose a work, as Rachel Blau DuPlessis puts it, "is to negotiate with these questions, what stories can be told? How can plots be resolved? What is felt to be narratable by both literary and social convention?" (1985, 3). Writing in a group situation meant that the trying out of the various subject positions offered through narrative was a doubled process. Power, desire, gender, sexuality, race, nationality, culture, and class as the mediating ingredients for producing different forms of being women were struggled over by the group, both on behalf of the fictional video characters, as well as on their own behalfs within the politics of the group's dynamics. This double process positioned me in such a way as to be able to ask, What are the acceptable notions of female gendered identity being produced? What are the set of identifications the girls deem necessary to be recognized as successfully female? And how are these diverse positionings made variously available to different girls?

Discussion was one of our main group activities. Often loud and rowdy, sometimes intensely emotional, this talk produced many contradictory statements and positions on the various topics discussed. Reporting on what any girl or group of girls believe about any particular issues is, therefore, rendered impossible both pragmatically and epistemologically. As Frazer points out, a methodology using closed-schedule questionnaires or even in-depth interviews is more likely to elicit from respondents a unitary and articulated opinion, attitude, or belief (1992, 99). The discussion group elicited, instead, an uncertain negotiation of alternative positions which frequently remained unresolved. In refusing a position of straight reportage, my analytic stance is one that protests that there is even a fixed set of beliefs to report on. Instead I offer a theorizing of meandering discursive positions articulated in fantasy and in talk. In this way I seek to link the confrontation of the self-other relationship with an epistemological set of questions about theory and ethnography.

This rather messy methodology works against the positioning and representation of experience as seamless. It renders impossible a reading of the struggle involved in producing experience as something other than disorderly, discontinuous, and chaotic. Our discussions were in effect often narrations of experience. In particular the work on the video characters—the struggle to produce a character whose personality, background, and problem fit together—made visible the very work involved in creating experience as seamless and coherent.

To prepare for our own productions, I brought in a variety of teen magazines and blank tapes and encouraged the girls to record the television and radio programs and music and dance videos they watched at home. We looked at and listened to these together. My original intention had been to use these materials simply as a means to generate discussion about what we might consider for our productions. However, I discovered, after some pretty abysmal attempts at trying to initiate discussion by simply coming to the group with a list of topics, that these texts were an excellent medium for talking about and analyzing discourses of femininity. They provoked some of our most interesting discussions and proved to be a useful pedagogical tool for raising questions about the ways in which femininity is constructed through and represented in these texts, as well as how these representations inspire our ideas and beliefs.

Reading a cultural text, suggest Gilbert and Taylor, can be seen as a kind of dialogue between the text and a socially situated reader. A particular text will be read in relation to others—television programs, advertisements, magazines, and films—and also in the context of the everyday social relations of the viewer (1991, 47). Reading these texts, and the tellings which they provoked—personal stories of comparable events, similar stories they had read, heard, or seen elsewhere—provided an opportunity for the group to analyze both representational cultural texts and lived social relations. Using these as a form of both methodology and pedagogy meant that not only were some of the girls' cultural perspectives and the frameworks which they use to make sense of themselves taken into account, but that since they were much more familiar with this material than I was, something of a renegotiation of positions of competence and authority could take place between us.

The nature of our productions also helped to decentralize notions of expertise. The production of both a magazine and a video are cooperative enterprises for which a range of different skills are needed, creating a variety of ways in which participation might occur. To some extent the girls had greater skills and familiarity with the video camera than I did, since a few of their families had one at home. On the technical side, Kenisha became very adept at figuring out which wires had come loose or buttons needed readjusting, as the somewhat less than state-of-the-art school equipment repeatedly broke down. The girls seemed to enjoy this reversal of expert roles, commenting, "Look, Kenisha's teaching the teacher—again!" We all took turns doing the camera work and LeLy found this the aspect of production she particularly enjoyed. She worked hard on getting the right angle for the shot, playing with light and texture. Maria, who in relation to some of the other participants had, throughout many of the preparatory discussions, often been one of the more quiet and subdued group members, thrilled at her role as the flamboyant Crystal. Parading through the set, she conceived a possible future for herself on the stage.

As Cameron points out, doing this kind of a project with students requires that feminist researchers pay attention to both the research process as well as the research product (1992, 121). While this book may not be immediately accessible and quite possibly of absolutely no interest to the girls, both the magazine and the video were fully available to them. Everyone who participated received her own copy of both. Even so, the process of discussion and analysis was an important part of what we achieved together and may, in fact, be of more significance than what we actually produced.

Through critical and collaborative work a form of conversation evolved among us as a group that allowed us to engage in what Macpherson and Fine call "collective consciousness work" as a form of feminist methodology (1995, 201). Using such an approach, they argue, participants may engage in interpreting their own experiences in ways that reveal how these experiences have been shaped and influenced within and by social, cultural, political, and economic spheres of society. Part of the task of feminist work with girls is, according to Hudson, to create a space in which they might express their own experiential knowledge (1984, 52). Such a space may not only serve the purpose of struggling over what counts as legitimate knowledge, but also is an opportunity to engage with girls' experience in a practice that is both affirmative and critical (Giroux and McLaren 1992).

From my perspective, perhaps the most important achievement of the project—possibly the only one—was the group's developing ability to engage with each other in this kind of conversation. Within the context of this particular school, as I have already suggested and the girls acknowledged, it would not have been common for girls of different backgrounds to have talked to each other at all, and certainly not in this way and about these issues. I like to think that through this research approach, our group was eventually able to work, as Roman suggests, "towards a dialogic community that recognizes cultural differences and inequalities of power while nurturing democratic rapport and communication" (1993, 303).

The process of collectively analyzing the ways in which femininity is constructed at a personal level within a network of gendered social practices was a means through which the girls could become analysts of their own cultural and social practices. As Fine (1994) suggests, using this kind of methodology, rather than one using individual interviews, opens up the possibility of working to counter the myths of an individualized adolescence. It is an opportunity to forge a set of connections between personal experiences and political structures; across races, cultures, ages, and nationalities; and within an invented space, cramped between the discourses of normative femininity; and perhaps for some, a growing sense of how things might be otherwise.

Recent discussions of critical feminist pedagogy continue to highlight the difficulties involved in challenging gender relations (Davies 1989 and 1993; Gilbert and Taylor 1991; Harper 1995; Kenway and Willis 1998; Walkerdine 1990). Given the complexities involved in the construction of femininity and the power and pervasiveness of gender ideologies at personal and social levels, it is not surprising that effective challenges are difficult to identify and put into practice. Reconstructing femininity in new ways is difficult because it involves not only deconstructing dominant ideologies but also confronting investments in normative discourses of femininity.

Our group discussions about the discourses of femininity found within the cultural texts we read, as well as in lived experience, could be construed as an attempt to deconstruct these discourses. Through these discussions a questioning process was initiated about not only how gender, race, nationality, sexuality, and class shape our own subjectivities, but also how these categories are generally understood as natural and inevitable. Informed by aspects of critical theory, these strategies are a means of exploring how social forces shape subjectivity and how these processes can be challenged through critical reflection and action. As Giroux suggests, critical reflection may be useful as a strategy to reconceive the ways in which everyday taken-for-granted common sense practices that are usually treated as givens "must be viewed within historical and social relations that are produced and socially constructed" (1984, 322).

Similarly, Shor writes of the importance of helping students to "extra-ordinarily" reexperience the ordinary. He makes the important point that, though his critical pedagogy is situated in the themes and experiences of the students, the aim is not merely to exploit or endorse the given but seek to transcend it, "[W]e gain a distance from the given by abstracting it from its familiar surroundings and studying it in unfamiliar ways, until our perceptions of it and society are challenged" (1987, 104).

Taylor suggests that in addition to these strategies of critique and deconstruction, a pedagogy with an agenda for social change should include the opportunity for students to become cultural producers in their own right. Such a program offers the possibility for students to play with dominant cultural representations and become involved in producing new alternative versions (1993, 139). This may be a useful way in which to complement strategies for change within the broader political, economic, and social structures. For as Alice Walker suggests, "[T]he absence of models in literature as in life . . . is an occupational hazard for the artist, simply because models in art, in behaviour, in growth of spirit and intellect— even if rejected—enrich and enlarge one's view of existence" (1983, 4).

Writing new visions, selves, and subjectivities into being was not a task that was easily accomplished within the group. Competing agendas—the school's demand for a program in which girls would participate, the girls' interests and concerns about the context in which their productions would be viewed, and my own attempts at balancing what I often found to be the conflicting agendas of both researcher and teacher—often worked against these goals. I came up against the same roadblocks again and again, and when this happened I would catch myself wondering if we were getting anywhere.

April 20, 1995
Notes On Fieldnotes

In looking back over my fieldnotes of the last little while I am taken aback, dismayed to find that so many of my entries seem to begin with "Didn't get anywhere again today." My concern is not only about all the time spent with seemingly few results for all the effort, but also about how I have construed that effort. It is as if I am expecting this project and its critical goals to be something—like a route on a map which can be measured for time and distance travelled with an anticipated time of arrival that can be calculated. This is clearly a mistake.

I am thinking again of David Massengill's song.[11] He starts off with "When I went out to change the world, I thought this old world would come around" and at the end of the song, first singing gently and than louder and perhaps a little angrily, he repeats several times, "I wanted to join the revolution, but I couldn't find a parking place." . . .

At the time, I enjoyed the irony. It spoke to my frustrations with my project, with what I thought was my problem in being unable to settle not only on a way, a method of provoking change but also not knowing for sure what those changes should look like. However, the song also points out that there is a certain amount of humor to be found in the irreducible limitations found in the midst of these kinds of freedom projects.[12]

Now, I wonder if the lack of a parking place is perhaps not a problem but rather something to strive for. It is a useful metaphor—a reminder that in doing a critical project, one probably shouldn't get too comfortable, too parked with one set of ideas of what changes are necessary and right as well as one way to go about doing it for all time.

Not parking leaves open the possibility of unanticipated side trips, detours, and yes, maybe even going around in circles if necessary. So, perhaps getting somewhere in a linear, mappable fashion is not possible. But it does not necessarily mean distance hasn't been travelled—perhaps it is not a definitive arrival that should be the goal. . . .

NOTES TOWARDS A POLITICS OF ARRIVAL:
NEW ETHNOGRAPHIC STORIES

Rather than a simple, single arrival on the scene of ethnographic enquiry my arrivals have, like my conversation with LeLy in the school gym, been variously interrupted, intercepted, and deferred. And while we know that a good ethnography has a discernable beginning, middle, and end these notions of time are blurred here. Not only does the nature of the experiment in thought undertaken obscure this kind of strict periodization, but the fact that traces of this experiment exist in the form of the videotape guarantees the impossibility of securing conventional ethnographic time. As a result my ethnographic stories and stories of ethnography are a negotiation of multiple beginnings, departures, and returns. To narrate such a story requires tellings of discrepant versions and ongoing negotiations of varied arrivals, as well as stories of the subtler insights of everyday journeyings—journeyings within and between the various and at times competing geographies, agendas, ethnographic registers of time, and political, methodological, epistemological, and ethical concerns that I have begun to outline in this chapter.

The partial nature of my arrivals serves to suggest an approach to journeying in the territories I have laid out. It is a travelling technique that insists on a certain open-endedness, incompleteness, uncertainty, and ambivalence. As a result, although the project's aims and implications may look clearer and somewhat more coherent to me now than they did at the time, in this book I attempt a writing strategy that, like my various research methods, is one in which "curiosity is not overwhelmed by coherence" (Tsing 1993, 33).

While my aim in claiming this strategy may be, at least in part, to unsettle any assumption that research subjects, data, and ethnographer are stable enough to be thematically labelled, sorted, categorized, captured, and fixed on paper, fixing does, of course, happen anyway. This approach then, marks the need to explore the ethical, political, and epistemological dimensions of ethnographic research as integral parts of producing knowledge about others, precisely because the conceptual ordering of experience structures intelligibility and unintelligibility, what is sayable and what will be left out. At the same time it acknowledges that how ethnographic inquiry is organized, constituted, and accomplished will, to a large degree, determine the form and substance of claims it is able to make (Simon and Dippo 1986, 196), resulting in an anxious fixing, unfixing and refixing.

As an ethnography that attempts to map the discursive positions of femininity and girls' identificatory practices within them, this book is constructed of stories from a number of sources, school administrators, teachers, myself as researcher, and most abundantly from the girls who participated in the program. Among my dilemmas in the retelling of these stories here, for a purpose and in a context that is vastly different from the ones in which they were originally told, is how to write about these lives so as to resist a too easy assimilation of the phenomenon of interest by given analytic, ready-made concepts. That is, my concern is with how to represent the various experiences, voices, and differences of these lives without reconstituting normatively fixed categories and identities.

Just as the girls have their models for what makes a story recognizable as a story, I too draw from various models in refashioning our conversations, activities, wonderings, and wanderings into a text and in the process constituting myself as a certain kind of storyteller. I draw, for example, on a rich tradition of ethnographies of educational sites which take up questions of identity from a range of perspectives and disciplines[13] on the emerging and contested field of girl studies,[14] on criticism of ethnography[15] and on various attempts to transfigure ethnographic writing[16] as well as on the recent flurry of feminist writings on questions of subjectivity.[17] There I have found how various sociological, anthropological, and feminist agendas make possible certain kinds of tellings of lives. What then are some of the forms these new ethnographic stories take? More specifically, as Britzman asks, "[W]hat does post-structuralist theory 'do' to ethnographic writing?" (1995, 229). Relatedly, what kinds of possibilities exist for writing of lives so as to constitute others as less other?

The critiques that began in the 1980s have spawned a profusion of concepts and visions for new ethnographic forms. In combination with poststructuralist theories that "disrupt any desire for a seamless narrative, a cohesive identity, or a mimetic representation" (Britzman 1995, 232), ethnographic authority is, according to Britzman, being challenged on at least three different levels, the authority of empiricism, the authority of language, and the authority of reading or understanding.

This challenge is changing the understanding of the general character of what ethnography is about. There is, according to Marcus, no sense of discovery in the classic sense in contemporary ethnography. Rather than "being first," these new ethnographic forms are interested in exploring the complex ways in which their subject matter has been constituted through diverse representations (Marcus 1994, 571), in destabilizing the givenness of objects (Game 1991, 20), and in theorizing the modes of intelligibility that constitute subjects (Britzman 1995, 235). Thus, new questions are asked of qualitative data, questions that are not necessarily interested in seeking causal determinations or direct access to experience. Rather they are formulated to investigate, as Simon and Dippo outline, the character and basis of social practices that organize, regulate, and legitimate specific ways of being, communicating, and acting (1986, 197).

These new questions have produced a shift in ethnographic practice that includes a much more demanding sort of depth than the modality for getting at certain functionalist, agreed upon topics of investigation. It is a kind of depth that challenges sensibility and ideas about subjectivity, personhood, and knowledge. This leads, Marcus acknowledges, to much greater pressure on what methodologically and personally was required of the ethnographer in the past (Marcus 1998, 247).

Accommodating new questions and modes of inquiry has also entailed a move away from realist accounts towards the writing of more inventive texts (Denzin 1997; Marcus 1994). In attempting to reflect the social conditions of postmodernity among subjects (and ethnographers), as well as to confront postmodernist styles of knowledge production, these texts trouble the relationship between the real and the representational, reflecting back to their readers the problems of inquiry at the same time as inquiry is conducted (Lather 1996, 2). In no longer allowing us to constitute ourselves as ethnographers in relation to subjects with quite the same sense of assurance as was previously possible, these texts also challenge the fixed alterities—self-other—of classic ethnographic texts (Tsing 1993, 33).

This set of concerns has, as Marcus outlines, been taken up most explicitly in a trend of ethnographic writing concerned with the shaping and transformation of identities (of one's subjects, of their social systems, of the nation-states with which they are associated, and of the ethnographer) (1998, 59). For Marcus, what distinguishes these works from realist ethnography is their experimentation with sensibilities and techniques such as reflexivity, pastiche, and dialogism, and a more explicit tolerance for the uncertain conditions of their own production. Rather than referencing a totality in the form of a literal situated community or semiotic code as cultural structure, the revised project of ethnography, he suggests, focuses on "how distinctive identities [individual and collective] are created from turbulence, fragments, intercultural reference, and the localized intensification of global possibilities and associations" (1998, 62).

In outlining her own project about identities in an "out-of-the-way place," Tsing (1993) argues that her examination of the idea of marginality—its pragmatics and imaginaries—within the traditional mise-en-scène of fieldwork refuses the traditional analytic distinction between theory and ethnography. This coalescence, she suggests, stimulates critical awareness of the assumptions of research and writing, a strategy which Ann Game argues rejects the distinction between representation and the real by disrupting the research model which sees theory operating as a hypothesis to be tested through research (1991, 27). My own attempts at such a disruption are reflected in the very structure of this book: separating neither theory from method, nor theory from data in its divisions of chapters, I also attempt to resist a theoretical separation of analyst from the object of study.

One of the further distinguishing features of a "messy text" is its "many sit-edness" (Marcus 1994, 567), making possible both the representation of many different voices, as well as the many voices of a single individual—voices that are, according to Britzman, "contingent on shifting relationships among the words spoken, the practices constructed, and the communities within which interaction takes place" (1991, 12). A consideration of voices as contingent and relational rather than singular works to get at the cultural and social frameworks of participants without suggesting their homogeneity. At the same time it allows for a consideration of how identities may be plural, contradictory, partial, and strategic. It shows that although the terms of discourses may be set (and include several and sometimes contradictory discourses) within these limits, "people do contest interpretations of what is happening, strategize, make choices, struggle with others, make conflicting statements, argue about points of view on the same events, undergo ups and downs in various relationships and changes in circumstance and desire" (Abu-Lughod 1991, 153). What is made possible, therefore, is a textual means of representing how identifications happen within a social practice, rather than just making theoretical assertions that they do.

With this possibility the interest of any particular story shifts from a stake in producing truth claims to one in which what is sought after is an understanding of differences within and among stories of experience, how they are told, and what it is that structures the telling and retelling (Brodkey 1987). As I have already suggested, reading these stories is not, therefore, about discovering the truth of a specific experience, but rather about gauging the processes of subject constitution in the articulation of individual with master narratives (Viswasnaran 1994, 50). The category "experience" is understood here as a means of reading ideological contradictions which leaves the boundaries of the object and subjects of study contingently open and allows for the derivation and negotiation of an analytic framework to emerge from discourse and from mappings within the sites in which the object of study is defined and among which it circulates.

This is a strategy that is intended to counter the exoticizing techniques of conventional ethnographies, while at the same time raising questions about representational authority, the constitutive constraints of representation, and the possibilities for other means of attending to difference. It seeks to accomplish this through holding in tension the ethnographic project's need for analytical categories with an understanding that the object of study always exceeds its analytic circumscription. Since the interpretative framework, the conceptual apparatus, and the naming of its object always remain partially unsolved (Marcus 1994, 567) with this approach, difference can never be fully consumed, conquered, or experienced, and any attempt at understanding is always suspicious of its own imperial tendencies.

Difference, Trinh Minh Ha writes, "is that which undermines the very idea of identity, differing to infinity the layers of totality which form I. . . . This is not to say that the historical I can be obscured and ignored and that differentiation cannot be made, but that I is not unitary, culture has never been monolithic and is always more or less in relation to a judging subject" (1990, 375). The conception of identity and humanity that emerges here is one that exists in and around and across and between difference, rather than on either side of a self/other dichotomy. Such an approach attempts to be highly attentive to (and respectful of) difference, but is also wary of the tendency to essentialize it (Rabinow 1986, 258).

Thus, the potential for uniting an analytical with an ethical project is seen to lie in rendering obsolete the view of the utterly detached observer who looks down from on high and replacing it with the depiction of a process of understanding that is embedded in a particular series of interactions. Social analysis becomes a relational form of understanding in which both researcher and researched are engaged and there is no pretence that these encounters and the knowledge they convey are either transparent or innocent (Kondo 1986, 85).

Towards meeting this goal and reflecting the messy methodology on which it rests, I build my "messy text" from layers of stories that do not necessarily fit together easily or well. Constructed from several different perspectives, these stories include disparate investments in varying and competing discourses of femininity by the school, the girls, me, and popular culture, as well as those we fashioned together through our discussions and in our creation of the video characters. As such, stories of hegemonic femininity intermingle with those struggling to undermine and replace them, and stories of the real are mixed in with fantasies of the imaginary. In placing these representations of femininity together, marking them all as data to be analyzed, my aim is, in part, to challenge the empirical positivities of subjectivity.

In a decanonizing criticism of colonial writing practices, Homi Bhabha offers an interesting approach to thinking about this challenge. He suggests that the so-called transparency of realism "is best read in the photographic sense in which a transparency is also always a negative, processed into visibility through technologies of reversal, enlargement, lighting, editing, projection not as a source but a re-source of light" (1986, 171). In terms of reading the identificatory practices of femininity, this challenge to realism prevents identity from ever approximating the status of an ontological given. Instead, identity becomes like the transparency, a negative processed into being through technologies of self, those ongoing dialectical movements between self and other, subject and object, inside and outside (Crapanzano 1992; Fuss 1995).

The critique initiated in the 1980s has inspired different forms of research questions, relations, and expectations from the ethnographic base. For feminists particularly concerned with the ethical issues of antiessentialism, positioning has been articulated as an epistemological act that works to set limits on textual authority at the same time as it recognizes the need for a system of viewing experience that simultaneously allows for difference and connection within the production of meaning. Donna Haraway (1988), for example, advances the case for a critical feminist epistemology that finds its stakes in limited location and "situated knowledge."

Positioning transforms the study of differences, formerly defined in opposition to an invisible self by displacing it with a "constantly mobile, recalibrating practice of positioning in terms of the ethnographer's shifting affinities for, affiliations with, as well as alienations from, those with whom she interacts at different sites" and thus constituting a distinctly different sense of "doing research" (Marcus 1998, 97). The process of knowing is therefore understood to take place within a complex collaboration between ethnographer and informants. As a result, there is a need to include both the response of the observed to their experience of surveillance, or as Rosaldo suggests, how the ethnographer is perceived by those studied (1989, 206).

Positioning thus becomes a means of recognizing that knowledge emerges from particular configurations of power, and as such the retelling of another's story can only ever be a partial one, bound not only by one's perspective but also by the exigencies of what can and cannot be told, what can and cannot be known. The suggestion that all stories are incomplete therefore requires responses (and thus engagement) from other readers positioned differently. A confrontation with the plays of power in the processes of interpretation is, as a result, required from both ethnographers and their readers.

Thus, it is holding two terms in tension—the desire to know and the desire to represent—that gives ethnographers the means, as Spivak suggests, to "question the authority of the investigating subject without paralysing her, persistently transforming conditions of impossibility into possibility" (1987, 200).

CHAPTER 3

Crystal's Story:
The Bad Girl Within

"Is everyone ready? Okay, places, everyone!" LeLy shouts. "Come on people! We haven't got all day!" "Oh my god, that thing is heavy," Fanny complains not for the first time today, as she picks up the video camera. "If this were a real movie, I wouldn't have to hold this the whole time. We'd have one of those things for the camera to go on."

"Cheap, this school is so cheap, man." Mai slowly gets up, removes the last vestiges of our lunch break from the table that will now form the center of the video set and leaves Maria peering at her image in the monitor. Staring back at her is Crystal, the character she plays. Maria makes some adjustments to her makeup and hair and then adjusts the adjustments. LeLy and Mai roll their eyes at each other. This is not the first time they have been kept waiting by the exigencies of Maria's hair and lipstick. Maria looks up. "Okay, okay!" She is enjoying herself. "I'm ready." "Ready? Aaaand action!" LeLy calls out.

We have spent months together developing the characters whose stories make up the video—working out the intricate details of plots, scenes, dialogue, wardrobe and props necessary to represent girls' lives. We have lived with these fictional characters for so long that when we speak of them, it is almost as if they are also bona fide members of our lunch group. And in the years following our work together, long after the girls claim to have forgotten them, these characters continue to haunt these pages, my life, and my thinking.

But in the last few weeks of the school year, back when the characters were what brought us together as a group, we are making all our plotting and planning concrete by translating it onto videotape. Throughout these long months we have accomplished most of our work in the minutes squeezed out of the girls' lunch hour, but for this last stage of the project I have negotiated their way out of a full

61

day and half of classes. Energy and spirits are high on the first day of taping. It seems the months we have spent planning and learning to work together will culminate in a smooth end to our project. We work quickly and efficiently. By the second day, however, the energy, excitement, and goodwill of all of us have begun to wane; animation gives way to old patterns of soporiferous bickering, and to fatigue.

CRYSTAL'S STORY:
NARRATING THE SELF THROUGH ROMANCE

The camera pans the small bright room and then slowly zooms in to focus on Crystal seated at a table. Head bent low, she is writing furiously. As the camera moves in, it offers a detailed study of her body; jeans, simple white T-shirt, glasses, hair pulled back into a ponytail. The shot comes to a rest on the table and fixes on the object of her intense attention: a diary.

Crystal's story is conveyed through several of these diary scenarios, which are interspersed throughout the video. The scenarios show the character in several different locations: lounging in her bedroom, sitting in the family living room, and cross-legged on the back steps of the school. These are some of the important social and spatial contexts in which girls' subjectivities are shaped and lived. In each scenario, the camera pays special attention to her posture, her clothes, and her hair, which progressively change. As the story unfolds, the T-shirt, jeans, glasses, and ponytail are replaced by a close fitting body suit, tight pants, high heels, contact lenses, and loose hair.

Looking contemplatively into the camera, Crystal pauses in her writing and tells her story:

June 5, 1995
Dear Diary,
   I'm so confused! I really don't know what to do. My brain is going to explode! I'm tired of trying to be good.
   I don't understand my parents—why do they have to separate us? They don't know how I feel.
   This is the situation. I met Matt a year ago—the first time I went to the community center. He was playing football. I was hanging out with my friends. He was my cousin's friend. The next week we all went to the movies together. One of my friends (Tori) told him I had a crush on him. He stared at me. I decided to go for it. I asked him, "Is there anyone sitting here?" And that's how we started to talk. We exchanged phone numbers. A few days later I called and that's how it all started.

June 6, 1995
Dear Diary,

We got into a big fight again! My parents say my marks are dropping. They expect me to be a straight-A student. Anyways I'm still getting As with only a few A minuses. Why can't they give me a break? They're putting their highest hopes on me, now that my sister Cindy is gone. It's so hard trying to be what they want me to be. Why can't I be myself? It's not fair!

I think they might be getting suspicious about Matt. They're asking questions about who I was calling, where I was going, who I was hanging out with, what was I doing. I hate it when they do that—I'm not two years old!

Just because he's black—I know they wouldn't let me go out with him. They don't want me going out until I'm 16—and they are prejudiced against black people.

June 7, 1995
Dear Diary,

Matt is so incredible—he's everything I ever dreamed of. People stare at us in a strange way. I know that what they're thinking is black and white shouldn't really be together but we really don't care.

The other day the neighbors saw us together. I'm afraid they're going to tell my parents.

June 8, 1995
Dear Diary,

I got home from school and my parents were in the family room waiting for me. They looked angry. I never saw them that angry before. They started to scream. I burst out crying.

"Who was that guy you were with?" "Why were you hanging out with him"? "Don't you care about your reputation?" We got into a big fight. Now I don't know what to do!

There are many stories to tell about Crystal and the girls who created her. In being a story about a good/bad girl, Crystal's tale may be read as a working out of the interdependent discursive structures that are required to make both positions intelligible ones. The story interweaves several different, often contradictory threads: romance, sex, parents, childhood, adulthood, nationality, and racism, each of which evokes its own stories, lying beyond the text. The thread of romance functions as a language through which the story can be read and made sense of. Like the classic romance plot, the story has as its primary focus the developing heterosexual love relation (Duplessis 1985; Radway 1984). Many studies show romance to be a central theme in the popular cultural texts which are part of girls' everyday lives. For example, romance novels are currently the most popular genre of literature read by teenage girls in the United States, Canada, England,

and Australia (Taylor 1991; Willinsky and Hunniford 1993). It is perhaps not surprising, therefore, that romance features in much of the girls' story writing. While
some have argued that girls' use of this genre in their writing tends to reflect the
narrow range of discourses about gender available through romance literature and
thus is a genre that limits attempts to write outside of patriarchal conventions
(Gilbert 1988), others suggest that young girls may use the romance genre as a
place from which to critically explore gendered identities (Moss 1989). Crystal's
is a story which complicates this debate. Like the romance stories and comics that
serve as preparation for girls' entry into positions in heterosexuality (Christian-
Smith 1990; Walkerdine 1990), the writing and performance of Crystal's story
may be read as an investigation into how discourses of femininity delimit the necessity of this entry into heterosexuality in order to be recognized as properly female (Butler 1993; Davies 1993; Griffin 1982; Rossiter 1994; Rubin 1984).
However, it is a story that not only outlines the series of artful maneuvers in and
around discourses of femininity and sexuality necessary for this entry, but also
questions and plays on by which and whose terms this entry may be accomplished. Romance therefore may be acting here as an introductory code word signalling permission for a discussion of desire: an amalgam of sex, power, pleasure,
and danger.

Spun together, the interwoven threads of Crystal's story tell a tale of a girl
who is "tired of being good" and the possible consequences and meanings this
state of affairs may engender. The announcement of the intention to engage in a
discussion about desire makes Crystal's goodness always already suspect, for to be
good within normative discourses of femininity usually means that a girl's desire
is left unspoken or spoken only in whispers (Fine 1988; Tolman 1994).

As the misunderstood ("They don't know how I feel") and unjustly treated
heroine ("It's not fair!"), Crystal's situation is typical of the condition of heroines
within conventional romance stories (Walkerdine 1990, 95). But her ambiguous
status as a good girl reflects a certain shift within this and other genres' representations of emergent modes of femininity. While generally in romance literature female characters were clearly either good or bad (Christian-Smith 1990,
1993; McRobbie 1982; Tinkler 1995; Walkerdine 1990), McRobbie suggests that
the last fifteen years has seen a discursive explosion around what constitutes femininity and its ambiguous relationship to feminism (1994b, 158). While McRobbie goes so far as to claim that in the teen magazines of the 1990s, romance is an
empty category, Mareike Herrmann suggests that within these same magazines,
the hegemony of the good girl is not completely undone (1998, 230).

For girls reading conventional romance literature, conscious identifications
could be made with protagonists who were properly good, but the bad character

might have also offered the unconscious mind a vehicle for the expression of what
has traditionally been socially and culturally forbidden to girls: anger, desire for
power, and control over one's own life (Walkerdine 1990). In some variations of
the form, the binary categories may still exist, but they might be blurred by being
embodied in a single character. For example, Ann Kaplan suggests that Madonna's
rock video *Material Girl* does this by the simultaneous telling of two stories. While
the sound track frames the story of a good girl, the visual images create an opposing story about a bad one (1987, 125). In other variations, such as those found
within popular fiction, the woman may be the sexual initiator (a sign of the bad
girl), but because she also wants marriage and babies, the socially transgressive
fantasy is rendered perfectly feminine (Kaplan 1986, 160).

It is therefore Crystal's ambiguous positioning within the binary pair that
makes her story an interesting one. This discussion, which took place as the group
began to settle on the kind of character we were writing into being, suggests that
positioning Crystal in this way was intentional:

1 Marnina: So let's talk about Crystal. [Ruffling through notes] Let's
               see, we were saying last time, that she wants to be a—
2 Fanny: who's Crystal?
3 Marnina: . . . . good girl but she doesn't want to be—
4 Lan: a good girl like.
5 Maria: Yeah, she wants to be good, just that she doesn't know
               how to be good without being bad. Like to their rules.
               Like not bad in a bad sense, like just whatever they think
               is bad. (Trans. 04/11/95)

In her comment that Crystal "doesn't know how to be good without being
bad," Maria suggests that Crystal is not simply good or bad, rather she is a good
girl who cannot always be good. She is struggling with the competing definitions
of both good and bad and the contradictory demands of her that these entail. She
is a self that in trying to live these contradictions is divided.

While the ways in which the girls constitute "good" and "bad" remain to
be seen, it is possible that their positioning of Crystal in this way may have
served them as a means to investigate their own struggles and competing desires—the desires that they may consciously or unconsciously realize will have to
be, or have already been, suppressed if they are to realize themselves as correctly
heterosexually female. Walkerdine uses the concept of splitting (borrowed from
Kleinian psychoanalysis), to suggest that good and bad elements of the ego may
exist in fantasy as split off from each other. She suggests that the desire to

constitute oneself as good means repressing the reviled parts of the self and projecting them onto an Other (1990, 151). The mechanism of repression is, as Butler (1990) makes clear, a culturally contradictory enterprise that is at once prohibitive and generative. Thus, it is possible to see how what is being played out by the good and bad female characters in teenage romance literature, and is perhaps being played with and resisted in the creation of Crystal, is this phantasmatic splitting.

As the group watched and talked about an episode of *Sweet Valley High*, a popular television show and book series that many of the girls watched and read avidly, they seemed to express an identification with and desire for elements of both of what the good/bad binary offers. The books and television show set up the good/bad binary through the central characters of the series, the identical teenaged Wakefield twins: Elizabeth the good sister and Jessica the not-so-good. This opposition is played out by juxtaposing Jessica's aggressive expression of sexuality with Elizabeth's more demure self-presentation. Like the evil and good female characters within teenage romance literature, the trope of the twin is one that is often used in literature to symbolize the other within the self (Ling 1992, 312). The double is symptomatic of a crisis in self which is the consequence of the conscious ego's denial of recognition of a part of the self. It is possible that the crisis in self that is being played out here is what Davies calls the contradictory imperatives to be a good woman, that is, to be sexually active without negating ones goodness (1992, 61). Profound unease about violating the bounds of traditional femininity, Vance suggests, may be caused by a woman's experience of desire, as it signals the giving up of vigilance and control, the responsibility of a proper woman (1984, 5).

In our discussions about the twins, the girls named the two different kinds of femininity represented by each of them respectively as romantic and sexy.

1	Tevy:	Do you think they look the same?
2	Marnina:	Pretty much, do you?
3	Mai:	Jessica looks better than Elizabeth.
4	Tevy:	No, Elizabeth.
		. . . .
5	Marnina:	If you could be, just say in your dreams which one would you rather be?
6	Lan:	Ah, none of them for me.
7	Charlene:	Both of them mixed together. Cut a piece, put it in a jar, cut another piece put it in a jar and stir them up. [laughter]
8	Marnina:	And which pieces would you want?
9	Kenisha:	Both of them—a piece of both of them.

10 Charlene:	Like make both of them together and make them one person.

. . .

11 LeLy:	Sometimes sexy and sometimes romantic or something like that.
12 Charlene:	A part nice and a bad part or whatever.
13 Annie:	There's two sides to everyone, like there's a bad side and a good side—
14 Lan:	there's only a bad side to Fanny. (Trans. 02/28/95)

In embodying both the good girl and the bad Crystal is the imperfect mix-and-match offspring of the girls' desire. Her story therefore offers a means not only of analyzing how the girls identify good and bad within normative discourses of femininity, but also of exploring what may lurk within good girls. It is a story that explores where and how badness may emerge, as well as how different positions within the good girl/bad girl dichotomy may be socially, materially, and psychically produced, understood and lived (Walkerdine 1990, 105).

Before moving onto a more detailed discussion of the story, I want to briefly discuss the girls' use of the diary format. Using the diary as a narrative device was a strategy that the group developed to help overcome some of the logistical problems we faced. Among others, these problems included the absence of male actors to represent the figure of Crystal's boyfriend and adults to play her parents. But the use of the diary also helped overcome the dilemma of how to represent some of the riskier activities planned for Crystal.

1 Marnina:	Okay, let's try to think of a scene where Crystal is going to be, where we're going to see some of these issues.
2 LeLy:	Okay, probably her parents walk by the park and see her with that guy making out or something like that.
3 Fanny:	Kissing—pretend.
4 Mai:	Where are we going to find a guy to kiss her? No, I'm talking about lots of guys would want to kiss you, but would *you* let them kiss you? And where are we going to find a guy?
5 Fanny:	I don't think so! A guy would kiss Maria!
6 Mai:	Lots of guys would kiss Maria!
7 Kenisha:	Just kissing her on the cheek—
8 Mai:	But would Maria let them kiss?
9 LeLy:	Exactly! Shut up! Okay, I know one.
10 Kenisha:	On the cheek, Maria, only there!
11 Maria:	NO! . . .
12 LeLy:	She can sit there and write her diary. (Trans. 06/05/95)

The image of the lone diarist also appealed to the girls as a means of conveying what they considered to be a common experience of girls: that is, the sense of extreme isolation and aloneness, even while in the midst of family and friends. In using the diary as a narrative strategy, the girls are making use of a literary form that is commonly associated with female literary expression. In fact, the publication of girls' diaries became something of an industry in the nineteenth and early twentieth centuries and the content of these were used by psychologists for their studies of child development. Thus, girls' diaries have played a part in shaping and defining the ways in which girls were and continue to be seen and understood (Steedman 1982, 68-69). The diary-writing young woman is also often used as a motif in literature to communicate a feminine concern with the inner world, emotions, and the private sphere more generally (Gilbert and Taylor 1991, 105). While the inner world is a preoccupation in Crystal's diary, many of the visual representations depicted focus on the outer world of appearances and how they might be read. What better form than the diary could there be, therefore, for telling a story that explores the contentious relationship of the inner world of a girl's desires and the attendant pleasures and dangers of the outer manifestation of those desires—a story which tells of the bad girl always already in the good girl and waiting/threatening to emerge?

SCENES OF DESIRE: THE BAD GIRL WITHIN

In a provocative reworking of Freud's oft quoted question, "What does woman want?" Jessica Benjamin asks, "Do women want?" or "Does woman *have* a desire?" (1988, 86-87). This is a question that radically disturbs Freud's theory of female sexuality as being primarily characterized by lack—lack of the very emblem and embodiment of desire, and that which men possess: the phallus. In Freudian theory, women's renunciation of sexual subjectivity and acceptance of object status are the foundational characteristics of the feminine. Hence, the radical disturbance of Benjamin's question is in the shifting of attention from conceptualizing women as the object of desire, what is wanted, to the subject, she who desires. Fashioning Crystal's story of romance out of scraps and relics from romanticism, modernism, television sitcoms, and feminism, the focus of the girls inquiry is on the desiring girl. It is a process in which they both name those recognitions of themselves within notions of femininity that are constituted through phallogocentric discourse and use this knowledge to explore and construct discourses through which they might be recognized in other ways. The result is something of a "double-coded" narrative, or a narrative that mobilizes at least two different dimensions simultaneously (McCarthy and Dimitraidis 2000, 65). Organized here into four scenes of recognition, each exploring the social, cultural, and material practices by which the individual constitutes and recognizes herself as a subject within discourse structures of femininity, this double-coded narrative entails simultaneous acts of fantasy, recognition, creation, acceptance, rebellion, and accommodation.

What is striking to me as I reread and work with the transcripts of Crystal's story is how palpable the girls' level of engagement is. Unlike several of the other characters' stories, here almost everyone seems invested in telling a piece of the story of heterosexuality. However, at times this interest seems to also be about an investment in disrupting the romantic story line. Fanny's contributions are particularly interesting in this regard, as she uses different occasions to move both in and out of disrupting and promoting the traditional story line, interrupting the narrative and her friends' and my authority to fashion it. This propensity for disruption is perhaps what earns Fanny the kind of distancing derisive comment frequently made by other group members in reference to her. Lan's "There's only a bad side to Fanny" exemplifies the genre, and as we will see throughout the transcripts, the effect of this sort of commentary is often to assign Fanny to a space outside the group. It is a mechanism that, as Bauman (1993, 162) suggests, may be used to defuse a certain aporia: group members may be seeking to distance themselves in order to be able to sustain a more comfortable cognitive space for themselves, in this instance within hegemonic discourses of heterosexuality.

Fanny's disruptions were particularly acute as we discussed Matt, the romantic hero, and what Crystal's attraction to him was about.

1	Marnina:	Okay, so what's with this guy? What does she like about him?
2	LeLy:	He's a real gentleman, you know how he treat her and everything.
3	Mai:	Yeah, he listens to her opinion and everything.
4	Fanny:	Yeah, he's really ugly too. . . .
5	Mai:	He likes only one person, Crystal. That's like he's so special to her.
6	Marnina:	Oh, so you mean he's like loyal to her.
7	Fanny:	Loyal—[laughs] is he a dog? . . .
8	Mai:	Oh, can we say he's a football player?
9	LeLy:	Oh, football, yeah there.
10	Fanny:	Football, what a geek. Aren't football people used to be stupid and stuff?
11	Kenisha:	No, they're not!
12	Fanny:	They get hit in the head too much? (Trans. 06/05/95)

Despite Fanny's unremitting interference, the romantic story line prevails and Matt is established as the exclusive object of Crystal's desire. Heterosexuality thus becomes the privileged form of pleasure and desire in the text. In Judith Butler's (1990) terms, this absence of other sexual practices constitutes a discursive route reinforcing the heterosexual hegemony. But as the group's creative efforts continued, this hegemony was unsettled by the expression, if not legitimation, of other possibilities of desire.

1	Mai:	[writing] "Never saw them that angry before"—What's wrong? She's like staring at me.
2	LeLy:	CAUSE YOU ARE ATTRACTIVE!!
3	Fanny:	Maria's lesbian.
4	LeLy:	[laughing] When did you become Kenisha's girl friend? [Kenisha plays the lesbian character in the video.]
5	Kenisha:	[Laughing; to Maria:] Are you okay?
6	Maria:	Yeah.
7	Fanny:	You're staring at Mai.
8	Mai:	This girl is staring, staring, not saying.
9	Maria:	I'm just thinking!
10	LeLy:	She's ATTRACTIVE, I told you!
11	Kenisha:	Like as if something is wrong with what we're saying.
12	Maria:	I just focus on something and than oohh my mind goes wandering off somewhere. (Trans. 06/06/95)

It seems the story of heterosexuality is a story that is unwriting itself even as it is being written. And while neither decided nor in question, it is possible that what we have here is a moment of slippage between identification and desire, between desiring and being the girl. And yet, while the contours of this romantic tale may be tenuous, its borders, as I will demonstrate, are recognizable by boundaries which are policed by a discipline of containment, a certain ordering of the body, and the gaze of others.

SCENE 1. SUBJECTIVITY AND FEMININITY

With its careful outlining of the context, locale, and circumstances of the initial sighting of Matt, as well as the subsequent first date, the question the first segment of the romance story asks about its key character is, How might entering into a heterosexual relationship be orchestrated? The issues that the girls, none of whom say they have as of yet dated themselves, seem to be interested in working through include When and where does a girl meet a guy? How might interest in a guy be appropriately signalled? What are the qualities that will attract a guy? And how will a girl's behavior be read? Essential for establishing Crystal as a subject within the romantic story line, addressing these questions involves a detailed conjugation of the feminine grammar of desire.

While the girls agree that the potential for romance is all over the place—at the movies, walking to school, at the community center—our discussions reveal several tensions in the group about the nature of the character who will be involved in this romantic experience. Current throughout the writing process, this disagreement over the achievement of oneself as a girl within the romantic story line has much to say about the good/bad girl boundary, the girls' own ambiguous relationships to negative and positive fantasies, power and powerlessness, and agency and passivity. Here, Kenisha is the most adamant about introducing nonconventional elements to the romantic tale, while LeLy's, Fanny's, and Mai's positions are each more contradictory. They juggle traditional and innovative elements, shifting from excitement, concession, and opposition in and amongst themselves, for and against ideas old and new.

1	LeLy:	Okay, can they meet in the movie or something like that?
2	Kenisha:	No, that's the first date. Like they met because she's popular in school, right? And then she meets some friends—
3	LeLy:	she's normal; she's not popular.
4	Kenisha:	She's not popular but—
5	Mai:	what's your point?
6	Kenisha:	She's normal. She's in-between, like sometimes she's with the popular, sometimes she's with . . . then she gets to meet some of the—
7	LeLy:	or—
8	Kenisha:	high school guys and stuff like that.
9	Mai:	It's a rainy day, right? [laughter]
10	LeLy:	Mai, that's—
11	Kenisha:	that's an old story.
12	LeLy:	that's an old thing story. [laughs]
13	Fanny:	(sarcastically) It's a rainy day, we bumped into each other—
14	LeLy:	[picking up on the sarcasm] oh yeah, and than he picked me up when I fell down.
15	Mai:	Oh maybe. Oh never mind. Oh yeah, she's new in the neighbourhood, right? She's finding her way to the school, right? But she doesn't know where, so she asks him, "Oh, where's this?" Oh never mind! (Trans. 06/05/95)

Although Mai (5) and LeLy (3) are dismissive of Kenisha's suggestion that Crystal should be a popular girl (Mai asks, "What's your point?"), the point is in fact a very important one. The popular-normal-nerd classification system, as I will discuss in more detail in chapter 4, is one of the ways in which schools organize subjectivities and it is also an organizing factor within the teenage romance genre as well. Kenisha's argument seems to be that if Crystal were popular, her meeting of Matt could be explained by her greater and easier access to guys, especially older high school guys (2, 6, 8) through her many friends. However, since holding a position of popularity within a school's social hierarchy also means accruing visibility, influence, and power (Canaan 1987; Eckert 1989; Eder 1995; Hudak 1993; Kinney 1993), creating a character that is popular suggests a girl who is an active subject in her own right.

Within traditional teen romance stories, this active subjectivity is rarely granted to heroines. Christian-Smith argues that many of these stories involve a transformation of the heroine from a "Cinderella in the corner" to a more confident, desirable potential girlfriend. It is through the power of romance and by virtue of the heroine's association with the hero-boyfriend that the heroine is transformed and gains recognition as a "somebody" (Christian-Smith 1990, 89). This conventional form of the romantic tale may be seen to reflect the ways in which women have no position within the patriarchal symbolic order, except in relation to men (Weedon 1987, 54).

Thus, Kenisha's concept of Crystal seems to disrupt this narrative by suggesting that a girl's value is not dependent on her affiliation with boys. It is, on the contrary, the popularity acquired in her own right, before she has even encountered Matt, that both provides her with the opportunity to meet him and makes her a likely prospective girl friend (2, 6, 8).

There is also a way of reading LeLy's suggestion that Crystal should be "normal" (3) as a kind of attempt at rewriting normative discourses of femininity. LeLy's own lack of popularity and access to positions of recognition within the school was a constant thorn in her side and the topic of many of our exchanges that year we worked on the video. Thus, her suggestion that Crystal is merely normal might be about a desire to see the opening up of possibilities for being "somebody" to more than just girls who are popular. In this version, since there is no suggestion that Crystal will become popular as a result of her relationship with Matt, subjectivity as a romantic heroine is granted to girls for having qualities that extend beyond the very restrictive qualifications of the popular girl.

In contrast Mai tries on two different occasions (9, 15) to introduce storylines which position the romantic heroine as vulnerable, and it is through this feminine vulnerability that she is able to attract a man. "It's a rainy day," she suggests almost like the formulaic, "It was a dark and stormy night." The others know the story she is proposing even before she has provided any of the details: dangerous and mysterious things could happen to a girl who is out on her own. While LeLy, Kenisha, and Fanny mock and reject this story of female vulnerability as an old one and therefore not of interest, Mai makes a second attempt to introduce the theme. She describes a heroine who is lost and needs help finding her way. In both instances the heroine displays a certain passivity and her subjectivity is realized through the power of the male's heroism and sexuality. This second time, Mai concedes of her own accord (15) and the suggestion is dropped.

Eventually we agree on a plausible context in which Crystal meets Matt (initially at the community center and then later at the movies) and that she gains access to him as her cousin's friend. This seems to be something of a compromise on the popular-normal issue. However, the underlying tension of feminine subjectivity surfaces again as we work on how the romance will be initiated. In the discussion that follows, I open by reminding the group that we had discussed having a powerful aspect to each of our characters and I make a suggestion of how this might work within the heterosexual storyline we have formulated for Crystal. The impetus to introduce powerful aspects to each of the characters came from a discussion the group had about how the television programs we were watching together usually position girls as weak or powerless in relation to men. Lan pointed out that our own project was not dissimilar, as each of our character's stories were up until that point "only about problems." Attempting to write strong characters was also part of my own critical agenda of trying to introduce possibilities for female subjectivities that go beyond normative discourses of femininity.

1 Marnina:	We also want to have girls who are active and powerful right? Is she interested in him and she makes the first move? Can we do that?
2 Mai:	If you want to. Cause, if she's shy—
3 Kenisha:	she's not shy! Is she—
4 LeLy:	what kind of person she have?
5 Kenisha:	She's a strong person. Didn't you guys said that?
6 Marnina:	Yeah, we said she was strong.
7 Kenisha:	She gets to do whatever she wants. Like she goes to him—
8 LeLy:	she have her own opinion—
9 Kenisha:	like at the football game with her friends like she goes up to him. She's always near to him and stuff and than she . . . she walk up to him and than she said "hi" and than she introduce herself and stuff, and then they start talking, she give him her number and whatever.
10 Fanny:	[sarcastically] Oh my god, she gives him the phone number!

11 Kenisha: Yeah!
12 Marnina: Okay good, does everyone agree that makes sense?
13 A few: Yeah.
14 LeLy: It's not always the guy that stands up and says "hi" to the girl—
15 Kenisha: but she's strong so she can do whatever she wants-
16 Fanny: if you're not a strong person I don't think you'd go up.
17 Kenisha: Go after a guy.
18 Fanny: If she was like a shy person she wouldn't go up.
19 LeLy: Let's put it into a sentence. Marnina, help us! Give us a head start.
20 Marnina: Like Kenisha was saying . . . something like "the next week, we all went out to the movies together." Is that all right, Kish?
21 Kenisha: Yeah.
22 Fanny: That's cool, get to go to the movies.
23 Marnina: So he doesn't notice her, but she likes him so she approaches him.
24 A few: Yeah.
25 Mai: That's what he like about her, like she does whatever she wants.
26 LeLy: Yeah, there.
27 Kenisha: Everything she wants she go for it.
28 Marnina: [writing] "The next week we went to the movies together—
29 Fanny: they pushed us together" or something like that.
30 Kenisha: NO!
31 Mai: "One of my friends told him I had a crush on him."
32 LeLy: "My stupid friend," because she feel so embarrassed at that time you know. Like it could be someone from the group, like Tori or something like that.
33 Mai: Hey, why didn't I think of that? [She plays Tori.]
34 LeLy: Cause you don't have a brain, remember? (Trans. 06/05/95)

Once again it seems there is a tension within the group about Crystal's status as a feminine subject. At one extreme is Kenisha, who persists in seeking an agenetic positioning for Crystal outside traditional storylines. She insists on a character who is strong and who does "whatever she wants" (7, 15, 27). LeLy is agreeable to this and adds that what would make Crystal a strong character is having "her own opinion." She supports Kenisha's suggestion (14, 27) by adding that boys are not the only ones who can initiate dating etiquette. Mai, while initially reluctant to have the romance instigated by Crystal (2), eventually moves to suggest that it is precisely Crystal's initiative that makes her attractive to Matt (25). At the other extreme is Fanny. Here, she works hard to reestablish a more conventionally passive positioning for Crystal. She resists Kenisha's suggestions (10, 16, 18), seems to momentarily find the scenario an attractive one (22), but than offers a suggestion (29) which rapidly undoes Kenisha's work (accomplished with some support from me and the others) to get consensus on building a strong character. Although her concerns seemed, until this moment, to have been largely ignored by the rest of the group, the result of Fanny's contribution is a pulling back of the story line, renegotiating Crystal into a position of ambivalence. When Fanny suggests that it is Crystal's friends who "push them together" she effects a reopening of the question of the intelligibility of the agenetic good girl. Despite a protest from Kenisha (30), Mai (31) and LeLy (32) move this suggestion forward by adding not only that a friend announces her interest in Matt on her behalf, but that Crystal is embarrassed about this interest she feels.

This position of ambivalence acknowledges not only Crystal's desire and the social transgression its expression effects for the good girl, but also the more fluid feminine subjectivities and ways of making sense of female sexuality in the 1990s mass media. While Davies argues that the achievement of oneself as woman within the conventional romantic story line is not through being a subject of desire but rather an object (Davies 1992, 66), Shelley Budgeon notes that although not entirely unproblematic, figures like Madonna and Sharon Stone might offer girls alternative models for defining an active sexual subjectivity (1998, 137); that is, a way in which to reconcile agency and desire with femininity in ways that the gender division that has historically existed does not accommodate (Benjamin 1988, 122).

The intervention of Crystal's friend is perhaps one way in which to abate some of the anxiety that stems from straddling both the knowledge of her own desire and its repercussions for her (self-)identification as a good girl. That is, this may be a way in which she is able to avoid a breaching of the internal stricture to be a good girl. For, notwithstanding these alternative models, the hegemony of a good-girl femininity linked to passivity and squelched desire has not been entirely overthrown. In discussing the female characters in the popular television show *Beverly Hills 90210*, the girls use the descriptive "nasty" when referring to their numerous sexual liaisons and improvident activity. Many indicated that the only character they liked or approved of was Tori Spelling's character, Donna,[1] because at that time in the show's history, she had made a commitment to virginity until marriage (FN 05/04/95).

The ambivalence of this position must be understood, however, not only within the context of its ongoing relationship to the very constitution of heterosexuality (Holland et al. 1994, 27) but, also as the second scene will illustrate, as a product of the social consequences for not conforming to this series of dominant expectations.

SCENE 2. BODIES IN TROUBLE:
THE BAD GIRL MADE VISIBLE

> On Sundays try to walk like a lady and not like the slut you are so bent on becoming . . . this is how to hem a dress when you see the hem coming down and so to prevent yourself from looking like the slut I know you are so bent on becoming . . . this is how to behave in the presence of men who don't know you very well, and this way they won't recognize immediately the slut I have warned you against becoming. . . .
>
> —Jamaica Kincaid, "Girl"

Body movement, clothing, comportment, and behavior, the implied mother above instructs, are simultaneously the ways in which a girl may be known by others and the means by which she may betray herself. Betrayal, it seems, could happen at any time, since as the mother in Kincaid's story suggests, the body is a network of social signification, a meaningful and functional subject capable of being read or interpreted symptomatically, in terms of what it hides (Grosz 1990). The body is constantly threatening to reveal the desirous girl. The combined effect of this predicament for the good girl is the requirement of a constant awareness of the rules surrounding the use of the body, rules that involve not only prohibitions and constraints, but also pleasure and desire. A girl's production and repression of her body demands, therefore, a perpetual watchfulness that might best be summarized as a "regulation of the self" (Prendergast 1995, 209).

Crystal's story offers several different ways in which the body and its production may operate as a scene of recognition and as a site where identifications are made and refused. From the diary's opening line—"I'm so confused! I really don't know what to do. My brain is going to explode! I'm tired of being good"—Crystal's story links her state of mind, one of confusion, uncertainty and fatigue, with that of the dangerous condition of her body, a brain that is threatening to explode. Through the interwoven threads of sex, race, and parental surveillance, the story offers a means to analyze the relationship between the assumption of a sexual position that takes place not only through a heterosexualizing symbolic with its taboo on homosexuality, but through a complex set of racial injunctions which operate, in part, through the taboo on crossing racial boundaries. Such a reading offers a means by which one might begin to ask how race and sexuality converge such that one is constituted through the other. In Crystal's story the articulation of this convergence seems to find expression through the interrelated exigencies of regulating the self and the competing demands and struggles a girl encounters in the romantic inscription of her body (Gilbert 1992, 196).

Like the girl referenced by Kincaid, in Crystal's story the parental figure has a role to play in refereeing the body's regulation: through the disapproval of the black boyfriend, (and by implication of his presence the possibility of a sexual relationship), the insistence on high marks at school, the concern about reputation, and, as is outlined in this discussion, her clothing and bodily presentation.

1	Marnina:	So let's talk about Crystal. [Ruffling through notes] Let's see, we were saying last time, that she wants to be a—
2	Fanny:	who's Crystal?
3	Marnina:	. . . good girl but she doesn't want to be—
4	Lan:	a good girl like.
5	Maria:	Yeah, she wants to be good, just that she doesn't know how to be good without being bad. Like to their rules. Like not bad in a bad sense, like just whatever they think is bad.
6	Marnina:	Okay, so lets talk about some of the differences between what she thinks is good and what they think is bad. Like what she thinks is okay but they would call bad.
7	Maria:	Okay, like [pause] like going out, no . . . okay, like what's it called? Okay, so what am I thinking here? I'm getting myself all confused! Okay, so what she thinks is good and what her parents think is bad?
8	Lan:	Well, some of her clothes; she can start with clothes.
9	Maria:	Clothes, okay, like something too revealing, something like that? Like maybe a bodysuit.
10	Lan:	Yeah, and a swimming suit—a bikini—
11	Maria:	a swimming suit, exactly.
12	Lan:	Like a bikini is too revealing.
13	Maria:	A bikini, I mean it, my dad would never, he'd freak out before I wear a bikini.
14	Lan:	I don't like bikinis.
15	Fanny:	So nasty.
16	Lan:	I like wearing like a whole suit.
17	Maria:	I know.
18	Lan:	It feels more comfortable than bikini—
19	Maria:	you feel so empty—
20	Lan:	like when you wear a bikini it feels like your whole stomach is showing up, like your whole big fat stomach showing out. (Trans. 04/11/95)

The contradictory definitions of the good/bad girl is initially set up here through the regulation of Crystal's body and the clothing she wears. Clothes that are revealing are defined as good for Crystal's purposes, that is, gaining the attention of a guy. From a parent's perspective—and here Maria includes her own father (13)—clothes like bodysuits and bikinis are defined as revealing too much. The implication seems to be that a girl's desire is shaped through the opposing demands[2] of two important sets of relationships: relationships between daughters and parents, and relationships between women and men.

Angela McRobbie discusses how, from within family relationships, styles created in youth subcultures may be opportunities for resistance: "For many of us too, escaping from the family and its pressures to act like a real girl remains the first political experience" (McRobbie 1991, 49). Style of clothing may be a way to resist families' definitions of girls' identities. But the change enabled by this rejection replaces one set of constraints with another: the use of sexuality/pleasure to reject the family places young women squarely within the dictates of femininity (McRobbie 1991; Nava 1984).

Walkerdine outlines the second set of constraints, those imposed by the dictates of femininity that render women as the object of the male gaze. She suggests that there is a tremendous amount of work that goes into a covering over, not of an essential femininity but a different set of desires and organization of pleasures from those which can either clearly be articulated at the moment or are sanctioned in the practices in which femininity circulates as sign (Walkerdine 1990, 145). Perhaps, it is this form of constraint that Maria is referencing and protesting when she comments on the sensation of emptiness (19) associated with wearing a bikini.[3]

The girls' discussion above is suggestive of the very tight space girls have for maneuvering between these competing demands. It is perhaps illustrative of what Anyon (1982) calls girls' strategies of "resistance and accommodation" for dealing with the limited range of options available to them. Clothes that are revealing are identified as one of the ways in which a girl may be bad while trying to be good, yet almost as soon as the prospect is raised, Lan, Maria, and Fanny quickly move to a consensus among themselves which seems to position them alongside the parental view and against clothes that are too revealing. They refer to the distastefulness of these clothes (15), the experience of bodily discomfort (18), and a concern for a concealing of the body (19, 20). What started out as parental regulation shifts to a regulation of the self, as the girls participate in both a constructing and policing of the good/bad border. However, while parental regulation is formulated around the concern that one's body might entice desire, their own self-regulation is perhaps formulated around a different concern—the fear that it might not.[4] Both sets of concerns are very much rendered within patriarchal representations of the desirable body and how within this context clothes that are too revealing code certain messages onto the body that are read in particular ways by others.

On another occasion where we are discussing Crystal's wardrobe, other group members suggest possibilities for differing identificatory practices as the group rehearses some of the possible social meanings a girl's clothing may carry:

1	Lan:	. . . and tight clothes—Crystal could wear like really tight clothes.
2	Fanny:	Oh bad.
3	Kenisha:	It's not bad; it's good. She wear whatever clothes she want to.
4	Mai:	Like Jessica, eh? [the "bad" Sweet Valley High twin] I like how she dresses.
5	Kenisha:	Yeah, I like to see people with tight clothes. Sometimes they look really cool.
6	Lan:	With nice bodies though, people with nice bodies. Ugly bodies wear those things, they don't look good.
7	Kenisha:	Like you, right? [laughter] . . . [inaudible] not bad—bad in a good way.
8	Marnina:	What would be the good way?
7	Kenisha:	Like cool in a way; sexy.
8	Marnina:	So you mean sexy doesn't have to be bad—
9	Kenisha:	too sexy is good!
10	LeLy:	Too sexy—too slutty!
11	Kenisha:	Too slutty? It's not too sexy—too slutty!
12	Lan:	[to Tammy] [inaudible] . . . horny.
13	Tammy:	[to Lan] Desperate for it.
14	Marnina:	So if Crystal looked too sexy, you think it would mean she was desperate for it? Is there something wrong with that?
15	LeLy:	Nothing's wrong with it—
16	Mai:	it's just you're cheap.
17	LeLy:	Yeah, just giving people like a feeling that you're cheap.
18	Kenisha:	So that mean I'm cheap. I'm not cheap people!
19	Lan:	Cheap like what's her name? [inaudible]
20	Marnina:	Why is it do you think that being interested in guys and sex makes you cheap?
21	Mai:	We didn't say that!
22	LeLy:	We didn't say interested in guys—
23	Mai:	or sex.
24	Marnina:	Oh.
25	LeLy:	You know we didn't say that.

26 Marnina: No?
27 Mai: But like go around to guys even if they don't want it.
28 LeLy: Yeah.
29 Mai: Like having with that guy than just having with another
               guy.
30 LeLy: Yeah, that mean cheap for us, as a student, you know.
31 Marnina: Okay.
32 Lan: I'm cheap! I don't spend all my money on other people.
               (Trans. 02/28/95)

Through this discussion about the signification of tight clothes, several readings of the sexualized self are registered, covering the full range from good to bad. Kenisha articulates a position that is initially supported by Mai in which the wearing of tight clothes and more generally the sexual meaning attached to them can be a source of power and pleasure. Her reading works to build on her earlier concept of Crystal as a strong character—the girl who successfully combines subjectivity and femininity. Her statement, "She wear whatever clothes she want to" echoes her "She can do whatever she wants" discussed previously. It is interesting to note, however, that while both girls agree in theory that this is a position girls should have access to, neither initially goes so far as to identify this as a position for themselves, although that she actually does is clearly implied by Kenisha later in the discussion (18).

Despite Lan's caveat restricting a position of power and pleasure to only those girls with the "right kinds of bodies," Kenisha is able to reclaim her own definitional position by turning Lan's suggestion about which bodies might rightfully wear tight clothes back on her (7)—this notwithstanding the fact that Lan's body, being very thin, would by most standards meet the criteria of being a "nice body." Kenisha's move effectively dismisses any authoritative privilege Lan might have presumed and her participation in the conversation tapers off. However, when LeLy offers a strong counter position introducing the very negative connotations of slut as a way of reading the girl who wears tight clothes (10), Kenisha is not able to hold onto this recovered ground. The woman who advertises her sexual interest loses her value, becomes cheap (16, 17, 30). Mai, LeLy, and I disagree on the implications of this position (20, 21, 22, 23) and what it means about the kinds of desires a girl is entitled to assert. A little incensed by my reading of their position, they clarify the stance they have taken, arguing that interest in guys and sex is not what they take exception to, but rather acting on this interest excessively (29) and making a nuisance of oneself (27). It is interesting to note, however, that this is precisely the juncture at which the group's attempts at an agenetic positioning for Crystal troubles the familiar classificatory grid, creating an aporetic situation in the last scene.

It seems that despite one's intentions there is always a possibility of being read as overly zealous in one's sexual desire. For girls, the safe expression of this kind of interest involves the successful engineering of a very narrow gauge.

As the discussion continues, LeLy reinforces the validity of Mai's argument (30) with an interesting claim to student status. Within the dynamics of the group and in particular the researcher-researched relationship, the mobilization of the category of student works in contradictory ways. On the one hand the category of student calls up the context of the school environment in which we are working, where this is a status that is shared by the girls. It evokes the related signifier of age and the age groupings by which students are sorted into grades and classrooms on the assumption of shared knowledge and experience. This is a naming which, while uniting the other group members across their varied differences and, in particular, ignoring Kenisha's quite contrary statements, serves to highlight one of the differences between them and me. It may have been intended as a reminder to me of this difference and a bid for acknowledgment as to why our understanding of this issue might be dissimilar. However, it is also possible that since I had often drawn on my own status as a student, for example to explain my presence in the group, and it was in fact the way I usually referred to myself, her referencing of it here could also serve as something of an admonishment to me, a pointing out of a status we share across our other differences, and therefore may be an attempt to draw me into agreeing with their conclusions. Both possibilities suggest an attempt to manage and contain the differences between us.

The will to sameness is a move which Macpherson and Fine also note in their research with a group of girls whose differences cross race, class, and ethnicity categories. They suggest that the suppression of difference operates to limit the exposure of deficits and fracturing of the group. Labelling this a Sameness Discourse, they suggest that this discursive strategy works to limit not only discussion about social inequalities and differences of power (both of which were operative in the researcher-researched relationship), but also the possibilities for where critical subjectivities might flourish, shift, and be explored (1995, 184). To some extent the Sameness Discourse seems to function here within our group dynamic. In our attempts to manage the differences that could threaten the cohesiveness of the group—a cohesiveness which was tenuous at the best of times—calling up the category of student focuses on sameness and the norm of Us and Our ways of seeing things. The discourse provides group membership through an identification with Us, suppressing differences within Us, while denying or making difficult identification with others. Macpherson and Fine suggest that the introduction of a discourse of difference that challenges sameness offers a means of destabilizing knowledge and identity. When differences are recognized, they argue, a discourse of plural meanings may open up new identificatory possibilities (1995, 187).

Lan's playful pun on the word "cheap" works to introduce plural meanings of the concept of cheapness and in doing so dispels the tension over boundaries of group membership. Referring back to Mai and LeLy's definition of cheap and Kenisha's counter argument, Lan announces that she herself is cheap for reasons other than those inferred already (32). In doing so she rejoins the discussion she had been summarily dismissed from, while at the same time completely shifting the terms of the conversation.

Similar to the discussion of the previous scene, Kenisha's contribution to this exchange marks her as somewhat distinctive from other group members. While she seems relatively unconcerned about the differences of opinion which appear to divide her from other group members, in this next exchange she justifies her position. Referring to how people dress in her country (Grenada), she mobilizes a sense of national identity, countering the connotation of slut as worked up by the rest of the group. In response, the other girls draw on their understanding of the Vietnamese context by suggesting how the wearing of revealing clothes might have different meanings, depending on the setting.

1	Kenisha:	I don't get the difference between bad girls, what you guys are calling bad girls.
2	Mai:	oh we're talking about—
3	Kenisha:	so what do you do when you do bad? Like rob somebody?
4	Marnina:	Well, that is one way of looking at it, but I think what we were talking about when we were saying "bad" is about the way a girl is thought of as being bad if she's too interested in sex and how she uses her body and the kinds of clothes she wears.
5	Kenisha:	In my country, most people dress like that.
6	Mai:	I wonder why; it's so hot! Your country is so hot, you're not going to wear thick clothes like this, right?
7	Kenisha:	Uh? Who cares, you wear whatever clothes—
8	Lan:	Vietnam is hot and they don't wear clothes like that. They always wear those ugly ao dais.
9	Mai:	Because those material that are like thin.
10	LeLy:	yeah, the material's thin—
11	Mai:	and wind can blow on them.
12	Lan:	You can see through all of them. . . .
13	Mai:	Well sometimes, slutty doesn't have to wear tight clothes.
14	Marnina:	So is there anything else?
15	Mai:	I think cause how she act too. Bitchy. And how she talks and walks.
16	Maria:	Even the way she walks.
17	LeLy:	I know. (Trans. 02/28/95)

The naming of a home country to organize the various understandings that displays of the body held for the group draws attention to the girls' status as members of immigrant communities in Canada. What the group seems to be doing here is something of an accounting of and working out of the differences in the discourses of femininity[5] as they might apply in the countries that inform their pasts and presents. In trying to make room for Kenisha's position on tight clothes without implicating her as slutty, and perhaps as an attempt at a further reconciliation with me after I reassert a definition of "bad" (4), of which we have already disagreed on the implications Mai not only attempts to find different possible meanings for the wearing of revealing clothes divested of sexual connotation (6), but also suggests additional criteria for reading the slut (14). Thus, bitchy behavior and manner of walking and talking are added to the repertoire. The implication here is that the term "slut" in fact bears little relation to a girl's actual sexual activity, but that all kinds of social behavior have a potential to be interpreted for their sexual significance (Hirschon 1993; Lees 1993; Lesko 1988). A girl must, therefore, be constantly conscious of how she conducts herself and of how her conduct might be read.

Maintaining a modest, heterosexual, feminine reputation seems to require that young women construct their bodies as passive both in the expression of their sexual desire and relatedly in their body's very materiality (Holland et al 1994, 25). This construction involves women in a contradictory relationship with their material bodies. The successful presentation of self as feminine involves, as Dorothy Smith (1988) outlines, an artful, skilled, and learned series of work processes applied to the body's surfaces. And yet, while the achievement of normative femininity seems to be largely centered on defining the self through the body and its appearance (Ardener 1978; Bartkey 1990; Lesko 1988; Young 1980), Smith observes that for a woman participating in the practices of femininity a distinctive relation to self arises—a relation to self as object of work (Smith 1988, 47). The result is, as Emily Martin shows, that women tend to see their bodies as separated from themselves—as detached, fragmented, alienated, and needing to be controlled (Martin 1989, 89). A woman comes to regard her body as other, as the object of another's gaze, rather than as a "living manifestation of action and intention" of her own (Young 1989, 155). Women's relationship to their bodies, it seems, is complex and paradoxical, moving simultaneously between embodiment and disembodiment—between both that which is me and that which is not me.

In the discussion that follows, the girls narrate with some hilarity a series of stories about girls' bodies as they are represented as a regular feature of YM, a teen magazine many of them read. As the discussion moves from magazine stories to a relating of their own stories of the body, the girls' talk demonstrates both the intertwining relationship between the symbolic production of gender and the

shaping of the experience of the body itself as well as the disciplinary attention
that must go into the feminine production of the body.

1 Hanh: In YM, there's, you know, the "Say Anything," there one
                 about, uh, and this girl went swimming—

2 Samantha: oh yeah, like embarrassing moments.

3 Hanh: Yeah, and than she went swimming down the water slide
                 and than she got a wedgie. And she was picking out her
                 wedgie and than she picked out her tampon and—

4 Mai: Uh?

5 Hanh: And then the lifeguard said like really loudly in front of
                 everybody, he goes, "Excuse me, can you dispose that?"
                 and she was like really embarrassed.

6 Mai: Oh, my god! Oh my god!

7 Samantha: Okay, this girl is in a plane, right? And she had a body-
                 suit on, but it doesn't undo at the bottom, so she had to
                 take it off like this? [indicates removing it from the top]
                 She's on the toilet and the plane jerked, the door
                 opened, she fell out and her bodysuit was like this
                 [demonstrating she's not clothed] and she was in the
                 middle of the hallway!

8 Mai: Oh! [sympathetic murmurs and surprise]

9 Hanh: There's this really gross one when, umm, this girl was
                 having turkey dinner and then afterward she coughed
                 and than a piece of phlegm fell out and it went into her
                 aunt's plate and her aunt ate it [laughter] and it was so
                 gross and she got so embarrassed she ran out, ran away
                 from the dinner table.

10 Mai: Oh my god!

11 Lan: I feel sorry for Tevy.

12 Marnina: Why's that?

13 Lan: She got her period during school.

14 Mai: Nine.

15 Lan: Her first one, it was during school. And everyone could
                 see it and everything or something like that?

16 Mai: no, she's nine years old. She was nine years old when she
                 got it—

17 Lan: and then she asked the teacher to go home and teacher
                 let her.

18 Marnina: Ummm, that is too bad.

19 Mai: So, I had it in school too.

20 LeLy: Yeah, no big deal.

21	Lan:	So, I didn't get mine yet.
22	Mai:	Big deal.
23	Maria:	I got mine during a rainstorm, weird.
24	Marnina:	Where were you?
25	Maria:	I was in the middle of the street [laughter] It's true! I got home all soaking wet. I was picking up my brother—
26	Lan:	[referring to Hanh] She got hers at home.
27	Hanh:	No, I got it in [inaudible] at four o'clock.
28	LeLy:	Where? Home or school?
29	Hanh:	Four o'clock, March twenty-first.
30	LeLy:	Wow! How can you remember so clearly?
31	Marnina:	Yeah, that is neat that you remember so clearly.
32	Hanh:	Cause it was this year. (Trans. 12/05/95)

As each of the girls contributes a story of the body—one they have read about, a friend's or their own—their talk seems to be a collaborative telling of the embarrassment a body out of control may engender. However, the object of their story is not simply one of deterring the possibility of a humiliating situation. Rather, it seems to be a narration of the related processes of both how the gendering of women's bodies is accomplished through the requirement of its control and how bodily control is read by the girls as one means of becoming a recognisably appropriate and valued subject (Davies et al. 2001). It appears a girl must be in a perpetual and exhaustive state of vigilance to contain her body. In their tendencies towards unpleasant and unplanned emissions, what should be kept hidden might become exposed, inside-outside, private-public. This is very clearly illustrated in the recitation of precise times and places the girls furnish about their own periods. According to Lovering (1997, 77), this is a very common feature of girls' accounts of their first menstruation and she argues it exemplifies girls' concern and preoccupation with managing their bodies. It is possible that beyond the embarrassment of being caught unprepared, unbounded, and discharging material, bodies are socially problematic because letting particular aspects of the body emerge is to be unfeminine. That is, the physical manifestation of material bodies disrupts the disciplined disembodiment of femininity (Holland et al. 1994, 33).

The efforts involved in constructing the passive feminine body do not simply constitute the corporeal as the social in an easy way. Women have to spend a good deal of time and effort in the skilled management of their bodies in order to make them socially presentable. Bartkey (1990, 72) argues that ideal femininity requires such 'radical transformation' that virtually every woman is bound to fail. As the girls' discussion above illustrates, the certainty of failure means that a girl's body is always already a body in trouble.

Female subjectivity, Bartkey suggests, is constituted in a significant measure in and through the disciplinary practices that construct the feminine body (1990, 78). Power enters the picture in the form of girls' continuous struggle to control and contain their bodies—its posture, gestures, appetite, and the appearance of both its visible and invisible parts, which may be read for the correct application of the rules of prohibition and constraint, pleasure and desire. In the writing of Crystal's story, style of dress and manner of talking and behaving have been identified as some of the means by which the social mapping of discourses of femininity on the body takes place. Each of these significations works through a discipline of constraint and possibility to simultaneously produce the good girl and repress the excesses of the bad. However, as we have already seen, such a mapping may be highly particularized and depends in part on which body and where it is located in place and time. Neither Grenadian nor Vietnamese, Crystal, like Maria who portrays her, is a Portuguese immigrant living in Toronto. Although there is perhaps little in the final version of the story which overtly marks her as such, at least some of the underlying issues chosen for inclusion in the story were intended by the group as a portrayal of the specific dilemmas faced by a Portuguese girl. In particular, the contradictory demands involved in producing the body of a good daughter who obeys her parents' prohibition on dating and the desire to constitute oneself as properly female through entering into a heterosexual relationship, while a dilemma well known to and often discussed by the girls of Asian backgrounds, were felt to have dimensions that were particular to Maria, the only Portuguese girl who regularly attended the group.

In the midst of discussing how the group would portray this dilemma for Crystal, Maria takes the opportunity to grapple with some of the seemingly irreconcilable expectations she herself faces over this issue. The question of what can and cannot be spoken, what can and cannot be expressed, is raised throughout her response and, as I will show momentarily, is linked with the larger question raised in Crystal's story of the dangerous yet potentially powerful repercussions of public exposure of both colour and desire.

1	Marnina:	Is part of what her parents want her to be good about about being a good Portuguese girl?
2	Maria:	Exactly. They want me to marry a Portuguese guy and I don't want to marry a Portuguese guy. Cause please, I don't need that attitude from him like I get from my father.
3	Marnina:	What attitude do you mean?
4	Maria:	Well, he expects me to clean the house, wash the dishes, do my homework, get good grades, get a job, find a hus-

band and everything all at one time. Not all at one time, but what is it called? He doesn't want anyone—he would expect my husband—ahhhh. [stops] Okay, I'm trying to say something. I'm trying to put into words here.

5 Marnina: You're doing a good job—

6 Maria: it's hard—hard to get, because my father thinks so old fashioned, my mom even says so, okay? My mom tells me, "I'm sorry honey, but your father is really old fashioned, bear with us right now." Cause my mom, okay, okay she's old fashioned too and she does expect me to clean, cook, and have a job and all that stuff but at least she'll let me—I don't know, she knows that like her father was not strict with her. Her father let her do lots of things, right? And she knows that I'm having a hard time when my father doesn't let me go out to a friend's. Like she could go out. She dated when she was fourteen. She—I don't know. She did anyways, but it was with my father. [laughter] "Don't expect that from me," I told her. Anyways, but yeah, like she understands that I like to go out, I like to have my own friends, I like to talk about boys, I like to go to dances, but my father doesn't understand that. When I told him I was going to the dance, he made such a big deal, he thought I was ready to leave with a boy or something like that. Now he gets too nuts, I think. He overreacts. . . .

7 Fanny: Oh, my god! Do they want you to be a virgin for the rest of your life?

8 Maria: Yes!

9 Lan: No, they might set her up without her knowing.

10 Maria: They expect me to get married without going out on a date— [laughs]

11 Fanny: oh my god!

12 Maria: how they expect me to do this—

13 Lan: you know how they do this—they set the person up for you, you don't even know him.

14 Maria: I'm not going to marry any person that my dad sets for me, or my mom, excuse me! That is so old fashioned!

15 Fanny: I would go, "Excuse me dad." You know what you say? You say this to your dad: "Excuse me dad, this is the 90s."

16 Maria: You don't talk to my dad like that. Don't even tell him it's the 90s.

17 Fanny: Why?

18 Maria: Cause he gets this lecture about what I did, blahblah-
               blah [inaudible]. You don't talk back to my dad, you can't
               express your point of view cause he won't listen, nothing
               like that, cause he'll just lecture you and I don't really
               want to get any lectures—
19 Fanny: oh god, lock him up—
20 Maria: you know why? Because I'm a good girl! (Trans.
               04/11/95)

In the terms Maria lays out, terms for which words are hard to find (and yet she obviously has much to say on the matter), being a good Portuguese girl entails the pressure of performing a seemingly endless series of tasks within both the domestic and public spheres, as well as marriage to a man from within the Portuguese community (2, 4). She positions herself contradictorily within these terms by at the outset anticipating her adamant refusal to marry a Portuguese man (2), while at the same time claiming knowledge of herself as a good girl who does not talk back to her father (20). As the discussion continues, the focus of her quandary shifts from whom it is she will marry, to a question of how it will be possible for her to marry at all, given her parents' (and her father's in particular) restrictions on her activities (10, 12). It seems the perplexing question of how to be good (entering into a heterosexual marriage) without being bad (expressing and acting on heterosexual desire) leaves only objectionable old-fashioned options as possibilities (14). For Maria, trying to constitute herself as a modern Portuguese girl of the 1990s, the question of simultaneously achieving both goodness and an entry into heterosexuality forces the question of the very possibility of this discursive positioning ("Do they want you to be a virgin for the rest of your life?").

This tension finds expression in Crystal's story and is made particular to her self-identity as Portuguese through the body that is the object of her desire—a boyfriend who is black and not Portuguese. The presence of black men is quite a common feature within the romance fiction genre and has held particular meanings, depending on the historical period and location. For example, during the interwar period in British magazines for girls, foreign black men were often the villains of romance stories. Tinkler argues that during this period race riots were high on the media's agenda and while the economic dimensions underlying the racial conflict were not mentioned in the stories for girls, these concerns found expression in the figure of the black man as villain and sexual threat to white British girls (Tinkler 1995, 173).

Black men appeared regularly in the romance stories that a number of the girls in the group wrote, and obviously the use of this image carried different meanings for particular girls, depending on their own racialized positionings. In view of these different positionings, the negotiation of possible meaning presented a particularly complicated challenge, for both me and them within the context of the group's collective writing process. At a certain point in the discussion about Matt, after establishing Crystal's attraction to him as being a feature of his looks, "gentlemanliness," and role as football star, the group decided to weave into the story line Crystal's parental objection to the relationship. A dramatic shift in discourses ensued that included, as the girls themselves acknowledged, some of the stereotypical racist linkages between black masculinity and violence. Noticing Kenisha had withdrawn from the conversation, disturbed that this might be due to the mobilization of this oppressive discourse, and concerned about its implications for her and relations within the group, I (ineffectively) attempted to create a space in the conversation in which her perspective might be centered: "What do you think, Kenisha? What does he think about her parents not letting—" Her brusque response, "I don't know, I never had a boyfriend before" (Trans. 06/05/95), was, I think a refusal to engage. Among its many other possible meanings, for me, the difficulties of this moment also highlight the complexities of my role as researcher/group facilitator—the one more usually focussed on the collection of "unadulterated" data, the other on advancing a feminist, antiracist agenda. Of course, the more important issue is what meanings, if any, the moment had for Kenisha, and that is something I do not know. The use of the image of the black man in the story does, however, need to be further discussed in order to address the kinds of identifications that are finding expression through its repetition.

As a Portuguese girl, Crystal's crossing of not only the national-sexual border but also the racial-sexual border, transgresses good girl boundaries on many different levels, and becomes a dense transfer point for a discussion about relations of power, sexuality, and desire:

> "Just because he's black—I know they wouldn't let me go out with him. They don't want me going out until I'm 16 and they are prejudiced against black people."

This segment of Crystal's diary reiterates one of the central themes of her story: the structuring of a girl's desire as a force that is shaped, as we have already seen, within and between the oppositional demands of family relationships and those with men. Or as Mai formulates it, "We're thinking, is she going to break up with the guy or is she going to go against her parents?" (Trans. 06/05/95). Unlike the situation previously discussed around her clothing, Crystal's expression of "desire in opposition" works here to suggest some possibilities for identificatory practices which offer some potential for the shifting of and resistance to relations of power and powerlessness.

In the discussion that follows, the group begins to analyze some of the objections Crystal's parent's might make to her relationship with Matt and moves into an attempt at both developing Matt's character and a further understanding of Crystal's attraction to him.

1 LeLy: Okay, her parents think that he's using her to like have sex and stuff like that. That's how she get into an argue with her parents. She told her parents that he's not, but her parents just think that you're so young, you don't know the real world and everything like that—

2 Fanny: yeah, sure, stupid parents. . . .

3 Fanny: He drives a motorcycle. Like he's in a motorcycle gang and he drives really fast. They think he's violent and—

4 Maria: no, he's kind, he's caring, he's nice. He may be black but—

5 Lan: Hey as long as he's nice to me.

6 Maria: He's a really nice guy. They sometimes get stereotyped, they all have to be in gangs or something like that. This one, he's really nice and he cares about me and everything—about *me*! [laughs] Crystal! (Trans. 04/11/95)

The eroticization of the forbidden has, of course, historically structured white racist relations with black people. On one level, Matt's blackness may be working in the text in ways similar to that in which cultural representation of male black bodies have often been configured: as bodies that are saturated with sexuality and violence (hooks 1992; JanMohamed 1992, 104). It is possible that sex, the unspoken but implied within the final text, is understood as present in part through Matt's blackness. The question of lifelong virginity is answered implicitly.

As I previously suggested, it could be argued that the girls in using this representation of black men are reproducing an ideology that has racist repercussions. It is possible that for certain group members this could have been what was at work. However, Crystal's crossing of the racial-sexual border also offers the possibility for, as Macpherson suggests, a radical rewriting of "the grammar of the hetero sentence: who's desiring subject and who's desirable object in sex" (1997, 290). It does so in a number of ways. Firstly, in countering the imagined parental anxious claims that Matt's interest in Crystal is simply as a sexual object, the girls may be protesting socially prevalent assumptions about female sexuality that sets up girls as primarily the victims of male sexuality, rather than as sexual subjects in their own right (Fine, 1988). Relatedly, the argument between Crystal and her parents may also be about a contest over how the real world is imagined. That is, partaking in sex is often considered to be an activity reserved for the world of those who have reached fully adult (and married) status. Young girls are presumed to not only not be engaged in sexual activity but are also defined as being uninterested in it (Eder 1995; Tolman 1994). Matt's blackness may be serving a function not unlike that of the bad girls in teen romance stories in that an active sexuality is made present through a projection onto an other. But unlike the good/bad girl split, the fact of Matt's blackness also renders Crystal's own desire visible, both asserting her entitlement to the adult world of sex and establishing her status as a desiring subject. Finally, while blackness no doubt functions as a very particular sign in other nonwhite communities, it is also possible that as girls who, with the exception of Maria, cannot position themselves within whiteness, there may be a certain identification with aspects of the marginality and denigration represented by Matt's blackness. Their insistence on the desirability of Matt as a sexual and romantic partner may, therefore, also be working as an attempt to position themselves as desirable subjects.

Crystal's desire is set up here not only as a force that is in opposition to parental attempts to define the proper conduct of her adolescent body, but also as a force that works both within and against racism. She writes,

"People stare at us in a strange way. I know what they are thinking. Black and white shouldn't really be together, but we really don't care."

The fact that Matt is black and Crystal is white draws attention to them—people stare, neighbors see them and report to her parents. I am reminded again of Foucault's Panopticon (1979). And yet this time, while there is clearly an acute awareness of being looked at or of being the object of surveillance, Crystal is defiant of social dictates. She refuses the gaze:

"We really don't care."

In the discussion above, both Maria and Lan clearly identify this as a position they themselves might occupy, becoming in their talk the girl who is attracted to a guy who is both Black and caring even while elsewhere they talk of their own parent's reaction should this situation ever materialize: "That's what they would do. Don't call me dad or mommy any more" (Trans. 04/11/95).

Perhaps it is in this demonstration of the power of a deliberate display that the group achieves some success in inventing Crystal as a strong character and in so doing rewriting normative discourses of femininity. It is in this risk taking, articulated at once as a racial crossing and expression of sexual desire, that the potential for disrupting the hegemonic grammar of subjects and objects in sex may be found. Perhaps what is in play in the girls' romance stories featuring Black men is an expression of an identification with the desiring subject that is both repeated and disavowed.

This should be the end of the chapter. As a stopping place, however, it is much too final.

SCENE 3. NECESSARY FAILURES: DISRUPTING THE GOOD GIRL STORY

Crystal's is not the only good/bad girl story. Nor is she the only girl with a story to tell that offers possibilities for the analysis of identifications and different trajectories of recognition, misrecognition, and rerecognition. Running throughout her story, both inside and outside, is a parallel story or series of stories that have been present but repressed in my telling of Crystal's story thus far. They now threaten a disruption.

Disruptive stories (like the disruptive bodies we have already encountered and will reencounter in this scene, in perhaps another guise) may open social analysis to new conversations, expanding and unbalancing the ideas rendered dominant by the contours in which familiar subjects are rendered recognizable; subjects like girls and researchers. Rather than concealing the workings of how subjects are rendered intelligible and naturalizing the effects, disruptive stories and stories of disruption are useful (and exciting) to the extent of their potential to reveal the strands and tensions webbed in the intricate and shaky fabric with which identities are imagined, stabilized, and reinvented. What is being disrupted here, therefore, is not merely a story half-told, but also the very categories of identification used to fashion the gendered identities of those who have featured in that telling.

The group has decided to meet after school as a bit of a going away event for Mai and Tammy, who are leaving with their mother to spend a month in Vietnam visiting their grandmother who is ill and soon to die. The plan was to meet and go skating after school, but when the appointed day arrives it proves to be a dark and rainy one; the ice on the outdoor rink at City Hall we figure will probably be covered by water. We will have to come up with another plan. Always a complicated process, coming up with a group activity outside school means having to take into consideration both lack of money and spaces available for young people to congregate, factors that rule out suggestions of going shopping or over to one of their families' houses. While Mai and Tammy collect their homework from their various teachers, the group slowly assembles. Pearl, who does not attend our regular lunchtime meetings is the first to join me.

Pearl could easily be mistaken for several years older than the thirteen that she actually is. It is not just her well-developed body; she also displays a certain sophistication and poise that I have not seen much evidence of in the repertoires of the other girls. The stance she often takes in relation to me is as my peer, or even senior. "And how's school going?" she almost always asks me when our paths cross. "Still doing well?" And yet at the same time she also regularly engages me in discussion, as she does on this day, that might be considered more typically adolescent, thus, marking me as *her* peer.

"I think my skin is my best feature. What do you think—hair, nose, eyes, teeth?" "What about Mai, what do you think her best features are? How about Lan, Kieu?" "Who do you think is the prettiest girl in the school?" "For me," she continues, "I'd probably say it's Mai. She really has her own style—with the hausers she wears." My own appearance does not escape appraisal either: "You're pretty—but, well it's just that your hair, it's too frizzy. And oh, oh," she says leaning across the table we are seated at and picking up a handful of my hair for closer inspection. "You have got a lot of split ends. I mean it, you should try using gel; your hair wouldn't be so frizzy." "It's the rain," I agree. "My hair always frizzes up in the rain."

Through this simple exchange about hair, clothes, skin we establish shared experiences; we speak a common language based on implicit understandings. I am completely drawn in. Through her positioning of me as an insider and my willing acceptance of this positioning of myself, this girl talk creates a female community which binds us together as girls. We both know the rules of engagement, although it is true it has been some time since I have had reason to make use of them. I am so seduced by this created sense of belonging that I forget myself. When the conversation shifts and I am repositioned within it, I am caught between subjectivities and I slip on the rules.

"Do you think I'm a virgin?" she continues in her questioning. I had heard through the girls' grapevine that she had recently stayed out all night in a park with a guy she had just met. The story had caused quite a stir in the group (and raised some concerns about Pearl for me). I would not have been surprised to hear that she was not. "I don't know," I reply. "Well, I am," she says. "Some guys tried to touch my ass, asked me to have sex, but I'm too young—only when I'm eighteen— eighteen is probably the right age. Don't you think?" "Eighteen sounds about right," I agree. "How about you?" she asks without missing a beat. "You a virgin?" "Nope." I don't stop to think about where I am (in the school library) and who my audience is (by now Pearl and I have been joined by several other girls. Hanging onto the margins of what had been a dialogue are now Lan, Trinh and Kieu).

Trinh and Lan rush in, "You eighteen, yet?" "Marnina, I'm shocked at you!" They have broken out of the margins. "Oh, I'm old—a lot older than eighteen." I am also rushing, as I begin to register some tingling of realization of what I might have done. "How old, how old are you again?" There is an urgency to the question. "I'm thirty—just turned thirty." This is territory we have already covered many times and I am now wondering about their "forgetting." "Then forty—forty is the right age to have sex," Lan pronounces. I am both amused and beginning to regret the direction this conversation seems to be taking. "Was it rape, or did you want to?" Lan continues. "No, no, I wanted to," I say, thinking I am reassuring her. "Oh, because if some guy forced you, I swear I would find that guy and kill him!" "What was it like?" Pearl asks. "What's the guy's name? What school does he go to?" Lan's questions come at me rapid-fire and I feel besieged.

When the full group gathers and our noisy discussion about what to do for our good-bye event looks like it will be irresolvable I offer to treat everyone to donuts at the corner donut shop. ("Don't waste your money," Pearl admonishes me. "You need it for your education.") Catching my eye across the table, as on several occasions that afternoon, Lan shakes her head and says, "Marnina, I'm really shocked at you." Regret. Confusion. Teasing? Amusement. Doubt. Rises, passes, dies away, settles in.

The injunction to be a given gender, argues Judith Butler, "produces necessary failures, a variety of incoherent configurations that in their multiplicity exceed and defy the injunction by which they are generated" (1990, 145). These failures, Butler goes on to suggest, are produced because of the ways in which gendered subjects are constituted, that is, through discursive routes which "signify a multiplicity of guarantees in response to a variety of different demands all at once."

I am not quite sure what to make of Lan's understanding of me. Yet I regard the story above as a story of necessary failures in the production of stable, homogenous gendered subjects. It is a story that illustrates, on the one hand, the failure of boundaries between good/bad, girl/woman, group member/researcher categories and, on the other, the processes of inclusion, exclusion, repression, and erasure that seek to mend these boundaries. I might have considered this an idiosyncratic reading of me unique to Lan if the story had not echoed almost a year later. Giggling and nervous, Mai and LeLy say they have a question to ask me. It is a Sunday afternoon and we are in the cosmetics department of a large department store, after having spent some time at the public library working on their speeches for the school's speech contest. Each is nudging the other to ask it; clearly they have discussed this between themselves as they both seem to know what the question is. I am pretty sure I know what the question is as well, but wait until one of them finally manages to get it out. Among the perfume, eye shadow, and lip gloss, with people scurrying all around us, Mai says so quickly I almost miss it, "Lan says you're not a virgin, but we didn't believe her."

There it was again. Not only had Lan clearly considered this a story worth telling the others, but it had obviously had the same effect on them as it seemed to have had on Lan: disrupting the notion of who they assumed I was. My efforts at engaging them in a conversation about what they made of the news were met with shrugs and averted eyes. By now we are at the subway. I try again to get a sense of their response. "Is it because I'm not married?" I ask. "No," Mai says vaguely as they get their subway tokens out. "No, we just didn't think you were like that—we didn't think you were that kind of person." Leaving me standing at the token booth, they pass through the subway doors and disappear into the crowd.

In the gap between what is said and what is thought, what is stated and what is implied, the fluid, flexible, and hybrid identifications in play for both the girls and myself are revealed in the contradictory ways Lan, Mai, and LeLy, on the one hand, and Pearl, on the other, position themselves in relation to me, and the way I position myself in relation to them in this story. There is a sense of co-herence disrupted, as knowledge "forgotten" erupts to dispel the image of the uni-fied community of girls. The work involved in creating this community, as I have already alluded to and will discuss in more detail momentarily, is in part accom-plished in this story through our girl talk. However, the fact that this talk had the effect it did can also be attributed to the ongoing work in which we engaged, ne-gotiating the subtle, and not-so-subtle, shifting and complex samenesses and differences that mediated our experiences as group members.[6]

By revealing knowledge and experience of sex, I slipped on the girl talk rules, transgressing both one of the primary defining features of girl/woman, child/adult boundaries (Davies 1993; Thorne 1995) and a presumed under-standing of me as a good girl. In response to my transgression, Lan tries through-out our conversation to reposition me as a good girl and therefore nonsexual. She does this by suggesting that the definition of girlhood should be extended to age forty, thus placing me well within its boundaries. In doing so she refutes my at-tempts to claim my age as a passport out of the good/bad dichotomy. Instead, she proceeds to offer me a different way out by suggesting I might have been forced into a sexed position by having been raped. When this too fails, she asks for the name and school of the guy involved—as if the event we are discussing had oc-curred the other day, around the corner, rather than the more likely scenario of sometime around the time she was being born, on the other side of the world. Her response focuses attention on my ambiguous status: unmarried, without children or visible means of employment, owning neither a car nor a house, I carry very few of the signs of adulthood in Canadian society. However, Lan's response also seems a refusal to recognize the many differences between us, as she works hard to mend the breach in imagined community through her efforts at stabilizing me in her understanding.

In contrast, in my conversation with Pearl, our shifting positions seem less problematic. Our girl talk is accomplished in such a way so as not to preclude recognition of ourselves as sexual beings. In fact, it might have even worked to accomplish this, as our attention to body parts and interest in products that signify our bodies as gendered female are also some of those that might mark us as heterosexually desirable (or not). Perhaps her goal all along was to establish this common ground as a means of moving towards her "real" interest in me—a potential source of information about sex. "What's it like?" she asks. In the months that follow, she uses this opening she has created with me to both candidly ask more explicit questions on this issue and to fill me in on any developments in her relationship with her older boyfriend.

In relation to Pearl my shifting between positions is also accomplished relatively easily, although not without some contradictions ripe with irony. I try to provide her with the information she is asking for, feeling a certain responsibility and concern about her, realizing it may be possible that I am the only adult who is aware of her activities ("My parents would kill me!" she tells me). But I am also conscious as I provide her with information about contraception and later on accompany her (when she asks) to an appointment I have made for her with a friend who is a counsellor at a birth control clinic, that I am crossing all the usual boundaries recommended for the role of researcher. Uncomfortable with the knowledge that I am aiding her in something her parents would completely disapprove of, aware that there is a possibility I am jeopardizing my position in the school should her parents or any of the school authorities find out, and realizing that there's a chance I am also risking relations with other girls in the group who know of and have made their disapproval of Pearl's activity clear, doing otherwise seems to involve equally complicated ethical dilemmas. These revolve around some of the debates within feminist research discussed in the last chapter. As I suggested there, the social position of researcher is not a unitary one and is instead composed of a mixture of several other social relationships. Having regularly drawn on these other more easily recognizable social positions—friend/sometime source of advice/willing audience to problems—and having been taken up on this positioning, in this instance by Pearl, not to follow through seemed to me to be a retreat into the (nonexistent) unitary position of researcher. Such a course of action, it seemed to me, while easier in many ways, would leave us both with something less than integrity and could in some ways be construed as a betrayal. To complicate matters a little further, my own understandings of myself also included a juggling of my roles outside the research relationship, that is as a sometime employee of a feminist health organization advocating around women's reproductive health.

While this story reveals some aspects about Pearl, Lan, Mai, and LeLy, it also uncovers some of the dynamics of desire involved in researcher-researched relationships and how these are implicated in knowledge production. One of the tenets of feminist research is attention to creating relationships with informants that facilitate and encourage the free flow of information between researchers and researched. Yet throughout this series of events I caught myself wondering and worrying about how much of myself I could show without risking a disidentification that could result in the dissolving of the group.[7] Feminist researchers have written much less about this as a possible outcome of feminist research practices.[8] Furthermore, my concern with provoking a disidentification made clearer to me how much of the work involved in establishing and maintaining the group as an entity, as well as individual relationships within it, involved playing on identificatory practices through significations of samenesses and differences. This story, then, of both the linked production of me as a recognizable good girl/good researcher, and the investments in this positioning, raises interesting questions about the meanings and interplay of this identification on our work together in shaping the story of that other good/bad girl, Crystal.

It is worth noting, however, this conversation which took place in the context of one of our group discussions about Crystal:

1 Lan:	Oh, you know what, Marnina?
2 Marnina:	What?
3 Lan:	There's a girl on TV, on a talk show, she's ten years old and she had sex already—a couple of hundred times!
4 Marnina:	You saw that on TV, did you?
5 Kenisha:	I know somebody in this school here just [inaudible] and had sex already.
6 Mai:	I know too. So what?
7 LeLy:	What's the big deal about that?
8 Kenisha:	There is a big deal in this, man!
9 Mai:	It's not you that's having it, right?
10 LeLy:	I know.
11 Kenisha:	Oh my god, but they're so small!
12 Lan:	Yeah, that girl is ten years old. She's even taller than me.
13 Mai:	Maybe she's mature enough already.
14 LeLy:	Yeah.
15 Lan:	She's only ten years old!
16 Mai:	But she might look mature. That show, right? She looks like she's eighteen, right? Remember, that show we were watching?
17 Tammy:	Geraldo? Okay, its like these teens who like this girl— there was a party or something like that—
18 LeLy:	oh you told her already—
19 Tammy:	and these two were like sisters and you know how they were like good girls in the daytime, but they party at night? They wear these like sluttish clothes? This very

short shorts, right? And they wear like something like a
bra, right? And their brother came and they started crying and everything, saying how come they're doing this
and everything—oh and oh—I forgot what I was going to
say, ask Mai.

20 Mai: I told you already.
21 Marnina: Humm, I forget how it ended. What did the mother say?
22 Mai: The mother's still crying.
23 Tammy: The mother said she's ashamed and everything. She was
                 sitting in the back and Geraldo told her to come out.
                 She's like, "No"—and they ask her why and she goes,
                 "Oh I'm too ashamed to go out," and stuff like that.
                 (Trans. 02/28/95)

Inquiring into the question, when is it alright to have sex? various possibilities are raised here: age, maturity, size. This discussion not only restrings
many of the threads of Crystal's story—good girls, bad girls, parents, and bodies—it also weaves them together in ways that illustrate how unfixed and unpre-
dictable their (our) positions are. In this outright rivalry of competing stories
about the partaking in sex by TV talk show guests and peers, the girls vie both
to establish themselves as knowledgeable and expert on the subject in relation
to me and to each other, as well as to manage how and on what terms this talk
will be accomplished. There seem to be some rather dramatic shifts from previous positions on the question posed above, as the crush to claim a piece of the
story to tell escalates. For example, Mai and LeLy unite (as they often do) against
Kenisha, Lan, and Tammy, at times belligerent and at others almost conde-
scending; they insinuate that the others are childish or naive for even considering it an issue worthy of discussion. Mai in particular questions Kenisha's right
to make any claims to this story, in a move that is perhaps protective of Pearl,
her on-again, off-again best friend and quite possibly the girl at school that Kenisha references. This leaves Kenisha taking a stance that might be characterized as less permissive ("There is a big deal in this") and thus quite a different
position for her, compared to the "She can do whatever she wants" of previous
sections of this chapter.

Like the bodies in trouble we have already considered, this story illustrates the excesses of categories such as "girls" and "researchers," and the incoherent configurations and unexpected disruptions excess may provoke.
Disconcerting to both the girls' and my attempts to stabilize our understandings of each other, to produce ourselves and each other as coherent, this seems
to be, in the end, an ethnographic story that insists on the necessary failure of
identificatory practices.

SCENE 4. GOOD GIRLS AND THE DISAVOWAL OF SELF

Good girls are produced, as Crystal's story and the "scenes of recognition" it offers have illustrated thus far, through an intricate interplay between relations of self and other, mediated through expressions and suppressions of desire. How these are negotiated is the central dilemma of Crystal's story. With its closing statement, "Now I don't know what to do!" Crystal's diary seems to end with no clear resolution to her problem. While this inconclusive ending signals the very impossibility of definitively solving this puzzle, it may also be seen as a gesture towards an attempt on the part of the writers of this story to trouble and perhaps even refuse the usual ways in which the interplay of relations of self to other works within the stories of girls' lives. Thus, it is the self that is the site of this fourth and final "scene of recognition" of Crystal's story.

The self that I am interested in investigating makes her appearance in the diary at one of the moments where Crystal outlines and contests her parents' objections to her partaking in a romantic relationship. She writes,

> We got into a big fight again! My parents say my marks are dropping. They expect me to be a straight-A student? Anyways, I'm still getting As with only a few A minuses. Why can't they give me a break? They're putting their highest hopes on me, now that my sister Cindy is gone. It's so hard trying to be what they want me to be. Why can't I be myself? It's not fair!

According to Valerie Walkerdine (1990, 96), the conditions for resolution of the plot within romance stories written for working-class girls are usually met through the overwhelming characteristic of the good heroine: her selflessness. Confronted with difficult and cruel circumstances, these heroines never get angry. Rather, they triumph over these conditions through the psychic organization of emotions and the selfless production of good deeds. In the stories Walkerdine analyzes, selflessness is contrasted with selfishness, anger, greed, and jealousy. These qualities signify as wholly negative and are therefore not to be displayed or ever sanctioned. Any thought for the self, any wanting, longing, desire, or anger is in this way produced within the text as bad and unacceptable. It is a view of self which exists only for and through others and which is so central to the production of femininity and female heterosexuality (Skeggs 1997; Walkerdine, 1990).

Angry, fighting, yearning, and wilful, the self that emerges in the last segment of Crystal's diary seems anything but the prescribed good heroine of the romance genre. Like the instance of parental objection I have already discussed around the issue of racial difference, this is another moment where desire in opposition is produced through the juxtaposition of parental obstacles to Crystal's entry into heterosexuality. As we have seen, the production of gendered subjectivity takes place in historically specific and socially variable arrangements. This moment of desire in opposition, I think, opens up the possibility for a further inquiry into some of the specific class and social circumstances in which girls are made good. For while it may not be transparent in the final text, this segment of the diary was intended to make Crystal's struggles with goodness recognizable as those of a girl whose working-class family has immigrated to Canada. Thus, it is the part played by the "technologies of the social" (Abel 1990, 184) in the regulation of desire that I want to tease out of this moment and the contested self that is produced there.

In her historical portrayal of some of the processes by which good working-class women are formed, Carolyn Steedman (1986, 105), following Alice Miller (1983), highlights how desire may be reproduced through a particular feature of relationships between mothers and daughters. Mothers, she suggests, may enter into a love relation with the child, whereby the child becomes a version of herself, someone through whom she may live and achieve all her hopes, lost through the exigences of living in difficult economic circumstances and the years spent raising children. In this way, she argues, there comes into existence daughters who are "intelligent, alert, attentive, extremely sensitive and (because they are completely attuned to her well-being) entirely at the mother's disposal and ready for her use" (1983, 29). It is in being the subject that a mother is endlessly striving to produce as ideal, one she herself can never be, Steedman writes, that a daughter comes to know that "you are not quite yourself, but someone else: someone else has paid the price for you, and you have to pay it back" (1986, 105). The "burden of being good," evolves into a sense of economic and emotional obligation and reciprocation whereby another's desires are taken on as one's own. What is being depicted here appears to be a relationship that is defined by a blurring of the boundaries between self and other—a relationship, as is symbolized in Crystal's name, that commands an evacuation of self.

It is, I think, this command to selflessness that the girls are negotiating both in the moment of desire in opposition produced on Crystal's behalf, as well as on their own behalfs, in the discussion that follows. In the girls' story and in their talk of their own families, it is usually relationships with parents, rather than specifically those with mothers, that seem to be portrayed. It is quite possible that this emphasis could suggest that there is a somewhat different dynamic at work in the family structures of these girls, the majority of whom, in fact, live in extended family households and not in nuclear families. But it is also not altogether clear who the term "parents" encompasses. For example, when it eventually occurred to me to ask, I found that when LeLy used the term "my parents," she was referring to her mother and grandmother, although her father also resided with them in the household. In this conversation they seem to be processing and protesting among themselves the sense that what is owed to parents is one's very self.

1 Maria: . . . they had you and like, like—
2 Fanny: they made you.
3 LeLy: Exactly, they think like, sometimes like I get into an
                argue with them, they say, "You used to be so goody-
                goody," and—
4 Fanny: that's different. That's a totally different story.
5 LeLy: No, it's not. Like, I don't know.
6 Marnina: It sounds like you're saying that you don't want them to
                be disappointed in you, but at the same time that—
7 LeLy: yeah.
8 Fanny: [inaudible] want you to be goody-goody—
9 Marnina: you can't be—
10 LeLy: yeah, exactly.
11 Maria: It's impossible—
12 LeLy: they expect you to be a certain person—
13 Maria: [inaudible] that they expect you to be, because you're
                your own person. (Trans. 05/31/95)

In the struggle to sort through the competing conceptions of self and how that self will be specified, echoes of "how to be good without being bad" reverberate here. A tension is set up whereby parental expectations are pitted against contesting desires of their own that also include wanting to be found good. This tension may be associated with one of the challenges girls face in attempting to constitute themselves as subjects within both discourses of Western liberal individuality and femininity. As many have argued, the dominant ideas of what constitutes an adult individual have been formulated around a masculine ideal (Benjamin 1988; Gilligan 1982; Hollway 1984; Johnson 1993; Wyn and White 1996). While this discourse emphasizes autonomy and self-sufficiency (being your own person), constituting oneself within hegemonic discourses of femininity requires demonstrating connection achieved through relationship management, particularly within heterosexual relations (Benjamin 1988). Moreover, within certain class cultures this relationship management may be centrally focused on one's extended family, particularly same-sex relations among females of that family. This polarity, Benjamin suggests, contributes to prevailing divisions between public and private spheres and is the social vehicle of gender domination. However, while it is possible to see here the dynamic of how desire may be reproduced through its articulation at once as obligation to another and as one's own, the content of these desires has to be further delineated and examined. As Steedman explains "[I]n the social world, it is the social people want" (1986, 106).

Caught between the expectations, fears, and plans projected onto her by her parents and the exigences of entering into a heterosexual relationship, the social

enters Crystal's diary through the signification of As and A minuses, the requirement to achieve in school with its underlying subtext of the family's future security
and prosperity. Romance is presented as an obstacle to being able to fulfil this
obligation—an obligation that weighs all the more on her since her older sister
Cindy has already broken this same contract by moving in with her boyfriend,
against her parents' wishes. With her statement, "Now all their hopes are on me,"
Crystal suggests that more is riding on her grades than merely her own academic
achievements.

In the romance stories that Walkerdine analyzes, she found that the heroines of these stories are often presented as doing very well at school. In explaining
this somewhat surprising phenomenon, Walkerdine suggests that one of the reasons academic accomplishment is acceptable, especially in the early and middle
grades, is because it is seen as something that is for others, something that makes
parents proud (1990, 97). For working-class girls, Walkerdine continues, success
at school may be associated with a possible route to upward mobility and plays
into a kind of good girl femininity (1990, 148), a theme which will be explored in
more depth in the next chapter.

For these girls—these daughters of refugees and immigrants—to take on
their mothers' desires suggests the necessity of more than a passing acquain-
tance with the hardships of lives disrupted and transplanted, of sacrifices made
on someone else's account. Speaking of their own mothers' longing to return
home, Tammy and Mai, for example, explain that the family remains in Canada
for the possibilities this country offers to themselves and their brothers: education and future prospects. In grades six and seven, respectively, they have already completed more schooling than either of their parents. Delivering
success at school is understood as compensation for hardship and sacrifice, as
well as a promise of economic stability and a better life for the whole family—it
is something that is owed. As LeLy comments about her grades, 80s and 90s
earned in a language she did not even speak three years earlier, "It's kind of a
trade. If you give me a certain thing, I have to pay you back a certain thing"
(Trans. 05/31/95).

However, the chain of signification of good grades leading to good jobs in
the public sphere and upward mobility is not an unfettered one. Associated with
it is a tension over competing expectations of successfully fulfilling dominantly defined definitions of female roles within the other privileged site of adult life: the
private sphere of the family. For Maria, reconciling these expectations means that
the issue of grades raises not a sense of debt but rather a painful sense of longing
and confusion. Her concerns reopen the question of how a good working-class immigrant girl is made recognizable to include the closely related question of what it
is she gains recognition for.

1 Maria:	Like mine's totally the opposite. Like OK, . . . I have a mixed feelings about my grades because my parents, I have a feeling that they care but then they don't care. Cause they care about my like, okay, they care, they want me to pass school and everything, get a good job and all that stuff but also be a housewife. That's why I'm getting mixed up with this. Because they say they want me to get a good job, but than I [deep sigh] mix it up because like they give me the impression that they want me to stay home, like cook, clean all that stuff. . . . Okay, like my last report card was like the best report card I've gotten from, since I came here, right? It was my best report card, because I got almost—well you saw my report card.
2 Marnina:	Yeah, it was a great report card.
3 Maria:	Yeah, I thought it was good. Because I know I'm not smart, so I can't expect myself—I'm not going to put myself through [inaudible] so like getting all As because I know I can't do that, but I got pretty good and I'm happy. Like, I get home, my parents go, "Oh, that's good."
4 Fanny:	That's all?
5 Maria:	Like they don't feel interested. You mean I try all this, I've been trying to make you guys proud of me and you go, "That's good?" Like sometimes I think they feel more happy when I clean the house, like when I do something at home good, like bake a cake, or something like that good, instead of my grades!
6 LeLy:	Which one you're feeling more like you want to do?
7 Maria:	I want to get better grades. I get like [sighs . . .] I get really sad and then I don't talk to them and then they say that I'm like—
8 Marnina:	being difficult.
9 Maria:	Yeah, being difficult. But it's not because . . . they expect me to be like . . . get a good job . . . but then they don't help me. Like some of the things I know I could do better, but I wish they would say to me, like say, "Oh that's good honey, but you can do better, I know you can." But they don't. As long as I don't get all C's . . . well they give me the impression that they don't care. I don't know if they care or not. (Trans. 05/31/95)

Carolyn Steedman explains that if a daughter is able to make the desires projected onto her by her mother her own, then the social world itself may provide her with some measure of their quality and validity and help her to stand to one side,

momentarily detached from her mother's longing (1986, 106). For the girls, however, this resolution does not seem to be a fully satisfactory one for either their character or themselves. Instead, a somewhat different possibility is offered to Maria by
LeLy in the group discussion above, and in the moment of desire in opposition the
girls create for Crystal.

"Why can't I be myself?" writes Crystal in her diary, and "Which one you're
feeling more like you want to do?" LeLy asks Maria. The former a proclamation of
self-instituted being, the latter an invitation to take up this option, both seem to
suggest a working against the command to selflessness and the disavowal of self.
This setting of boundaries around the self protests the view of self as completely
able to absorb the agendas of others. And yet, because there seems to be no other
negotiable position with respect to family expectations, and given the overwhelming and contradictory demands of being good, such a position cannot be anything
other than an ambivalent one. Whereas the negotiation of heterosexual relations
seems coded with shifting representations of romance, and a more open field of
possibilities (in no small measure due to feminist discourse), here the internally
contradictory behaviors defining goodness (good grades/homemaking), means
that being good is manifestly impossible without simultaneously being bad.

CHAPTER 4

Tori's Story:
Becoming Somebody

The bell rings. Two girls sit around a table, eating. It's lunch time. They are engaged in an animated conversation. A third girl joins them—looking gloomy, walking slowly, Tori makes her entrance.

Girl 1:	*So what's up?*
Tori:	*Nothing really.*
Girl 2:	*Something wrong?*
Tori:	*I don't want to talk about it.*
Girl 1:	*You can tell us.*
Tori:	*Okay, I have a problem. It's a school problem. Not about homework or anything, right? It's just that I feel like a nerd. I'm so ugly.*

Fast forward to the next segment featuring Tori. Tile floor, blue stalls—it's the girls' washroom. Dance music can be heard coming from some distance away. Tori's feet are visible from underneath one of the stalls, surrounded by articles of clothing. She addresses the two girls waiting on the other side of the stall.

Tori:	*I feel so uncomfortable in these clothes!*
Girl 1:	*Come on!*
Girl 2 :	*Don't be chicken!*
Tori:	*Promise not to laugh?*
Girl 1:	*Okay.*

The door opens and Tori cautiously exits the stall. PAUSE.

Having retrieved the video from its storage place in the back of my filing cabinet, I am watching the scenario unfold from a distance of three years—or is it four? I am further from those girls now, from Mai, who plays Tori, and the others. Three years ago I knew them, not uncomplicatedly, as girls, working-class students, immigrants whose family histories brought them to this city from the far reaches of the globe. Talking on the phone recently to the girl I am calling LeLy, I learn that she and Mai are studying to pass a test for their drivers' licences. That makes them at least sixteen. A moment of disjuncture. If they are sixteen, then who are the twelve- and thirteen-year-olds I encounter daily as I work through my piles of transcripts? The question takes me back to a time when I, slightly older than they are now, had by chance come across the Hare Krishna annual fall festival at the base of Mount Royal in Montreal. Standing in front of a crowd of curious onlookers, a man is discoursing on reincarnation. In response to a question from someone in the audience, he pointedly asks, "Well, if you don't believe in reincarnation, then just where do you think your baby body is?" Bodies extracted from and wandering through time.

Rewinding to what things seemed to have meant then, playing with what I need to make them mean now (so as to fit between the covers of this book), fast-forwarding to anticipate how others will read, make sense of, and evaluate it, ethnographic writing performs the contradictory move of securing wandering bodies by extracting them from time. But even with my finger pressing the pause button, keeping the girls static at thirteen, I am having trouble fixing identities and meanings. Perhaps what I am confessing here is that however I choose to write about back then, I am forced to reflect that time in the flickering of that old school video monitor that keeps breaking down—that is in fragments that fail to completely mirror the bodies in front of the camera. Reader: reconcile yourself to the inevitability of missing bits.

PLAY. *Gasps, as Tori exits the stall.*
Girl 1:   *You look great!*
Tori: *You sure?*
Girl 1:   *Positive. No one will recognize you! Sit down. I'm going to do*
                    this hair of yours, and it's going to be wonderful!

With her new clothes and restyled hair, a metamorphosis transpires—the nerd is transformed into the popular girl. Yes, Tori's is a story of a kind of reincarnation. Such stories, like the romance genre the girls used to tell Crystal's story discussed in chapter 2, are also a device commonly used in the narration of women's lives. Often using the rags-to-riches formula, women's transformations in these fictional accounts may be physical, moral, or linguistic.[1] Their successful accomplishment is usually followed by women's traditional reward: the love of an eligible man. Transformation and romance stories are, therefore, closely linked.

Cameron suggests that transformation stories are also what is being promised in the lengthy tradition of self-improvement literature specifically addressed to women, as well as in the perennially popular makeover feature in women's magazines (1995, 172). Playing on both desire and guilt, the seductiveness of this formula, Cameron argues, goes to the heart of a powerful fantasy for women in consumerist cultures. Transformation, however, figures in an even older tradition of stories that significantly predates modern capitalism. In these stories, rather than a professional army of fashion consultants, hair stylists, and makeup artists, ugly ducklings become beautiful swans with only a wave of a magic wand. I am, of course referring to the fairy tale.

Like all stories of reincarnation, the one the girls created for Tori and the one I aim to tell here contain traces of other lives. I'll mention two. The first is summoned from within the fairy tale tradition. Cinderella's story is, according to Bruno Bettelheim (1976, 236), the best known and best-liked story of a girl's life of all time: she would not be left out. The story the girls created for Tori shares many significant elements with this tale of a kitchen maid turned princess. Perhaps this should not be surprising, as the story of Cinderella, with its 345 versions dating back to the seventeenth century (Luthi 1970), is quite possibly the archetypical story of feminine transformation.

The second is a different kind of story. A story that might have been, but is not quite. We gave her the name Kathy; however, her story cannot be accessed through the videotape. It's not there. Worked up as the character that Lan would play, she was not completely finished when Lan's participation in the group dropped off and we were short another actor to play the part. I outline her story now so that you'll recognize her when she makes her debut appearance here in this chapter. Or perhaps, if the other girls permit, I should let Lan tell it, as it was after all her idea.

1	Lan:	Kathy is a smart intelligent, who never gets guys. Cause you know, how guys like girls that are stupider than them?
2	Mai:	Some guys.
3	Lan:	And she's a straight-A student and guys avoid her.
4	Maria:	She already has everything for Kathy here!
5	Lan:	KATHY'S A BOLD INTELLIGENT!
6	LeLy:	Lan, enough! You know nothing about Kathy. (Trans. 04/05/95)

Well, never mind. LeLy's interference—communicating as it does more than a mere hint of a power/knowledge struggle—foreshadows one of the central themes of Tori's story. In any case, Lan will have other opportunities to say more about Kathy shortly. But for now she will have to wait as I outline the linkages between the various lives represented in and through these stories, their multiple and competing authorizings, and the purposes they will serve in this chapter. She won't have to wait too long.

The predicament of the nerd, as Tori defines it for her friends, is a school problem. The nerd popular categorization appears to be something of a cultural signature of North American schools. It pervades many popular culture exposés of adolescent life in film, television, and books, and it has also been the subject of academic studies documenting life in schools (Caanan 1994; Eckert 1989; Eder 1985, 1995; Kinney 1993; Schofield 1981). While the identities of nerds and popularity are often analyzed as individual and psychologized phenomena, the group's interest in working with these categories in the telling of Tori's story seems to me to go beyond the mere reproduction of these familiar and stereotypical representations. In gossipy news items that passed around the lunch table along with the food we shared; in angry reports of the latest experienced injustices; and in a series of letters LeLy and I exchanged that year we worked on the video together, this was an issue that clearly resonated with enormous emotional import. Often coupled with this theme was another: the refrain of teacher fairness. Together the topic of nerds and popularity may carry the forceful significance that it does because for the girls these categories encode some of the microsocial politics through which they negotiate the multiple and competing regimes of power and powerlessness that determine what it means to be a girl or to be a particular sort of girl.

Like the nerd, the smart girl is also a school story. Kathy's dilemma, as it is laid out by Lan, highlights the conflicting discursive positionings of the girl who is an A student. As it is impossible to simultaneously exhibit her intelligence and have her femininity recognized and confirmed by male attention, her story, like Tori's, raises important questions about what counts as valid and valued expressive forms of femininity (Hey 1997; Walkerdine 1990; Willis 1977).

Together Tori's and Kathy's stories detail an account in which the school emerges as a site that is intimately connected with, and strongly regulative of, a sense of social identity. In focusing attention on the issues of popularity and smartness, these stories rehearse some of the particular cultural forms and practices that embody the power/knowledge nexus through which identities are regulated, struggled over, and produced within schools. That is, popularity and smartness may socially symbolize, in both overlapping and distinctive ways, the cumulative effects of an organized production process of subjective value. While popularity may afford those who can successfully position themselves as such a certain kind of recognition and a measure of symbolic capital that is denied others, girls' displays of smartness, as I have already suggested, may carry both

rewards and risks. Scratch the surface and the refrain of fairness is revealed, en-
meshed in a complicated web of gender, race, and class relations, crystallizing in
story form a narration of the girls' schooling experience.

The writers of Tori's story—working-class, immigrant, Asian/black/white,
girls living in Toronto at the end of the twentieth century—occupy tenuous positions as subjects within discourses of schooling. Whether absent and/or marginalized[2] or present and misrepresented,[3] what is apparent is that they are positioned
as somehow lacking, inadequate, and falling short of some measure of what it
means to be a real child, adolescent, student, or girl.[4] These discourses, as I have
already demonstrated in chapter 2, were not only clearly in circulation at the
school attended by these girls, but were also called on as part of the rationale for
initiating the project on which this work is based.

For these girls (who neither considered themselves nor thought themselves
considered by others to be either smart or popular), perhaps what compelled the
creation of a video character whose story revolved around these themes was the opportunity of using Tori's story as a relay point to produce ways of engaging with
what was going on. It is possible that it afforded them an opportunity to both work
through their own positionings within this valuation system, as well as to fantasize
alternative positions and what these might promise for something else. However, it
is too simple to suggest that the girls' identification(s) with their character was a
completely straightforward one.

1	Lan:	Why does she want to be in the popular crowd in the first place?
2	Fanny:	Cause she's a nerd.
3	Mai:	Don't you want to be in the popular crowd?
4	Fanny:	I'm a nerd and I don't care.
5	LeLy:	Don't you want to be popular?
6	Kenisha:	No.
7	Lan:	I just want to be normal. (Trans. 23/05/95)

There is a suggestion here of an ambivalent identification in the way the girls' responses, clearly articulated from an outside position, move from acceptance to
resistance and refusal. Fanny's initial response to Lan's question (2) rehearses
what Corrigan understands as the privileging of preferred forms: "a desire to be
in 'those places' so designated so approved" (Corrigan 1987, 39). The only explanation required for why Tori wants to be popular is that she's a nerd (2). On
her own behalf, however, she refuses this desired place and Kenisha does the
same (4, 6). Perhaps, as Lan seems to be suggesting, the struggle for even meeting
the criteria of hegemonic definitions of normality takes on particular force when

one is, like these girls are, denied full access to dominant forms of cultural and social power (7).

However, as the discussion continues, this identificatory relationship with the idealized popular girl becomes significantly more complex when LeLy forcefully insists that the other girls, and Lan in particular, confront the privileges, power, pleasure, and excitement promised by inhabiting this desired place. Perhaps what is most important about the insights that are offered here is what they have to suggest about the workings of a hunger for positive identification within a history of experienced rejection (Wexler 1992).

8	LeLy:	Don't tell me no one in here want to be popular!
9	Kenisha:	What do you mean, "popular"? Popular sucks a lot.
10	LeLy:	In your heart, people!
11	Kenisha:	[mimicking] In your heart. You want to be popular. Popular sucks.
12	LeLy:	Okay, if you're taking Lidia and taking Fanny, who do you want to be? Lidia or Fanny?
13	Kenisha:	[laughing] Fanny.
14	LeLy:	IN YOUR FACE! Who don't want to be Lidia? She's smart, she's popular, she's pretty, who don't?
15	Maria:	[inaudible] . . . she's popular, she's smart, she's pretty.
16	Fanny:	I don't care. I don't want to be her, even if she's smart.
17	LeLy:	They're not being honest. Why bother? Who don't? Right, Maria?
18	Lan:	I want to be rich and famous [inaudible].
19	Kenisha:	What's so nice about Lidia?
20	Maria:	Exactly, popular.
21	Kenisha:	[teasing] Popular, she's pretty, she's a brainer, ahhhh.
22	Lan:	There, LeLy says she's a bitch.
23	Maria:	She is a bitch.
24	Fanny:	Horny, slut.
25	Lan:	Whoaa!
26	Mai:	But I don't think Lan's being honest here. She doesn't want to be Lidia. I'd rather be Lidia than Fanny too.
27	?:	Of course you would!
28	LeLy:	Okay, let's put it this way. Lan, would you rather be a famous singer star or be a garbage picker?
29	Lan:	Famous movie star!
30	LeLy:	There, IN YOUR FACE! Who wouldn't want to be popular? Just putting another looking, another angle, thing.
31	Lan:	I don't want to be garbage picker, yuck. Garbage picker smells, you know.

32 LeLy: I'm not talking about how they smell.
33 Mai: Movie star has more respect than garbage picker.
34 LeLy: You don't admit it one way. If you put it another way,
                 you'll admit it! (Trans. 23/05/95)

Trying out various tactics in her attempts to counter denials, teasing, and disavowals, LeLy works hard to get the other girls to concede their own desire for a position within popularity. Her strategies include initially using an abstraction of the category "popular," but this yields little capitulation from the others. She then tries another approach, making the concept more concrete by setting up a comparison between Fanny and Lidia who, within the localized context of their school, seem to epitomize the differences between the nerd and the popular girl. When this meets with only limited success, LeLy redoubles her efforts and introduces another contrasting associative pair—the famous movie star and the garbage picker. LeLy uses Lan's often expressed fascination with the world of Hollywood and its movie stars to finally win her argument.

Beyond their deployment to outmaneuver Lan, the split pair of the famous movie star and the garbage picker is interesting for how they are pitted against each other as symbolic antagonists in the struggle for recognition, visibility, and respect. Split images, appearing as they do in both the nerd/popular division in Tori's story and the good/bad girl of Crystal's, seem to be a device used by the girls to both define and evaluate competing discursive positions (Luttrell 1997; Walkerdine 1990). In this particular instance, the famous movie star opposed with the garbage picker is offered to Lan as a fantasy space in which she might imagine herself as a somebody (or not). In this way it is possible to see how particular girls may use fantasy as a positive identification within the limited terrain of self-production which is open to them. As people struggle in a world full of apparently glamorous options to "be somebody," fantasy is, according to Walkerdine, a pleasurable space in which subjects mythically satisfy their own needs (1997, 178). The famous movie star promises a lifestyle and presents a model of femininity which is both far from the mundane existence of the working-class school girl and, for most, also completely out of reach. Engaging in these kinds of fantasies might be considered practices of survival, because they are about managing to survive and even to prosper in difficult circumstances (McCarthy 1998; Walkerdine 1997). Perhaps the particular allure of the cultural fantasy of transformation stories might begin to be understood using these terms.

The famous movie star and garbage picker are also interesting for what they suggest about the classed dimensions of femininity embedded within the nerd/popular divide. Within the context of a discussion about popularity, the split pair establishes popularity as not only the route to forms of recognition, visibility, and respect within the school, but also as intimately connected with, and perhaps a symbolic analogy for, differential positions of power within class relations in a wider social context. There are, in fact, historic links between the achievement of popularity and those of middle-class ideals. Thompson argues that in the 1920s and 1930s parents and teachers encouraged the proliferation of adolescent social and extracurricular life with the underlying assumption that sociability prepared middle-class girls to be social assets in their futures as wives of businessmen and professionals (Thompson 1995, 48). The economic and political implications of the popular/unpopular split were considered a serious educational problem by social and political scientists as early as the 1920s. Since then, however, it does not seem to have been analyzed in these terms. According to Thompson, the apparatus of clubs, proms, and student government was thought to confer schools' institutional power on popular students, creating an elite and undermining what some believed should be the equality-building projects of schools. Seen by some as a function of class, it was argued that either popularity had to be abolished or its skills taught to all, as part of an education in the ways of middle-class life (Thompson 1995, 50).

This historical debate about popularity highlights both the contradictory and contested educational agendas of schools and the ways in which the production of particular identities is integral to these agendas. Schools seem to be expected to both confirm and challenge social divisions to control and regulate, and to be sites of social change and emancipation. However, perhaps the most interesting aspect of this debate is the way both positions in it pivot around a valuing of middle-class over working-class norms. Making a shift into a position of popularity may therefore be viewed as a move out of and into a series of related discursive and social relations, involving a complex of gendered, classed—and I will add heterosexual and racialized—positionings.

Pretty, smart and Portuguese, Lidia typifies for LeLy and the other girls the signifying repertoires and the interactional resources necessary for their accomplishment to access a position within popularity. However, when her name is invoked, rather than extracting the confessionary identifications that LeLy is seeking, this phantasmic reading of Lidia incites instead a sexualized attack. The politics of reputation (Bottomly 1979) seems to be deployed here as a very strong refusal of identification. Then again, perhaps this might be read not so much as a refusal of identification as a defense against it. That is, this denigration seems to construct a boundary between the girls and the popular girl Lidia; a boundary built from a particular structure of feeling: envy. Envy is, according to Cohen, an ambivalent structure of feeling. It involves the desire to possess certain idealized attributes of the other and the desire to destroy them because they signify what is felt to be lacking and impossible to attain (1992, 73).

This envious sexualized attack on Lidia's reputation, occurring as it does within the context of a discussion on popularity, may indicate an understanding, as we have already seen, of the ways in which popularity is the realization of a certain kind of femininity, one that involves compliance with white, middle-class, and heterosexual norms. At the same time, it may also signify both an acute desire for an identification with what is understood as a socially highly valued form of femininity, and a corresponding powerful fear of the losses such an identification might incur (Luttrell 1993; Unwin 1984; Walkerdine 1990). The ambivalent relationship to the popular girl, as I will outline in more detail later, seems therefore to be about a thwarted identification (Benjamin 1988, 111).

Tracing how the popular/nerd and smart girl positions are charted by the girls on the discourse map of femininity generated by the video project, this chapter not only explores the different and overlapping meanings of femininity and girlhood designated by these categories, but also begins to analyze the ways social selves emerge from particular contexts, specifically the school—through what Foucault terms the "capillary" network of power in knowledge regimes (1980, 93). Thus, on one level the story I tell here is about the practices of schooling involved in the social production of difference and the ways in which social meanings and systems of valuation work to make these differences recognizable. On another level, the story explores how these differences, in their contradictions and multiplicity, are lived and their meanings struggled over. In this fusion of themes, Tori's transformation story serves as a vehicle through which to explore difficult questions about the assignment of recognition, vulnerabilities to misrecognition, and the relations of spaces, places, things, and people in the intricate ongoing project of "becoming somebody" (Luttrell 1996; Rockhill, 1987; Wexler 1992).

NARRATING THE SELF FROM THE INSIDE OUT

As the three friends sit around the lunch table, Tori elaborates on the collection of problems indexed under her nerd status: "Why can everyone always, always judge you by the outside? Is this world a fairness world? . . . I thought about this question for a long time. I can't get the answer," she confides to them. Divided into two realms—inside and outside—the self she conceptualizes is represented as a spatial territory marked by the boundaries of the body. The outside, she seems to be suggesting, is visible, observable and therefore knowable to others, while the inside is hidden but somehow more authentic or real. Her problem seems to be in part a feature of a miscommunication. Not only does this division of the self invite the possibility that the outside may fail to properly represent the inside, but this may also occasion an unjust misrecognition by others.

In the last volume of *The History of Sexuality* (1980), Michel Foucault argues that it is not so much the sense of the self that is a development of the modern world, rather it is the location of the self that is new. Charles Taylor (1989, 1991, 1994), supports this view when he claims, after surveying the whole of Western philosophy, that what happened in the nineteenth century was a massive subjective turn. Understandings about identity, which he suggests had prior to this time been conceived of as originating from outside the individual, shifts inside. He calls this development "the world passed within." This spatial sense, what Steedman (1995) terms "interiority," entered into common sense understandings about the nature of the self, in part through discourses of psychoanalysis. These suggest, Flax argues (1990, 208), that there is something deep inside us, something bodily but at least partially knowable by consciousness. These discourses put forward an ideal of an individual, authentic self about which knowledge is possible. This self is seen and experienced as deep and foundational, created by the layering down and accretion of childhood experiences, our own history in a place inside (Steedman 1995, 12).

The girls are clearly drawing on these modernist discourses of the self to create their character, her problem, and the question of how she might be transformed. The question without an answer that Tori is asking suggests a theory of subjectivity that implicitly links discourses of recognition with those of identity, justice, and knowledge of the self. Identity is not simply a matter of self-identification but, rather, is also shaped by the recognition or its absence by important others (Benjamin 1988; Fanon 1967; Honneth 1996; Taylor 1994). Like the spatial remapping of identity, the linkage of these discourses is also a product of the modern age. Taylor (1994, 34) explains that with inwardly derived personal identity, recognition is not something that is enjoyed a priori. It has to be won through a dialogical exchange with others. He argues that what has come about with the modern age is not the need for recognition but, as Tori personifies, the conditions in which the attempt to gain recognition can fail.

As Taylor (1989) suggests, the important question to ask about the conception of the self produced through these overlapping discourses concerns the shape of the life stories it allows the girls to tell about their character and about themselves.[5] What are the experiences that are mediated as an effect of a subjectivity constituted in and through these terms? How are these discourses implicated in the intersubjective relations of schooling and the practical relation to self that is realized within these relations? How are these discourses implicated in producing the regulative norms at work in the process of "becoming somebody"?

As they attempt to grapple with these questions the girls' use of the simple narrative form of the fairy tale seems a particularly provocative choice. Identified by some as assisting readers, particularly children, in bridging the immense gap between inner experiences and the outside world, fairy tales are thought to help with the integration of the rational order with the illogic of the unconscious (Bettelheim 1976; Spence 1995; Steedman 1986). The fairy tale, Steedman suggests, is one of the places where a child's understanding of herself as part of the world may be established. In its turn, this social understanding helps interpret the inner landscape (1986, 143). It seems, therefore, that the fairy tale is a very useful narrative tool with which to enter into considerations of not only how outside class, race, and gendered discourses are reconfigured as the inside of girls' subjective and intersubjective relations, but also how the interaction between the two organize and produce the terrain where recognition is enabled or hindered.

Traditional fairy tales are also interesting from the perspective of the kinds of identifications they facilitate. These are very often stories in which women and girls are active agents, rather than merely secondary supporting characters. Commenting on Hans Christian Anderson's propensity for presenting so many dramas where women are dazzling and powerful, witches, queens, and fairies, Steedman suggests that he uses women, the final outsiders, to write his own outcast working-class life drama. Not only does this offer his readers a rare reversal of a common transformation of gender in reading, whereby girls have to read themselves as boys in order to become active heroines in the text (Steedman 1986, 143), but the stories also consist of a detailed study of how reviled outsiders may become valued insiders. The linkages between gender and class transformations necessary for the successful achievement of this kind of project play a central role in Tori's story and will become important aspects of my analysis of it. In terms of the group's ongoing consideration of how to introduce powerful elements for each of our female characters, these concerns of the fairy tale form, combined with Tori's specific dilemma, created as we shall see, some interesting challenges.

Relatedly, among the many themes that fairy tales often take up is a concern with outlining a program for an improved future (Bettelheim 1976, 73). Concentrating as they do on the process of change, rather than describing the exact details of the final outcome, the traditional fairy tale offers the writers of Tori's story many relevant suggestions for how to narratively realize the promise encapsulated in the women's magazine makeover cliché, the "new you." More specifically, what this form engenders is a focus on the process of transformation—the process that is at the heart of Tori's attempted refashioning of her self from nerd into popular girl.

SCENES OF TRANSFORMATION

The conventions of various genres, Pam Gilbert argues, furnish particular choices about story progression, about the organization of events in a narrative, and about the functions of actors. Since genres are recognizable social language conventions, they provide something of an index to cultural values and assumptions held within a society at a particular time. Embedded in each of the structural narrative elements of a story are, therefore, implicit understandings about gendered subjects. Gilbert suggests (following Cohan and Shires 1988) that a focus on narrative construction is a powerful way of uncovering social constructions of gender (1992, 190-191).

An analysis of the transformation genre as a narrative construction offers distinct and interesting insights into prevailing discourses of gender and the identifications these make possible. At the most rudimentary organizational level, the stories that fall into this classification present a series of problems whose solutions are revealed through the transformative process. Mediated in terms of morality (good versus bad), through visual motifs (a glass slipper, a new set of clothes), physical characteristics (beauty/ugliness), the transformation in these stories repetitiously lays down, in various guises, that which is considered socially and culturally ideal in terms of gender, sexuality, race, and class. However, constructing and making sense of the structure of the narrative in a gendered way requires a particular set of writing and reading practices which rely on dominant discourses of femininity to make the sequence of incidents resulting in the transformation seem meaningful and possible. In writing Tori's story, therefore, the girls are drawing on both their competence in the transformation narrative and in their knowledge of the social relations of the school, with all the associated dimensions of gender, race, and class, to name the operative categories, as well as to justify specific courses of action.

In uncovering the narrative construction of the story, I use a reading strategy, outlined by Pam Gilbert (1992), which involves identifying the organization of progressive transformations of events in the narrative, alternately moving between the various constituting features of nerd and popular identities. Thus, my analysis multiplies the concept of transformation to incorporate not only the intention of the narrative but also its very design and structure. According to Cohan and Shires, these are organized in two ways—on both horizontal and vertical axes:

> A story . . . syntagmatically places events in a sequence to organize signifying relations of addition and combination, thereby operating like metonymy in a linguistic structure. Moreover, events in a story do not "simply happen" in a syntagmatic chain but are structured paradigmatically as well. A story paradigmatically replaces one event with another to organize signifying relations of selection and substitution, thereby operating like metaphor in a linguistic structure. For purposes of analysis, then, a story can be segmented into events, and events can be distinguished from each other (and

so identified as signifiers) according to the way in which the story sets them in a structure of syntagmatic and paradigmatic relations. (1988, 54)

Mediated through a double matrix of words and images, action and sign, the paradigmatic transformations in Tori's story may be seen to unfold as follows. Tori does not look right: she has not yet learned how to inscribe her self so that she may be recognized as the kind of girl she wishes to be. Consequently she seeks help from her friends who have certain skills and experience in this regard; she will need to strategize around the many barriers in the way of achieving her goals; she will need to select an occasion and a location in which to both publicly display and test the successfulness of her transformation. This paradigmatic structure may be seen to closely follow the basic formula for transformation stories as it is laid out in that archetypical story of the genre, Cinderella. As summarized by Jo Spence, the sequence may be characterized as a perceived lack on the part of the female protagonist, intervention of an outside agent, and a resolution to the lack (1995, 63).

The syntagmatic structure of Tori's story is organized into three distinct video segments. Each segment features Tori and her two friends in different school settings: the lunchroom, the girls' washroom, and the gym. Supported by the dialogue between characters and a visual vocabulary of props, wardrobe, and hairstyle, these shifts in location propel the narrative's forward movement and signal the various stages of Tori's transformation. As a result, the transformations appear to take place in a logical and natural sequencing order, making it possible to interpret them in particular social ways (Gilbert 1992).

The three segments that make up the syntagmatic structure of the story are arranged around the anticipation of, preparation for, and participation in a school dance. The actuality of a school dance scheduled to take place around the time the videotaping was planned prompted the group to incorporate it into Tori's story—a decision which served to perhaps inadvertently further strengthen the resemblance of our protagonist's tale to that of her prototype Cinderella. But, just as relevant, school dances may also have served for the girls many of the same purposes they designed this particular one to perform for Tori.

Intersecting the horizontal and vertical axis of the story's transformations, two scenes of recognition emerge. Generated in the production and performance of Tori's story, these scenes map the constitution of the categories nerd and popular and the sites in and through which the meanings attached to them are realized. Thus they illustrate how social institutions like schools organize groups through a distinctly spatial ordering of subjects. They are, in short, the means by which I investigate the questions I want to raise about identification, identity, and social power and at the same time they serve as our reentry back into Tori's story.

SCENE 1. FROM THE OUTSIDE IN:
(RE)DRESSING SOCIAL DIFFERENCE

On The Horizontal

Loosely based on the story concept and character development agreed upon in our group deliberations, the dialogue that Mai, Maria, and Kenisha are engaged in on behalf of Tori and her two friends is improvised rather than scripted. Watching the scenario around the lunch table unfolding, the discussion feels as if it harbors many undercurrents, any of which could, without much notice, carry it off in multiple directions, taking the story along with it. This prospect for conversational drift arises in part from the questions the girls are trying to advance, and the competing ways in which they may be interested in seeing them addressed. That is, the dual task of the first segment of Tori's story is to establish popularity and all that it confers as a desired place, as well as to situate Tori as somehow lacking what it takes to successfully occupy this position. This task is complicated by what we have already seen as the girls' ambiguous and conflicting relationships to popularity. In the following general discussion, the very differing knowledges, experiences, and investments the girls may be bringing to their representation of this desired place, as well as how Tori's problem is understood, are evident.

1	Mai:	I heard this interview. Popular people and nerds too. And nerds say, "Oh, we can't get along with popular people; they're too popular and we're scared," and stuff.
2	Kenisha:	Nobody's not nerd! Everybody's just people! Just people.
3	Mai:	People get categorized, unfortunately.
4	Marnina:	So, how do these categories happen then? Of popular and not popular?
5	Kenisha:	This is what I just can't understand. How did they happen? Oh, my god! (Trans. 04/05/95)

Drawing on the authority of a well-liked local radio call-in show that several of the girls had separately heard the night before, and that she had tape recorded and given to me, Mai puts into commission the binary categories nerd and popular. Her emphasis on the problematics of intergroup interaction sets up an understanding of the differential privilege attached to the two categories, naturalizing the favorability of one position over the other. In referencing the radio show, where callers were asked to identify themselves as being either a nerd or a popular person, Mai authenticates the categories as real entities that always already exist in the world, beyond the local conditions of their school and the realm of fiction.

For Kenisha, however, the taken-for-grantedness of these categories does not seem at all straightforward. The way in which she uses the term "just people" questions assumptions about the existence of these categories and the way that they are differentially valued. In this context "just people" could, on the one hand, be calling on a rhetoric of normalcy. The expression may be understood as the deracialized human, that is, white, middle-class, Canadian, male norm against which these girls appear inherently aberrant, the unconditioned ideal of which they are doomed to fall short. It reiterates Lan's comment, "I just want to be normal." At the same time, it is also possible that Kenisha's protest may be about turning around this rhetoric to verbalize an oppositional view, namely that being "just people," without having to submit to an unwritten cultural/political agenda, should be everyone's birthright. She may be claiming entitlement to what comes uncontested to those in unmarked positions of power and with choices (Wong 1993, 180).

On the set, this dynamic plays out as follows in the three friends' first exchange:

Girl 1:	*So what's up?*
Tori:	*Nothing really.*
Girl 2:	*Something wrong?*
Tori:	*I don't want to talk about it.*
Girl 1:	*You can tell us.*
Tori:	*Okay, I have a problem. It's a school problem. Not about homework or anything, right? It's just that I feel like a nerd. I'm so ugly.*
Girl 1:	*Why, you're not a nerd.*
Tori:	*Yes, I am. Look at me right now! And you guys are so popular. How come? Like how come you guys can be so popular? I'm so ugly!*
Girl 1:	*Don't say that!*
Girl 2:	*Because you want to make yourself ugly.*

The girls quickly accomplish the positioning of each of the characters within the seemingly taken-for-granted binary and differentially privileged categories nerd and popular. The dialogue is supported by visual effects: Tori's body language, clothing, accessories, and speech pattern almost preempt her pronouncement, naming herself a nerd. She walks and talks tentatively, her head hanging down, shoulders hunched. Her hands are shoved into her pockets; an old beat-up and torn canvas book bag is slung over one shoulder. Nothing, however, screams "nerd" louder than her outfit. Her jeans sport cartoon character decals, which the girls considered childish. Even more incriminating, they do not fit properly. They hang well above her ankles. Her feet, in running shoes, look oversized as a result. Her blouse is tight in all the wrong places, the collar is choked up around her neck, and her wrists are as exposed as her ankles. Brushed off her face and tightly fastened into two short braids, her hair tops off this portrait of awkwardness.

Perhaps not unexpectedly, the girls' representation of Tori makes use of many familiar features available from stereotypical images of the nerd current at the time. While this raises the question of how it is that our lived fictions and the fictions in texts intersect and (in)form each other (Davies 1993, 151), it also emphasizes the reciprocality of identity, mediated through the economy of the look. Female subjectivity is achieved, as Angela Partington suggests, through learning-to-look as well as learning-to-be-looked-at (1991, 54). "Look at me," Tori instructs her friends when Girl 1 mildly protests the appropriateness of Tori's having named herself a nerd. She provides a further directive for how to read her otherness by drawing attention to the cumulative effect of her appearance—her ugliness. Just like in a fairy tale the girls' story uses archetypal characters with the visible attributes of beauty and ugliness to convey a set of social understandings around issues of belonging, worth, and worthlessness and dominant/subordinate relations. Moreover, it is within the economy of the look that these relations are secured. The nerd is set up here as spectacle, in contrast to the panoptical stance enjoyed by her popular peers. As McClintock argues, these two positions, variously available to those in subordinate and privileged social positions, have historically been a structural feature organizing and reinforcing hierarchical relations between social groups (1995, 122). She argues further that the internalization of the gaze of the voyeur offers a certain ambiguous power. It allows one to participate in the vicarious enjoyment of their power. Yet it also breeds a corresponding dependency on the one endowed with the social privilege of approval (1995, 157).

Thus Tori's lack is initially established by the failure of her body to acquiesce in the power of the social norm and the standard of this norm is made effective through the signifying relations of the gaze. While Tori's recognition of her otherness is represented as having occurred rather suddenly, the following discussion suggests, as Haug argues, that this kind of recognition occurs as a result of a long and detailed process of becoming familiar with normality (Haug et al. 1987, 118).

1 Samantha: If you wear something really bad and act cool, people don't like, they think you're a geek, you know? You wear something in style, which is a good, like . . . you present yourself well and everything all together, then they think of you as really cool and everything. What you wear and

		how you act with what you wear. What people think about you—you have to keep up an image.
2	Marnina:	What kind of work is involved in keeping up an image? What do you have to do?
3	Samantha:	Make sure you don't dress bad every day and how you style your hair and how you approach people.
4	Mai:	See if your clothes would match.
5	Samantha:	Wear like stuff that people like. If a lot of people wear a certain thing you should wear it too. But don't like press onto that you love the stuff, cause people will think that you're a biter.
6	Marnina:	A what?
7	A few:	Biter.
8	Marnina:	What is it?
9	Samantha:	Where you copy everybody. So, like you don't want to go too far in trying to fit in. You want to have a little bit of yourself. (Trans. 12/12/94)

Here the "loaded surfaces" (Hebdige 1979) of clothing and hairstyles seem to resonate with narratives about social acceptability and belonging. Using what appears to be "insider's" information on "what they think," Samantha outlines how girls may use the visible images offered by the normative rules of fashion to both identify and regulate the categories of sameness as normality against difference as other that seem to be one of the keys to social inclusion or exclusion. However, as the discussion about the biter's overzealous application of sameness illustrates, these rules are complicated by the fact that social meanings are multiple and cannot be guaranteed. They create an ambivalent task that cannot be easily tackled precisely because its two sides seemingly cancel each other. Rather than a mere duplication of the same, it seems that inclusion depends on the ability to produce an abstracted version of it. The skill seems to lie in successfully managing the contradictory imperatives to, on the one hand, demonstrate a thorough knowledge of the normative rules, while on the other hand to do so in such a way so as to reveal an individual and authentic self. Thus, the task is one of becoming an individual through belonging, for uniqueness has to be communicated and understood as such, and that means shared with others (Bauman 1991, 198).

This practiced knowledge is also rehearsed in a related way in the quite different advisory strategies offered by Tori's two friends and in the manner in which they are delivered. In the approach taken by Girl 1, who gently admonishes, "You're not a nerd," it is not the existence of the categories nerd and popular that is refuted, but instead the placement of Tori within the first category. The stress here seems to be on Girl 1's own expertise in being able to recognize normal, which she uses as a means to convince Tori of her mistake. She does so using a supportive and comforting tone which is maintained throughout most of the other video segments as well. It is a discursive strategy effectively used to establish herself as an authority by taking up a position as teacher or mother. As Walkerdine (1990) has noted, these closely related positions are often adopted by younger girls as sites of power in their play. Maria herself recognized her use of the strategy as girl 1, when, at one point during the filming, she interrupted herself, looked up from the talk around the table, and exclaimed with surprise and perhaps some dismay, "Oh, my god! I sound just like my mother!" (FN 06/14/95).

Girl 2 seems to take quite a different stance. Recalling elements of her "just people" argument, her response, "You want to make yourself ugly," seems a significantly less delicate resistance to Tori's self-positioning and to the nerd/popular division as inevitable. Through an appeal to a sense of individual responsibility and choice, she insists on the possibility of managing one's own movement from the nerd into the popular category, disrupting what Homi Bhabha calls "the concept of 'fixity' in the ideological construction of otherness" (1983, 18). This movement is achievable, she seems to argue, if one possesses both the desire to be like others or a desire for social integration and the knowledge necessary to make full membership claims—knowledge that she hints she herself already enjoys and, as we will see later, is willing, from another teacherly/motherly discursive positioning,[6] to impart to her friend.

Perhaps not surprisingly, this particular video segment proved extremely troublesome to shoot. We had to redo it more times than any other. Although she played the part beautifully, Mai was less than thrilled with her character. Every time she would catch a glimpse of herself in the video monitor as she walked onto the set, she would stop dead in her tracks, completely mortified at what she saw. The other girls would collapse hooting and laughing, getting louder and more rambunctious as Mai's annoyance with them increased. Despite her best efforts to maintain a scowl, Mai, too, would often crack up laughing. She did, indeed, look a ridiculous figure.

There is both humor and pain in the girls' responses to Mai's exaggerated rendition of the nerd. Their laughter implicates them; with it they include themselves. They acknowledge a self-recognition at the same time as they strive to distance themselves from this disturbing association. Stirring the story's undercurrents, creating conversational shifts and its changeable course, this play between difference and similitude underlies the series of multiple and competing identifications at work. How these identifications are produced and lived through the complexities of cultural, social, and material life is what drives Tori's story along its unreliable path and what provokes my query, "How do these categories happen?" echoed by Tori herself when she asks her friends, "how come you guys can be so popular?"

On the Vertical

The question, once asked, tilts the syntagmatic and paradigmatic axis of the story, marking the first step towards Tori's transformation. In posing the question, she actively pursues the knowledge necessary to take up a position within popularity. The pursuit denotes the moment where Tori's recognition of herself as deviating from the norm allows the standards on which that norm is founded to become truly effective (Haug 1987, 117). She desires that place. Her friends are invited to assume their positions as experts, the intervening outside agents who will assist her through the initiation rites granting her passage from nerd into popular girl.

Girl 2:	*If you like, get some new clothes.*
Tori:	*Yeah, I don't know. I'm so shy to go shopping by myself. I don't know which clothes match me and which not. And my mother always buys my clothes.*
Girl 2:	*Well, you have to tell her—*
Tori:	*I'm spending their money, so I have to do whatever they say.*
Girl 1:	*Yeah, you have to stand up for your rights here.*
Tori:	*I don't have that much confidence. You guys are strong. I'm not.*
Girl 2:	*How you felt like, you can do it. You know that. You know who you are.*
Tori:	*But what can a geek do?*
Girl 1:	*You're not a geek! How many times do we have to tell you?*
Tori:	*Yes, I am a geek! Not two people make a difference, when thousands of people call you a geek!*
Girl 1:	*Fine, we're going to change your appearance.*
Tori:	*If you guys change, I'll be a geek still.*
Girl 1:	*No you won't! Meet us after school today and we're going shopping. Tomorrow you'll be a whole new self!*

Just like Cinderella, Tori's prospects for rising above her humble beginnings are made provisional upon her ability to display the right moral and physical characteristics (Spence 1995, 63). New clothes combined with strength of character are named as the first step towards transformation. However, the happily-ever-after guaranteed in the fairy tale is hampered here by a rather intriguing series of challenges.

Powerless women have, according to Steedman (1986) and Skeggs (1997), always worked on their bodies, often the only bargaining power available. The prescription for new clothes is clearly such an effort, but it also does not relate exclusively to the body. Rather, the promise of new clothes lies in the relations they create between character and the body. The body becomes the pathway to truth about identity (Haug 1987, 83). The regulation of external appearance is suggested as a means to convey particular meanings relating to herself as a person: to display her inner qualities.

What new look replaced the too-tight blouse and too-short jeans when Tori hesitantly emerged from the stall in the school bathroom? Skipping ahead for a moment, past the shopping trip initiating the transformation, past the discussion of family relations which threatens to frustrate the whole project, past a reopened debate between fixed identities versus the possibilities for creating new selves, it seems appropriate to offer a glimpse of the reincarnated Tori here. Plain jeans, a simple red and white stripped T-shirt, black boots: from among the fashion styles current at the time, Tori's new look is, I agree, nondescript, to say the least. Writing of the significance of conventional clothing style, Hebdige says, "[U]ltimately, if nothing else, they are expressive of 'normality' as opposed to 'deviance' (i.e. they are distinguished by their relative invisibility, their appropriateness, their 'naturalness')" (1979, 101). Having shed the clothes that marked her difference, it is perhaps not that surprising that what Tori attempts to communicate with her new look is an effective claim to sameness, or "normal."

The complication arises for Tori when, as the shopping trip is discussed, the proposal for new clothes unleashes a circular debate about, on the one hand, relations between external appearance and inner qualities and, on the other hand, how identities are constituted and recognition won. While Tori's friends suggest that a new identity is possible through a changed appearance, Tori seems to have a significant amount of doubt about the effectiveness of the strategy: "I'll still be a geek." The emphasis on new clothes as a means of transformation stresses their effect as costume and appearance. What is set up then is a binary between artifice and authenticity (Harbord 1996, 101). Furthermore, when Tori claims that the problem is that she does not to have the strength of character to accomplish the task, her friend's reassurance consists of a suggestion that she rely on her own self knowledge: "You know who you are." Again Tori balks, insisting that her recognition of self comes from others, who see her as a geek: "Thousands of people call me a geek." The tension between the competing strategies outlined is the result of a replaying of inside/outside notions of identity that renders the external as somehow less authentic than one's inner true self. Yet it is a more certain method for winning recognition from others, recognition that is essential to successfully staking a desired identity claim.

In trying to strategize a credible process of transformation for Tori, the girls often turned to analyze both their own liminal positions and the positions of those they considered popular within their school. The ongoing task of positioning oneself within these kinds of relations requires a significant amount of interpretive work. As they do for Tori and her friends, in the following discussion the

girls attempt to explain the situation to me, illustrating the work involved in producing an appearance that is an instance of the right category rather than the
wrong one. Aware that there are some very real practical impediments in doing
so, here they use the category of "cool." Coolness and popularity, while not identical positions in the school lexicon of sociality, do seem to furnish those who inhabit them many similar advantages and both stand in oppositional relationships
to the nerd.

1	Tevy:	You know how fashion always changes? They always keep up with the fashion and things like that.
2	Marnina:	So that takes quite a bit of work, doesn't it?
3	Samantha:	Well sometimes like if clothes go out like really fast, like you've gone out shopping and bags full of stuff—like in-style stuff and then they're out, like the next day, it's sort of hard.
4	LeLy:	It's like Stacy, you know the Stacy from last year, remember?
5	Tevy:	Stacy, she is not cool!
6	LeLy:	Some kind like that.
7	Marnina:	What was she like LeLy?
8	Tevy:	Stacy, she's—
9	Marnina:	LeLy?
10	LeLy:	She's like, every time something new—she have her hair long, then fashion they're supposed to cut their hair like really shortly—like a guy and she cut it. Looking like a guy—I'd rather be not cool.
11	?:	Then you're a lesbian.
12	Samantha:	It's not exactly a guy cut though—
13	Tevy:	like the style—
14	Samantha:	I don't care. If I, I don't know if I am a lesbian. I don't think I am. [giggles] Like people can think what they want and that's the way they want to think about it, well then they're just going to have to live with it. (Trans. 12/12/94)

   While there may not be full agreement (4, 5, 6) on the exact reading of the
particulars of the embodiment of the cool girl, what is clearly highlighted here is the
central role played by class, race, and sexuality in the regulation of femininity and
in the production of otherness. In sharp contrast with Tori's original mismatched
outfit, made up of remnants of the girls' own outgrown and outfashioned
wardrobes, the cool girl with her shopping bags "full of stuff" is always on top of
new and rapidly changing fashion styles (1, 3). Accentuating the short-livedness of

these trends in a slightly mocking tone, Samantha's accounting of the unlimited buying power necessary to stay on top of them introduces the notion of class, usually an unspoken and unacknowledged explanation for why people end up in the social positions that they do, as a consequential element for accessing what she implies is a very desired place (3) (Connell et al. 1982; Luttrell 1993; Walkerdine 1990).

LeLy's comment about hairstyles, while also focusing on the changeability of fashion trends, is more interesting for what she indicates about the tensions and ambiguities these changes may mean for producing "appropriate" sexualized femininity (10). Here hairstyles are the manifestation of an assorted range of intersecting identities and social meanings that include gender, sexuality, and coolness. Girls whose hairstyles position them outside the normative representational order within and beyond the educational setting may encounter, as Tori has already discovered, a devaluation of embodiment (Haug 1987; Luke and Gore 1992). However, for LeLy the matter is more complicated than that. As she points out, and McRobbie confirms, in the context of the late 1980s and early 1990s the representational order was dominated by the idea of androgyny, which is reflected in fashion styles of the time (McRobbie 1994a, 148). The challenge arises when short hair, while being a sign that intends coolness, is also one that calls into question what LeLy and some of the other girls consider their gendered and heterosexual identities. This double-edged femininity seems to provoke an anxiety about the possibility of a sexual misrecognition.

And yet, the same concern does not seem to shake Samantha's confidence in the fashionable feminine identification she has spent such a lot of energy thinking about, if not yet exactly cultivating. Interestingly, in contrast to the previous discussion, where she seemed to argue that "what they think" is inextricable from any "cool" identity claims one can make, here Samantha reformulates the issue to one that is about individual rights of self-definition. At the same time, her discursive flirtation with a lesbian positioning momentarily destabilizes the norms, conventions, and expectations of femininity that she is both working to establish and trying to position herself within (14). Perhaps it is her embodiment as the only white, working-class girl in this discussion that makes it possible for her, more than any of the other girls, to consider risking sexual ambiguity in order to be able to make the identification with coolness. For her whiteness, unlike the other girls' racial positionings, allows her to make some claim to the norm, even if, as she implies early in the discussion, her class position may make it difficult to guarantee.

Class position also appears to be a contributing factor in Tori's skepticism about the success of the shopping expedition in winning her a position within popularity. Not only does she claim to lack the required skills and experience to select the right clothes, but she argues that her spending options are fully defined by her position within the family. "I'm spending their money, so I have to do whatever they say." Mai outlines what it is Tori may be being told to do and how this may be both impeding the shopping trip and contributing to her lowly status: "Well, cause she sees, umm, other people, like the girls go shopping, just for them, and like she's got to stay home and they're asking her, 'Oh, what did you buy?' and stuff like that. It's like 'Oh, I stayed home, washed the dishes.' And they're like this, 'Oh, what a geek!' and stuff like that" (Trans. 05/08/95).

In Spence's interpretation of the story of Cinderella, it is predominantly a story about class (1995, 64). Central to this claim is the way in which family and economic conflict, manifested through Cinderella's household labor, is resolved by a magical transformation that allows her true worth to be recognized and her successful taking up of a higher-class position through marriage. Cinderella motifs circulate in popular consciousness, Hey suggests, precisely because they connect to working-class girls' immersion in household labor (1997, 98). Tori's responsibilities at home obstruct her inclusion in the sociality of group shopping trips, one of the means by which girls both learn and participate in constructing gendered norms and meanings (Chapkis 1986; Chua 1992; Ganetz 1995). Certainly, carrying a significant workload within the family was familiar territory for each of the girls.

Maria, as we have already seen in chapter 3, was allowed very few excursions outside the house with the exception of going to school and family outings. At home, as she puts it, it's "'Maria do this, Maria do that, Maria do this, Maria you're so lazy, Maria do that, you never want to do anything.' It gets on my nerves!" (Trans. 04/11/95). Before her grandmother was able to join the family in Toronto through Immigration Canada's Family Reunification Programme, it was LeLy's responsibility to cook dinner for her family every night, for which she was paid twenty dollars a week (Trans. undated). Once her grandmother arrived to live with the family, LeLy was often charged with taking care of her at home (FN 07/13/94) and with accompanying her to medical appointments, where her translation skills were required. For other girls it was younger family members who were the recipients of their care giving. When Mai and her sister and mother were leaving to visit her grandmother in Vietnam for a month, the concern she expressed was not about missing schoolwork or her friends but for her younger brother's welfare while she was away. Among her other household chores, it was her responsibility to wake him in the morning for school, get him dressed, and cook breakfast for him and her other siblings (FN 01/28/94). These younger family members were frequent participants in our group outings, as the girls often baby-sat on weekends and after school. On one weekend group skating trip to City Hall, Lan was accompanied by both her baby brother and a very young cousin. Both about two years old, the toddlers kept the entire group busy chasing after them, searching for buckle-on skates that failed to stay attached to winter boots, and setting small, overturned, stuffed-in-snowsuit bodies upright. Lan was quickly exasperated with them, complaining, "I can't do anything with them here!" Before too long she angrily left, single-handedly returning home by street-car, her two charges in tow (FN 11/26/94).

Tori's friends respond to her protestations about family constraints by in-troducing a new discourse into the discussion: "You have to stand up for yourself" and "You're old enough to go and get your own clothes," they say. Shopping for oneself becomes a claim to the right to self-definition through the construction of one's own appearance and a marker of adult status (Skeggs 1997, 103). This dis-course of rights within the family is offered as a means to counter that of Cin-derella-the-family-drudge. Thus, part of the intervening role Tori's friends play in her initiation into popularity is teaching her about another way to name and think about relations in families. However, this new discourse also seems to be one that is based on a voluntarism which assumes that change can follow from subjects' recognizing and choosing to stand outside the conditions of their own regulation. Intensely individualist, it is a discourse embedded within a bourgeois order[7] that has little place for an understanding of regulation that is the product of scarcity of money with which to keep up with fashion trends and surviving harsh living conditions, in part by relying on daughters' household labor.[8]

The "whole new self" that Girl 1 suggests will materialize after the requisite shopping trip has been executed and the new clothes purchased also depends on another series of conditions to ensure recognizability. That is, Tori's difference is also manifested and made visible, through some of the social spaces available within the school. It is the ways in which some of these spaces organize relations of difference that the second scene of recognition will explore.

SCENE 2. (RE)SITUATING THE SELF IN SOCIAL SPACE

On the Horizontal

"A theatre of regulated performances" is how Philip Corrigan (1988, 151) characterizes the institution of schooling in his ground-breaking piece on the making of masculinities in schools. Capturing something of the extreme painfulness involved in the difficult work of gender, Corrigan suggests that in schools, as in any total institution, survival depends on understanding the cru-cial ecology of the ruling relations: what, who matters and to whom, when, how? And then, shaping, spacing, timing, and wording one's gendered body to *their* tunes. Is there any doubt left about the central role the school will play in Tori's transformation story?

It is the ideal body which operates as the classification device—the grammar through which all the arranging, dividing, sorting, comparing, contrasting, and yes, transforming is accomplished. While the ideal is, of course, never actually accomplished, "perfection is always postponed, causalities are heavy and the wounds for participating in this struggle are carried for a long, long time—perhaps forever" (Corrigan 1988, 153). Organized for the observation, regulation, and supervision of their subjects, schooling is, as Corrigan has pointed out, a project which embodies both transformation and regulation (1987, 159). And while it is true that the two are not always theorized as being part and parcel of the same kind of schooling project, holding them together and in tension with the question of how recognition might be won and lost in schools offers a reading of Tori's story that focusses on the relationship between schooling and the multiple and contradictory consequences for the production, authorization, and valuation of the identities it is instituted to manage (Foster 1996; Gordon 1996; Luttrell 1993).

The girls' efforts to create a narrative that would be hearable and seeable as a realistic portrayal of the identities of the nerd and popular girl—social categories whose meanings gain their currency primarily within the specific context of the school—entail a study of how subjects act upon, influence, and repel one another and are ultimately constituted within the social spaces of this institution. These spaces are represented in the story by the three different physical locations in which the various segments of Tori's story unfolds. They are, as I have already mentioned, among the visual cues that mark the plot's movement, tracing the stages of the transformation from nerd into popular girl. However, the use of the lunchroom, the bathroom, and the school gym to signify the process of transformation also throws into sharp relief how access to and use of public space is itself structured in conditions of difference (Adams 1994; Hey 1997; Gotfrit 1988; Gordon 1996).

Working like a crosscurrent with the first scene of recognition, the second scene makes the positions of the nerd and popular girl intelligible with an illustration of how identifications are formed in particular physical spaces that are always sociopolitical ones. Struggling to anchor the story's precarious agenda of transformation, the second scene overlaps and supports the first with an expansion of its focus on the dialogic of self-peer identifications. The dynamics here include the interdependent relationship between the social and discursive practices of the unofficial school (constructed by the students themselves), those of the more official school (produced by teachers and other school authorities), as well as those between the school and the wider community.

To begin to unravel the workings of these dynamics, a revisiting of the question, How do the categories nerd and popular happen? may be worthwhile. This question not only guides the writing into existence of Tori's character, but also my own attempts to analyze the practices the girls identify, so as to understand how subjects are produced within them. Drawing on popular culture depictions as well as on their own school experiences, what emerges in the girls' grappling with this question is a very interesting linkage between the signification of the categories nerd and popular and use of and access to various school spaces. However, as we will see, these signifying relations are also extremely unstable, which is precisely what makes them so interesting.

1 Maria:		Well, maybe they're smart or whatever. Maybe, because one of the things on the show yesterday was who was popular. Anyways, they started getting good grades in school and they weren't popular any more.
2 Mai:		Cause she had good grades, right? Like she played sports and stuff like that and she's good at it. And than her parents saying, "Oh, your grades dropping down" and after she didn't play sports that much, so she studies and stuff like that, and she has good grades and people are like this: "Oh, you're a brainer now." Like she's not that popular no more.
3 Samantha:		So if we're going to make her a nerd, she should be a brainer that doesn't like dress good.
4 LeLy:		[inaudible] goody-goody.
5 Fanny:		Not goody-goody!
6 Mai:		Well, yeah, because if you don't talk a lot you have no friends, so if you have no friends you always do your homework.
7 Tammy:		You act like good to the teacher. So you're the goody-goody. (Trans. 12/12/94)

In this foray into the question of the construction of nerd and popular categories, the smart girl finally fully reenters the story via the radio call-in show mentioned previously. Despite my best intentions, Kathy, and more importantly Lan, have been kept waiting longer than I anticipated would be necessary when I postponed the telling of their tale, back in the early pages of this chapter. The fault is not entirely mine. For as many have suggested, and the discussion above implies, the discourse map of femininity, as it currently exists, does not leave a lot of attractive room for the smart girl's story (Cohen 1996; Hey 1997; Walkerdine 1990). But here she has found her way into our tale in the guise of the nerd. Clearly, the stories of the nerd and the smart girl are closely related ones.

Drawing on the experience of a caller to the radio show, the girls underline how the categories' intelligibility is shaped by social, athletic, and classroom spaces within the school, which are constituted as a competitive marketplace for visibility, respect, and recognition (Dei and James 1998; Eckert 1989, 1993; Hudak 1993; McCarthy 1988; Thorne 1995). While the suggestion is that there is more than one arena in which to "become somebody," it seems that the achievement of success and status within one arena inhibits accomplishing the same in another. Furthermore, the forms of recognition and the kind of feminine "somebody" each engenders are considerably different.

The caller's story juxtaposes two possibilities for the winning of visibility, respect, and recognition: popularity versus smartness. Popularity, achieved through the social activity of sport and conversation, requires not only likability but also sufficient, well-managed visibility to draw the community's attention to that likability (Eckert 1993, 36). Visibility gained through school activity increases one's access to popularity and secures the recognition of what appears here to be mainly other students.

In contrast, the chain of associated meanings around smartness produced in the caller's story appears to be predominantly about a good girl femininity. The emphasis on the necessity of curtailing social activities to focus on academic achievement makes doing the management work that popularity requires an impossibility. This route seems to be understood as a more serious and responsible approach in that it is associated with the adult approval of parents and teachers. However, the response from friends differs rather significantly. From them, the caller's renewed studiousness wins her the label "brainer," a designation clearly not intended to flatter. It appears to be a regulative term, threatening social isolation from peers. With the linking of smartness and social exclusion, the nerd, in its most common characterisation within popular culture, is reproduced.

There is another dimension to the risks of making claims to space within the classroom through displays of smartness that I want to briefly introduce before returning to the girls' use of these meanings in their own story. If the nerd exemplifies wrong femininity because of her poor fashion sense, her smartness is certainly also deemed a contributing factor to her outsider status. Returning to Lan's interrupted attempt to outline Kathy's story, the debate that ensues between the girls as she does underscores the difficulties of simultaneously inhabiting a position of smartness and one of heterosexual femininity. At the same time, the discussion, pregnant with perplexing discursive plays, moves back and forth between a desire for and revulsion of both positions.

1 Lan: So what did I say about her? Oh yeah, and guys don't go
             near her cause she's so smart and everything. Okay,
             there's this really cute guy that she has a crush on, right?
             Okay?

  2 Mai: Why you love Kathy so much?
  3 Maria: Who's Kathy?
  4 Lan: My low life girl.
  5 Fanny: But he doesn't like her—
  6 Lan: no, we don't know if he likes her or not.
  7 Fanny: don't make him like her—
  8 Lan: but he doesn't talk to her a lot, so she figures it's because
                  she's too smart and that's—
  9 Kenisha: she's not—
 10 Lan: . . . why she starts like failing a couple of classes and
                  thing.
 11 Kenisha: Alright, okay.
 12 Lan: Cause guys don't like girls who are smarter than them.
 13 Mai: It's true, in magazine, I read it.
 14 Fanny: That's a stupid thing.
 15 Kenisha: Yeah, she's stupid if she did that just for a guy.
 16 Fanny: Yeah, make it end like she knows that the guy doesn't
                  like her so she starts working harder and harder and then
                  she gets better grades back.
 17 Mai: Or—
 18 Kenisha: or she could end with the guy.
 19 Fanny: I know another guy, instead of him another guy, but he's
                  smart.
 20 Kenisha: No, no, no! She could end up with the same guy, when
                  she start putting back school work is first, then she
                  might—
 21 Lan: Kathy's I.Q. You know what Kathy's I.Q. is?
 22 Marnina: What?
 23 Lan: 200.
 24 Kenisha: Yeah, right! . . .
 25 Marnina: So the brainer gets the guy?
 26 Kenisha: Brainer don't get the guy! In my country the brainer
                  doesn't get the guy!
 27 Marnina: No? What happens?
 28 Kenisha: What you have, they get the guy.
 29 Mai: It does usually happen, the girl that has money gets the
                  guy.
 30 LeLy: Yeah.
 31 Kenisha: The brainer could be, the brainer could have money too.
                  Like my sister she have money and lots of guys like her,
                  cause she goes to high school. In my country why they

think we have money because my mom is away and most
of my family is away and she sends money.

32	Lan:	I know one! I know one!
33	Marnina:	Go ahead.
34	Lan:	Okay, she ends up with the guy, but he tells her that he likes girls that are smart.
35	Kenisha:	Exactly.
36	Maria:	That's what I was thinking.
37	Marnina:	That's what Kenisha was saying.
38	Lan:	Oh.
39	Kenisha:	Ha, ha, ha! (Trans. 04/05/95)

Contradicting each other as well as themselves, the girls produce a story and a series of identifications that in their very incoherence reflects the splitting that is, according to Walkerdine, commonly the smart girl's central experience (1990, 46). The traditional storyline which finds Kathy renouncing her smartness to win male attention is both embraced as true (It's true, in magazine, I read it") and resisted ("That's a stupid thing"). Lan and Kenisha's positionings seem particularly paradoxical. Lan is, as Mai comments, enamored with her character (2, 21, 23) and yet is also extremely quick to repudiate her as well (4). Kenisha is both the most ardent proponent for an ending which allows Kathy a coherent sense of identity, permitting her the possibility to maintain a positive identification in the dimensions of both smartness and heterosexual femininity (18, 20, 31, 35), and the most dismissive of the credibility of this tack (11, 15, 26). Perhaps, as Walkerdine suggests, what is being acknowledged here by the girls is the play of difference, power, and desire within the practices which regulate and position subjects within these two dimensions. According to Walkerdine, the clever girl is positioned in pedagogical discourses as though she could and can inhabit a position of power, while she has to negotiate other practices in which her femininity is what is validated. While she is told that she can be successful, the painful recognition that is actually likely to result from the fear of loss of one or the other (her femininity, her success, or both) is a failure to be either, producing neurotic anxiety, depression, or worse (Walkerdine 1990, 46).

With an interesting reversal and an ironic twist on the conventional politics and economics of heterosexual success, Kenisha reconciles this contradiction for Kathy (and herself?) by introducing money and class as a mediating factor for Kathy's success. She is supported in this move by Mai. While it is possible that in the Grenadian context that she is referring to, the cultural understanding is that wealthy women attract good-looking men, in the North American context the reverse is generally understood to be a cultural truism. However, as her own family's situation illustrates, the organization of the international labor market which enlists women like Kenisha's mother to work at menial jobs in North American cities, while other family members are left at home, may contribute to this structuring of the heterosexual market. The perception by the community of the family as wealthy which assists what Kenisha claims are her sister's numerous victories in the heterosexual domain, is ironically possible only due to the sums of money her mother is able to send back to Grenada, from what is unlikely to be a sizable salary earned as a nurses' aide in Toronto.

Lan settles the contradictory demands of the two dimensions somewhat differently for herself. At a certain point in an ongoing back-and-forth playful conversation she and I often shared about the popular film critics Siskel and Ebert, she declared that she too would translate her love of movies into a career. "I'm not going to be married. I'm going to be a critic. I still have my heart set on that thing" (Trans. 04/05/95). She would fuss, "I won't have time to get married, I have to practice my thumbs up and down to be one of those critics. It takes four years of school to get a job like that. You sit in class and the teacher goes, "Okay, prepare your thumbs—now up! Now with a little more sensitivity!'" (FN 03/21/95). There is something of a critical edge to Lan's comedic commentary. While she appears to be embracing the route of smartness as a way out of the marriage market, her caricature of educational practices seems to also challenge the legitimacy of academic and professional qualifications. However, if the film critic idea did not pan out, she also had a backup plan that would similarly find her relieved of having to negotiate heterosexual femininity but not without pleasure in her life: "If I don't become a critic, I want to be a nun. I want to be a nun with a big screen TV in my house" (Trans. 01/24/95).

For the purposes of their own story the girls produce an interesting reworking of some of the signifying relations of smartness, popularity, and heterosexuality. Playing with various dimensions of the question of how to make oneself seen in school, they return compellingly to inquire into the difference that difference makes. That is, they return to a suspicion born out of their own experience that the capacity to mobilize resources and exploit the unequal reward system available through school spaces varies considerably according to the race, class, and gender of minority and majority students (Fine 1991; McCarthy 1988). Not merely a story of luminous personality, exceptional skill or unusual talent, the key to visibility and valuation in the school rests on access to certain forms of cultural capital usually associated with those who can position themselves in the dominant social groups. Furthermore, while popularity is commonly understood (and was presented above) as an element of unofficial school life that transpires among students, Tori's quest for popularity and what it might confer is imagined as a response to a failure of recognition within the official space of the classroom—a failure that, as Honneth (1996) suggests more generally, may result in a shrinking of horizons of both one's sense of unique value in the surrounding social world and the possibilities for developing a practical relation to self. Popularity is seen, therefore, as an alternate route to what seems to be a deep-seated desire for recognition, but not necessarily solely from a girl's peers. What is proposed is that teachers also read and make use of the organization of the nerd/popular continuum in their own interactions and evaluations of students. Tori's desire for a position within popularity is understood as a strategy for gaining the attention of the teacher. The specter of the teacher figure raises the question of not only how different school spaces are made differentially available to students and how the school itself participates in the construction and maintenance of the nerd/popular categories, their social meanings and material consequences, but also how the desire for recognition may be organizing my ethnographic relation with these students:

1 Marnina: Okay, how about . . . We also said that she had some trouble with teachers. What's that about?

2 LeLy: Teachers never trust her and everything.

3 Mai: Yeah, so that's why she puts herself down. She says, "Okay, forget about school then. I'd rather be popular then."

4 LeLy: Okay, yeah, okay. She's really, really smart, okay? But, teachers always never trust her, think that she's stupid, so that she try like, she keep on trying to make herself like smart and everything, but it never works for her—

5 Mai: so then she sees popular people and then she sees they trust them so much, so she's like this: "Fine, I'll try to be popular [inaudible]." (Trans. 05/08/95)

The articulation of Tori's situation as a failure to make herself smart is curious considering the representation of the nerd previously discussed, where smartness and nerdiness were read as very closely associated. This peculiarity opens up a series of interesting considerations about identificatory practices, space, and social difference. First, it suggests that the smart self is an active and conscious production, and then raises questions about the social and political limits of signifiability of gender, race, popularity, and smartness. But it also suggests an ambivalence about smartness that gestures towards a relationship between grades and being a good girl.

To begin to understand why it is that smartness as a strategy can never "work for her," it is important to both consider the difficulty girls have in gaining access to classroom space in which to perform their smartness (AAUW 1992; Delamont

1980; French and French 1993; Sadker and Sadker 1994; Stanworth 1984; Warren and Frantz-Lutzer 1994), and relatedly, to recognize that within the school context the forms of expression that signal smartness are structured around a very circumscribed repertoire of speech behavior (Corrigan 1988; Walkerdine 1990).

Citing a nexus of pedagogical practices linking the production of intellectual achievement, sexed bodies, and aspects of modern bourgeois individuality with rational argument, Walkerdine traces how this particular form of expression has come to be associated with real learning. She argues that while rational argument is understood as the pinnacle of intellectual achievement, its accomplishment requires girls to make a bid for power (a claim to the phallus), which, though not impossible, involves a risk, as we have already seen, to their femininity. Though this boundary negotiation may produce pain and anxiety, and often has the effect of rendering girls totally and definitively silent and thus unrecognizable as smart (Walkerdine, 1990), Crystal's story suggests, as I will discuss further in chapter 5, that these girls may be more open to the possibility of negotiating a new relationship between femininity and smartness.

Reconciling the necessity of speech displays, if they are to succeed in gaining the recognition they desire, with the threat and terror of being made visible in the classroom, in these next discussions the girls' talk highlights the struggle, conflict, and difficulty of operating within and between these practices.

1	Tammy:	Some people they know about, they know the questions. If they say, they're scared that it might be wrong—
2	LeLy:	the teacher may make kind of joke—
3	Tammy:	might say, "Oh how come they don't answer any questions?"
4	Fanny:	And she tells your parents, "Oh they don't cooper—they don't—
5	A few:	Participate!
6	Kenisha:	You know what she does sometimes? Like last time, my mom came to school, my report card. She tells my mom I don't answer any question in class. I don't do nothing in class; this is what she said! I just sit there. Too bad!
7	Maria:	She used to come? My mom used to sit down. "Maria does not pay attention enough; she's much too quiet in class, blah, blah, blah, blah, blah, blah. Then my mom will come and tell me, "Why are you quiet?" (Trans. 04/04/95)

1	Marnina:	So sometimes you know the answers but you don't want to say it in case it's wrong.

2	Kenisha:	The other day, I know the answer but I never say a word in front of the class; I doesn't want to talk. So she goes make me shame. I know the answer. I goes, "200 and something." [laughter] I said it the first time, then I go, "200 and something." I was really scared. I think sometimes it's wrong. I know sometimes she thinks it's wrong.
3	Marnina:	Is there ever a time when you want to answer a question and put your hand up?
4	LeLy:	When you're very, very sure, make sure.
5	Tammy:	There's a problem with me. If I think that's the answer, it's right. But if I put my hand up to say it, it's wrong.
6	Kenisha:	Sometimes I have my answer. Then when I put my hand and then they call me, they say, "Okay say it," and I say the answer. sometimes I say the wrong one. I had the right one in my head, and then I say the wrong one.
7	Mai:	Cause you get scared and you forget things, right? You're like shaking and stuff.
8	LeLy:	Yeah, you're shaking.
9	Mai:	Is she going to pick on you?
10	LeLy:	You're kind of scared, right, because when you say it wrong, the teacher is the one who make fun of you.
11	Tammy:	The cool people too. (Trans. 01/24/95)

Learning the rules of how to perform properly and acceptably is, as Corrigan claims, a painful and difficult procedure. The eliciting context of the school rewards correct forms of expression and ridicules, marginalizes, pathologizes, or punishes incorrect forms (Corrigan 1990, 158). The girls clearly acknowledge the expected forms and are familiar with the consequences when their capacity for displaying them is limited by their fear and anxiety should they get it wrong. However, as Tammy's last comment suggests, it is also possible that not all girls are positioned in identical ways within this system of knowledgability (Fordham 1993; Grant 1992; Jones 1993; Luttrell 1993). In fact, a whole series of complaints to this effect were often lodged by the girls under the epithet "teacher fairness," suggesting teacher approval of some forms of femininity over others. And as we will see in the last section of this chapter, the girls' critique of this system could also be scathing.

For Mai and LeLy, who were perhaps the most vocal on this issue, the struggle over knowledge, power, and recognition and its layered linkages to the social categories of nerd and popular was repeatedly explored through a particular incident that occurred one day in their Canadian history class. Almost as interesting as the event itself is their compulsion to retell it. The power of retells, as Hey suggests, is in the possibilities they create to deploy a range of cultural knowledge concerning self and other (1997, 109). Potential new meanings can be derived by revising interpretations or, as most often seemed the case with the recounting of this incident, shared understanding of the event's meaning can be reaffirmed, strengthening group bonds and identifications with certain collective identities. However, it is also possible that the particular force of this compulsion was intensified by my presence in the classroom on the day this episode happened to take place, highlighting once again the organization of the ethnographic relation around the desire for recognition. Interested, perhaps, in the possibility for vindication, or maybe simply in seeking confirmation for the legitimacy of their meaning making that my collusion might confer, the girls' retells often concluded with what seemed to be both reassurances to each other and instructions to me: "She's going to write it in her 'book,'" and "Write that in your book!" (FN 02/01/95). Now referring to my fieldnotes, I willingly comply by producing yet another retelling of the incident:

> The grade eight class were studying the 1885 Riel Rebellion today. The lesson began with the handing out of a fact sheet and a question sheet. Mr. Burns stood at a podium-like thing beside the popular enclave, and asked a student to read the first question. "Where was Louis Riel born?" After referring the class to the fact sheet for the answer, he called on Mai for her response. "The Red River Settlement," she answered. Mr. Burns indicated her answer was incorrect and asked someone else for the answer. Ali answered, "St. Boniface," which Mr Burns announced was the right answer. The class was then instructed to work in small groups and answer the rest of the questions in their notebooks. After a few moments, Lidia put her hand up and asked a question about the first answer. "The fact sheet says Red River Settlement. What should we put down?" Mr. Burns looked over the sheet and agreed, it did indeed. He announced to the class that the answer to the first question was "Red River Settlement," and directed the class to continue with their work. Mai and LeLy exchanged significant looks. LeLy leaned across her desk to where I was sitting a few seats away and said in a loud stage whisper, "Get our point?" (FN 05/01/95)

The incident illustrates the complexity of gender relations within the social space of the classroom and the ways in which the nerd and popular categories are mobilized by the girls to make meaning of the structural and political features organizing the struggle over knowledge, power, and recognition. What irks the girls is that the answer Mai provides is not trusted, nor is she credited when it is eventually accepted as correct. The teacher's failure denies Mai the positive visibility that answering a question correctly in class has the potential to deliver. Thus, the point to be gotten is not merely that from the girls' perspective the popular girls like Lidia enjoyed a favored relationship with the

teacher but, more importantly, that popularity was one of the conditions structuring teachers' recognition of smartness. And, as we have already seen, popularity also carries particular classed and racialized meanings, suggesting that
these may also be implicated in structuring the signification of smartness.

In controlling some of the available routes to the visibility that is essential
to developing a social identity in the school, teachers not only make use of the social categories nerd and popular, they also participate in manufacturing and
maintaining them. The dynamics involved in the staging of a school play in the
second year of my project highlights teachers' involvement in establishing this
contrasting directionality.

Titled *From Borders to Bridges*, the play was a schoolwide, year-end production that parents and other family members were invited into the school to watch.
It was designed to involve the entire school community. Besides the handful of
individual acting and dancing parts, every student participated, in that each grade
was assigned one of the songs in the show. However, as might be expected, it was
the limited number of speaking roles that were considered the most important
ones and were the most sought after. Here, Miss Wright, the teacher who directed
the play, describes what she took into account when she made her casting choices:

> One of the things I found interesting with *Borders and Bridges* is that stu-
> dents who stuck it out were the students who I don't really perceive as the
> "in crowd." And the ones who you would have—I would have thought
> would be stars dropped out. . . . I was thrilled that so many of the students
> who usually aren't in the light, you know were able to . . . whereas I say
> some of the really "in" students dropped in and dropped out. And that's
> even with me personally speaking with a few of them. Cause I felt they
> would be really a positive influence. . . . In fact I had cast most of the
> people—ended up with speaking roles weren't the ones I initially cast. And
> when the others dropped out then I—people who—you know all of them—
> Trinh was in it—Were you there that night? Did you get to see it? (Trans.
> 06/29/1994)

Teachers' jobs, as Connell et al. (1982, 185) point out, require them to
constantly put students in rank orders of merit through the assignment of
marks and by directing students to particular programs or streams. Thus, competitive, hierarchically organized schooling practices are used to produce an explanation for difference which is based on the results of its own effects. Miss
Wright's account makes use of precisely this kind of prophetic explanation.
While acknowledging the existing social classification system differentially cat-
egorizing students, she fails to recognize either its racialized features or how her

own practices both create and reinforce it. Initially casting the highly valued speaking parts with the in crowd, she provides these students with access to yet another forum in which their visibility works to define their position within the power relations of the school's social hierarchy. When the in crowd drops out, and these roles go by default to more marginalized students, the message of second best is hardly likely to have been lost on them.

All the more paradoxical, considering the play's progressive content about justice, equity, global cooperation, and peaceful conflict resolution, the production of *From Borders to Bridges* seemed to build more in the way of borders than bridges between the school's insiders and outsiders.

Rather than an individualized lack, the girls' own analysis makes the linkages between their collective identities and the difficulties they encounter in successfully positioning themselves within those desired places, so that they, too, might win the recognition they desperately seek. The girls' explanations for how the categories nerd and popular happen thus extend well beyond the walls of the school. In this debate, which became so intense that they conducted it from the vantage point of the tabletop, rather than from their chairs (FN 5/2/95), the importance of race as an organizing feature of the social spaces within the school is highlighted. However, its signification is quite complicated. It is compounded not only by the various nonwhite positions the girls claim, but also by their construction of a racialized geography existing outside the school, which at times contests dominant renderings of inclusions and exclusions, and insists on the destabilization of inside and outside meanings.

1	LeLy:	Like take this school, I think most of the popular people like they're, most of them are English popular, like Portuguese, Black—
2	Fanny:	[indicating Kenisha] hey, she's not—
3	Kenisha:	I'm popular for myself! I'm not popular in the school, but I'm popular wherever I come from.
4	LeLy:	I'm talking about Patricia, Lidia. Want me to point them out?
5	Mai:	They're outgoing too.
6	Kenisha:	I'M POPULAR WHEREVER I BE, okay not in school; I really don't [inaudible].
7	Marnina:	What about you?
8	Mai:	I'm not picking on my school, okay, cause there's the school and then there's the outside. Oriental popular outside, but not in school.
9	Marnina:	That's interesting. . . .
10	Mai:	You're telling me this school now—

11 LeLy:	I'm talking this school, so DON'T ARGUE WITH ME, MAI!
12 Fanny:	Another school oriental people are popular. Is it because other schools, it's because this part there's a lot of Portuguese people—
13 Mai:	yeah, she's right.
14 LeLy:	THAT'S WHAT I WANT TO SAY!
15 Fanny:	Too bad, ha, ha.
16 Mai:	If a school has community of oriental then oriental popular. Community is Portuguese then Portuguese popular.
17 LeLy:	It's because this area is Portuguese, that's why.
18 Marnina:	Maria is shaking her head.
19 Maria:	Not over here; that's on Ossington. That's Portuguese village over there.
20 LeLy:	It's Chinese in Chinatown.
21 Fanny:	Holy, so much!
22 Maria:	In Chinatown it's the same thing.
23 LeLy:	[inaudible] . . . Vietnamese in here, people here, but is there any popular people that Vietnamese people? NO! I don't see any. It's just because THIS IS THEIR WORLD—
24 Kenisha:	yeah—
25 LeLy:	it belong to them or something—
26 Mai:	no, don't say that—
27 Kenisha:	my father own the world. Did you know that, Marnina? MY FATHER OWN THE WORLD!
28 Maria:	We do not own the world, you guys!
29 LeLy:	What is it, Maria?
30 Maria:	WE DO NOT! (Trans. 05/02/95)

LeLy opens the conversation attempting to categorize the people considered popular in their school. She initially stipulates English, Portuguese, and Black (1), producing a list that mobilizes an Asian/non-Asian split. However, when Fanny points out a flaw in her argument by contending that while Kenisha may be Black she is not considered popular (2), LeLy particularizes her list by naming Patricia and Lidia, girls whose names are repeatedly invoked in our discussions about popularity and who are clearly identifiable as both Portuguese and white (4). Kenisha, as she has been seen to do before, refuses Fanny's positioning of her outside the category of popularity and, in doing so, resists both the very definition of popularity and the terms on which it might be won. First, she rejects requiring the recognition of others ("I'm popular for myself!") and then she modifies this by producing a place outside the school where she is recognized as such ("I'm popular wherever I come from"). This "outside the school" formulation is then used by

Mai to create a space, clearly unattainable inside the school, in which "oriental people" might also gain this recognition (8). As Cohen argues, perhaps the main defense for those who have been the victims of the perverse inclusion/exclusion games of powerful classification systems has been to construct an "imagined community of resistance" which cuts across existing internal divisions (1992, 73). Though, of course, as the geography of the city of Toronto shows with its many neighborhoods organized around ethnic communities, the construction of space within which marginalized identities may gain recognition is more than just an imaginary practice.

Once the girls establish an imagined place for themselves, they reopen the question of their outside status inside the school, ironically at the very same time as internal divisions within the group threaten to erupt with a quarrel over space inside the conversation (11, 14, 15). Nonetheless, together they work up a very sophisticated analysis, theorizing their marginalized positions within the school as an effect of the power relations that operate outside it. Beginning within the domain of their own neighborhood and expanding outwards to encompass other Toronto communities and finally the world, they draw a map divided into racialized territories, and make the linkages between the rationalities of social space and relations of power and social difference (12, 13, 16, 17, 22, 23) (Foster 1996; Goldberg 1993; Gordon 1996; Shilling 1991). However, within this framework, at least two different facets of the operation of power within and through racial geographies seem to be under consideration.

Initially, although there is some disagreement about the exact whereabouts of certain boundaries (19), Fanny, Maria, Mai, and LeLy agree on the necessity of a group's majority status within a bounded community to secure access to positions of power, or in their terms, popularity. LeLy then seems to take a somewhat different position, provoking strong disagreements from both Mai and Maria (26, 28, 30), and a response from Kenisha that remains unclear to me (27). With her revised claim, LeLy reinvokes the Asian/non-Asian split that she used to begin this discussion, suggesting that social relations within communities are not immune from global systems of domination. In contrast with non-Asians, racialized difference and racist oppression make highly doubtful the plausibility of Vietnamese people ever being intelligible as popular or powerful (23).

The rules of racial classification manifested here—rules that Fanon (1967) might refer to as "racial schema"—are represented through the girls' imagined geographies. In Fanon's terms, these classification systems position bodies in physical space, producing knowledge that articulates and reproduces an interpreted bodily image—an image that is "woven out of a thousand details, anecdotes, [and] stories" (1967, 35). The image that the girls depict through their geographies suggests that while the inclusion/exclusion boundaries of these rules may leave them inhabiting less than desired places, the meanings attributed to these positions are also contested ones.

Having been structurally positioned as dominant, Maria uses denial ("We do not own the world, you guys!"), as a strategy of disavowal. Kenisha's more ambiguous position in the conversation is reflected in her response ("My father own the world. Did you know that, Marnina? MY FATHER OWN THE WORLD!"). On the one hand, she may also consider herself to have been included in this structural position of dominance implied in LeLy's owning the world argument and is using sarcasm to also disavow her placement here. But, it is also possible that her comment is aimed at disrupting her exclusion from not only this position, but the very terms on which the conversation has thus far taken place. That is, she may be taking up this powerful insider position, to insert herself into what has thus far been a dichotomous Vietnamese-Portuguese comparison. While the intention of Kenisha's comment may be ambiguous, with it she is clearly calling on my authority as teacher-researcher to support what appears to be a bid for inclusion in the conversation, where her voice has until this point been little heard. Perhaps her forceful insistence on my attention here is a rejoinder to my failure earlier in the conversation to respond to her attempts to claim a position within popularity (3, 6, 7).[9] This time I do not miss my cue, and as the discussion continues we shift to a consideration of the position of Black students in the school. The result is a rethinking of the nerd/popular theory developed thus far, and the generation of yet another dimension to it.

31	Marnina:	It's interesting about who is popular in this school. You were saying that there are some Black people in the popular crowd. How does that work?
32	Kenisha:	Cause we—
33	LeLy:	I don't know—
34	Kenisha:	no, because you know—
35	Maria:	cause it's not a lot.
36	LeLy:	I'm not saying that; I'm not calling them—
37	Kenisha:	there's not a lot of Black people in this school, like you know—
38	Fanny:	hey, I see a few—
39	LeLy:	[inaudible] . . . black people and I don't know why, most of the popular music and singer is Black people. Is it?
40	Kenisha:	[starts to sing] (Trans. 05/02/95)

What is suggested here is that some Black students may be able to gain access to a contingent insider position that the Vietnamese and other Asian students cannot (Back 1993). The girls struggle for an explanation to account for this difference.

Their prior theory about the requirement of majority status to attain this access is not tenable in this case, as they all agree Black students are not a dominant presence in the school. LeLy offers a hesitant possibility that, again, looks outside the school to explain its internal social relations of power. She refers to the considerable current fascination, attraction, and influence in popular culture of Afro-Caribbean musical forms and stylistic innovations as a way to explain this phenomenon. Her analysis is shared by many school ethnographers and cultural commentators who have also noted that Black musical forms offer Black and other marginalized young people a means of renegotiating their marginalized institutional status (Back 1993; Gilroy 1987; Heller 1999; Rampton 1995; Rattansi 1992). Perhaps Kenisha's playful embrace here (40) of this set of powerful images signals an identification that is not similarly available to the other girls, and for which no equivalent for them seems to exist currently. It is possible that these images provide Kenisha with an alternative system of valuation. Because they also seem to carry some currency within the school, at least among students if not the staff and administration, they may assist her in countering the incessant devaluation she faces there.

Emerging from this discussion is a sense of how the structure of the social relations within the school, its racialized and gendered social and discursive configurations, are textured by factors outside it. At the same time the school itself may also provide a very important context in which hegemonic understandings of social difference may find localized expressions and legitimation (Connell et al. 1982; Mac an Ghaill 1995). In terms of the latter, Connell et al. point out how particularly potent this kind of reinforcement is with respect to how schools may participate in supporting divisions between sections of the working class, not only because it operates intimately within the neighborhood, inside the residential community, but also because it offers social meanings and definitions to kids well before they even enter the labor market (1982, 171). From the girls' discussions it seems that the operatings of the categories nerd and popular within the school served to corroborate and supplement what they already know about social divisions, their consequences, and their meanings existing outside the school, across both classed and racialized differences.

In negotiating the interplay of race and popularity in Tori's story, the girls encountered something of a complicated challenge. On the one hand, they were interested in representing the dynamic discussed above—the obstacles they felt particular collective identities may pose as a factor limiting access to positions of power within popularity. And on the other hand, they were clearly also highly invested in being able to portray the "just people" argument. That is, they assert the right to be seen and treated as individuals with complex facets, abilities, and potential. Indeed, the premise of transformation at the heart of Tori's story would seem to insist on this possibility. Juggling these two axioms, the girls produce an

"(ambiguously) non-hegemonic" racial positioning for Tori, to use Rachel Blau Du-
Plessis's (1985) phrase for contradictory subject positions. Her mother being Vietnamese and her father Anglo-Canadian, Tori is mixed race. This ambiguous
positioning, a means of addressing contradictory axiomatic narrative dictates, becomes a threshold place where social boundaries may be questioned, (re)config-
ured, and (re)articulated. The mixed-race girl flagrantly throws into question the
purity of binary raced categories—white and Asian, black and white, Asian and
black—and the bounded communities from which they might be expected to
emerge. Tori's mixed-race embodiment may therefore mark an uncertainty about
identity and play on the girls' own multiple and competing identifications with
the popular girl.

The girls articulate their own interest in this ambiguous position using an
entirely different framework. For them the significance of Tori's mixed-race position seems to lay within the moral and ethical considerations that the prospect of
her transformation might precipitate. To illustrate some of the features of these
considerations, the girls use one of the trials that those existing as other within
schools encounter daily. Tori explains:

Tori:	*But you guys don't understand.*
Girl 1:	*What do you mean? We're trying to understand.*
Tori:	*You guys are popular; no one makes fun of you. I'm not popu-lar. I'm a geek. Every second, every minute people make fun of me.*
Girl 2:	*They make fun of you, you don't bother. You laugh about it after.*
Tori:	*I try to laugh. After a while it really hurts my feelings, you know.*

This teasing which, as we will see momentarily, is highly racialized, is clearly
one of the social practices which regulates identities and signifies relations of
power between groups of students in the school. For a person whose racial position is ambiguous, who is interested in and for whom it might be possible to cross
the nerd/popular boundary, this practice poses an ethical and moral dilemma for
Tori's successful transformation. Within the politics of the group dynamics, the
discussion of this dilemma unleashes another order of crisis.

1 LeLy:	I was wondering, which way [inaudible] like sometimes they were trying to make fun of Chinese or Vietnamese people, right? Like what I'm talking about Tori is like you're in the middle. Like Portuguese people are talking about your own culture, and if you argue with them,

they start picking on you. If you go on with them you feel inside like you're making fun of your own country. So she have to decide—

2 Lan: but if she's half English and half Vietnamese and people can't tell you're real Vietnamese and they wouldn't make fun of you—

3 LeLy: cause the way she look, she look more like Vietnamese people, so in this community is Portuguese—don't look at me like that—so she don't fit in with them, so like you or not is depending on the way you look.

4 Fanny: How do you say people mixed in English?

5 Mai: I guess mixed.

6 Fanny: No, there's a politer way.

7 LeLy: Yeah, there's some word to it.

8 Fanny: My mom got the word in her English notebook.

9 Marnina: So for Tori, what do you think she should do?

10 Mai: Or let me give you an example. Let's say LeLy and Kenisha is popular and Lan is and Fanny isn't. You're gonna say, Fanny is so short, so brainless, so lazy because she's Chinese and she's so ugly cause she's Chinese.

11 Fanny: Yeah, sure!

12 LeLy: You Chinese people are so short, there!

13 Fanny: Oh, my god!

14 LeLy: If she argue she get picked on.

15 Mai: I'm not saying Portuguese is rude or anything, right?

16 LeLy: Yeah, I'm not saying—

17 Mai: but around here there's Portuguese people, even little kids, even little kids even make fun of Oriental people.

18 Fanny: I know.

19 Mai: Even little kids—

20 Mai: or another example, her and Fanny—

21 Fanny: DON'T TALK ABOUT ME! (Trans. 23/05/95)

Attempting and failing to find the truth of racialized identity within official texts (4, 5, 6, 7, 8) telling the story of the mixed-race girl complicates any notion of narrating identity as something that is cohesive and coherent. At first glance, however, their discussion seems to revolve precisely around the issue of how to identify the signifiers of "English" or "Vietnamese," as if their meaning could be exactly guaranteed. Only they soon find that this guarantee and the difficulty of the question of identity is exacerbated by a lack of proper language that threatens to implicate them in a contravening of the rules of politeness (6, 15). The complications of race seem to produce here a very uncomfortable in-betweenness that on

the one hand the body tries to master but any fixed meaning is continually undone through the social interaction that the mixed-race setting of this conversation occasions. For, although almost silent until the very end of the day's session,
both Maria and Kenisha were present for this discussion Their silence as much as
their participation is expressive of the ongoing challenges the group faced in con-
versing across our racialized differences and of the ongoing work the group undertook to investigate the various ways in which sex, race, and social difference
may be imagined

23 Marnina:	Before we end, I just want to hear from Maria, because she hasn't said much today. Are you okay?
24 Maria:	I don't want to defend, like [inaudible] like you guys are more right to defend, like [inaudible].
25 LeLy:	We're not telling you to defend them. We're just trying to make a point. If you think that's wrong, say it out.
26 Mai:	It's your culture; you can defend them. We could be wrong.
27 Marnina:	Well, if she doesn't—
28 Maria:	and I don't want to. That's why I'm quiet. So forget me today. I don't want to defend anyone right now, so—
29 LeLy:	my point is—
30 Mai:	we're just making a statement—
31 Maria:	They might be Portuguese, but I hate them. Doesn't mean I have to like them, just because they're Portuguese.
32 LeLy:	There! There, can we bring this situation in here? She's Portuguese, but she doesn't fit in with those Portuguese.
33 Maria:	I'm not saying that.
34 Marnina:	Some Portuguese, just like you might say some Viet-namese—
35 LeLy:	[indicating Mai] like this person, so ugly. (Trans. 23/05/95)

The moral and ethical dilemma around which this anxious exchange takes
place is also the query that is at the center of Tori's story: the layered effects of difference, social power, recognition, and the fantasies that both constitute social
identities and constantly undo them. More intriguingly, perhaps, both are also interested in exploring how the cultural and social resources available—in terms of
the identities that can be inhabited and the forms of identification enabled or disavowed—allow for greater or lesser ease in living through the contradiction and
complexity of racialized positions.

Above the girls suggest that the metamorphosis Tori dreams of is achievable
by way of what Butler calls the "trick of passing" (1993, 178). Her ambiguous

racial positioning means that she may be accepted by the popular Portuguese girls as one of their own. However, while the mobility afforded by this passing is certainly seductive for the power and privileges it confers, it seems to also come with an enormous cost. To be recognizable as popular in the terms the girls lay out also entails participating in the perverse exclusionary practices of using racist insults against Vietnamese girls. For Tori, doing so would mean having to disavow her own self and community. Or in the terms LeLy uses, having to "make fun of your own country." Relatedly, within the context of the group, Maria, who acknowledges the difference in the structural dominance of her position (23) through a language of "dis-identification with racism" (Mercer 1992), suggests that for her such a position also entails a certain disidentification with community (30).

To become acceptable to a racist society, Wong suggests, the marginalized outsider is presented with a cruel bind: one must reject an integral part of oneself (1993, 77). Cast in a position of ambivalence, the price of accepting the bait of social promotion and acceptance within this arrangement becomes, for Tori, first having to admit her own inferiority (Bauman 1991, 73).

It is no wonder that the girls seem to simultaneously long for and distrust the recognition, attention and power of the popular girl. In developing Tori's story, the girls return to analyze the splitting required of them in making the identification with the popular girl over and over. Significantly, such a splitting is also performed in the process of discussing these very exigencies. Ostensibly providing examples to illustrate their point, LeLy and Mai (re)stage the comparison of themselves to the ideal through a voicing of the racist criticisms of their peers. Alternately taking turns, they project these critical self-appraisals onto Fanny (2, 4, 20), who is positioned, even more blatantly than usual, as the repository of the group's ambivalence. Fanny's response seems to first protest the way in which these criticisms are used against Asians collectively (11, 13). Only later does she object to the way in which she is singled out as the personification of this critique and refuses to go along with the pretense of innocence assumed by the others (21).

Successfully producing oneself as a popular girl within the space of the school depends on the negotiation of an impossible array of identifications, which, as we will see again in the next stage of Tori's transformation process, seem to slip between sameness and difference, desire and aversion, recognition and misrecognition, and are variously invested in the certainty of fixity and the possibilities for choice. Moreover, in attending to the repetitions of these conflicts and contradictions, the ways in which they are lived as paradoxical moments of comedy and pain, complexity and crudeness, opens up the possibility for thinking about representations of gender and racial identities as sites of identitifcation where our fantasmatic ideals might be called into question, assessed, and perhaps reconfigured.

On the Vertical

When recognizability as smart proves to be something that is impossible for Tori to produce, she invests her efforts and energies in another school space in which it might be possible to "become somebody." Within the narrative, this spatialized turn from the classroom to a focus on the girls' washroom, the school gym, and the dance that is scheduled to take place there signals a paradigmatic shift in the signifying relations of gender, class, race, sexuality, and recognition in the story.

Tori:	*The dance is coming up. Like I want to dance with Scott, right? But, I know that he doesn't like me because I'm a geek and he's so popular.*
Girl 2:	*You think so?*
Tori:	*I know who I am; I'm just [sighs]—How much people change me, I'll still be a geek! I look like a geek and Scott will never dance with me!*

Like Cinderella's ball, the school dance becomes the culminating moment of Tori's transformation. At once social, heterosexual, and highly visible, the space of the dance offers more than the mere promise of romance. Rather, by using it in some quite specific ways, it offers Tori a means with which to attempt to distinguish herself as a popular girl and not a nerd. Heterosexual display becomes one of the distinctive signs which seem to promise full access to this space and to public recognition as a normal girl. As we will see momentarily, Tori is advised by her friends to initiate a heterosexual encounter by inviting Scott to dance. Interestingly enough, this advice is dispersed without any of the cautionary alarms that troubled Crystal's similar attempts in chapter 3.

However, as the dialogue above makes clear, while Tori's invested desire to be approved continues to retain its power, the question of the likelihood that she will be able to make the criteria is constantly reopened. In Cinderella's story, along with some magical help, the ball and the events leading up to it facilitate the smooth path of justice and the restoration of moral and social order (Spence 1995, 67). In Tori's case however, the restoration that Spence suggests ends a proper fairy tale appears to be perpetually postponed. Instead, the girls' story interrogates the moral and social order of the school through some very interesting inquiries into the dialectical relationship between the material organization of interiority and the cultural forms and modes of material production that are subjectively lived (de Lauretis 1984; Hey 1997; McLaren 1991).

Within the school, dances were an infrequent occurrence; in my first year there were three and in the second only one. Usually organized around a holiday or special occasion like Valentine's Day, their relative rarity served to accentuate their specialized status. Yet while the dance's occurrence outside the everyday of school life served to heighten the intensity of anticipation around it, as a social practice that has widespread currency, there was also much about its organization and form that were shaped both by certain institutionalized expectations and many of the everyday features of social life within the school. As such, the space of the school gym may be read like an atlas of identities, where the differential access to the visibility offered by the dance makes explicitly apparent the micropolitics of the inclusion/exclusion dynamics of the school's social hierarchies.

One of the routes to visibility offered by the event of a dance is the opportunity to be involved in its organization. An official dance committee was operational in one year, responsible for asking permission from the principal, booking a DJ, advertising, and selling tickets. On the day of the dance the organizers were very prominent. Looking official with clipboards and lists, they stood by the gym doors checking names, taking tickets, and making loud comments to everyone as they passed by into the gym. Among the principal's usual predance remarks about appropriate behavior and warnings about any abberations spelling the end of future dance privileges, she publicly thanked the dance committee, making special mention of the Valentine's decorations they had borrowed from the art room for the occasion. It was the way in which she concluded her remarks, asking everyone to clap in appreciation of the committee's efforts, that broke the stony silence of the girls with whom I stood. It seems that a bureaucratic misunderstanding had resulted in the replacement of an original dance committee struck at the beginning of the school year—which included LeLy, Mai, Trinh, and Tammy among its members—with another when a new principal arrived in January. Thus, once again the girls found themselves not only overlooked but audience to a laudation of the achievements of their nemesis Lidia, at the helm of the reconfigured committee (FN 02/10/95).

Just as in the case of Tori and her friends, for the girls, the days leading up to a dance were replete with talk of it and little else. Numerous discussions would take place about who among them would be going, for while dances were always scheduled to take place during the school day, for those who either did not have the two-dollar entry fee or who chose not to attend, there was also the option of going to the school library or simply skipping off. Thus, one's mere presence at the dance signalled an interest in or perhaps only a curiosity about what this space had to offer, but the collective nature of the decision making also seems to suggest that to some extent access to it was dependant on having a friend or a group with whom to attend.

This precondition for attendance also communicates something about both the social forms of the dance and the ways in which difference is made visible through the use of this space. For example, an unofficial gendered partitioning of the gym was a feature of every dance, with the boys taking the far side and the girls the side closest to the exit. Keeping to their distinct sides, except for when a slow tune was played, the girls and boys danced separately, the girls dancing in clusters of varying sizes and the boys dancing only one at a time, infrequently getting up to do some fancy steps while the other boys stood around watching, at which point the girls would also crowd in to see. Thus, in terms of volume of space, the girls as a whole tended to take up much more of the gym than the boys.[10] However, it also seems that the social hierarchies differentiating among groups of girls were reflected in their varying use of space in the gym. When not dancing, LeLy, Mai, Lan, Kenisha, Maria, and the others sat on the benches lining the wall by the door. They tended to dance in this marginal area, as well as at the back of the gym. In contrast, the group of girls considered popular occupied the benches bordering the boys' side of the gym and danced together there, which meant they were using the central floor space of the gym (FN 01/21/94; 02/10/95; 05/18/95).

Prior to actually appearing at the dance, however, a series of preparatory tasks were necessary that were also collectively accomplished. This preparation takes place in a prefatory space to that of the actual dance—the girls' bathroom. Congregating in the large outer vestibule to await Tori's dramatic exit from the stall, here her friends collaborate to provide Tori with both the fashion assistance she requires and some instructions on how to make proper use of the space of the dance so that she may be recognizable as popular.

In the first of two sequences in the washroom, Girl 1, playing the role of fairy godmother, pulls the instruments of magic from her large shoulder bag: hairbrush and comb, hair spray, eyeliner, eye shadow, mascara, lipstick, blush, sponges, Q-tips, and when her work is done, a long-handled mirror so that Tori can appraise her new self. Replicating a scene familiar not only for its widespread representation in teen girl movies, but also for the regularity with which the girls gave each other this kind of sensuous attention—climbing into each other's laps, brushing each other's hair, hanging onto each other's arms, hands, and necks—Girl 1 sets out with much apparent pleasure to "fix up" her friend.

Girl 1:	You look great!
Tori:	You sure?
Girl 1:	Positive. No one will recognize you. Sit down. I'm going to do this hair of yours and it's going to be wonderful!
[Girl 1 starts brushing out Tori's hair]	
Tori:	How am I supposed to act at the dance?
Girl 1:	Just go up to him and go, "Do you want to dance?"

Tori:	But I've never asked a guy to dance with me before.
Girl 1:	Want me to ask him for you?
Tori:	No, no, no! I'm embarrassed.
Girl 1:	You shouldn't be; you going to look wonderful! Oh, that looks good. [She finishes with the hair.] Here, now get ready for this! You're not going to know who you are! Hair spray, so that it holds. See, doesn't that look wonderful? [Hands her the mirror.]

The washroom, often considered something of a private or marginal space[11] is converted into a semipublic one for the purposes of Tori's transformation. There the girls produce useful (gendered) knowledge[12] and spend time together in one of the few places in the school where they might do so, away from boys and teachers. Capturing the way in which marginalized girls may be discursively productive in marginalized spaces (Hey 1997, 20), this video segment seems to emphasize the opportunities of this space rather than its limitations.

Just as Girl 1's work is completed, Girl 2 swaggers into the washroom and introduces Tori to one of the other material practices that could support her attempts to meet the conditions of recognizability as a popular girl. The marginal space of the washroom engenders in this second segment an opportunity for the production of important sources of information and counterinformation. It becomes a place in which to express affiliation with and opposition to certain collective identities, interests, values, and knowledge.

Girl 2:	Hey, what's up? Hey!! You look so cool, man! Just the way you look, not those pony tails! Want to smoke, man?
Girl 1:	Sure.
Tori:	Okay. [Takes a puff and coughs.]
Girl 2:	What's wrong? You okay? Don't you know how to smoke?
Tori:	Of course I know how to smoke!
[Two other girls walk into the washroom, look over at Tori, do a double take, and whisper loudly: The geeky girl!]	
Girl 1:	They're going to take a little time getting used to it.

Girl 2's intervention shifts the tone of things significantly. As we have already seen, in contrast to Girl 1's use of a gentle motherly discourse with which to assist Tori with her problem, Girl 2 has all along presented something of a tougher stance. Here this is accentuated even further through her choice of language and the introduction of the quasi illicit properties of cigarettes, smoked secretly in the washroom, contravening school rules. Cigarettes are commonly interpreted as a symbol of adulthood, sophistication, rebellion, or coolness

(Danesi 1994; Eckert 1989; Lloyd et al. 1998). Like new clothes, hairstyles, and heterosexuality, they are also displayable, and therein lies their value for Tori. Participation in the ritualized practices of smoking is an expression of category affiliation. Moreover, the risk factor, the collective strategizing to secure a place in which to do it, as well as the practice of sharing cigarettes solidifies this alliance, making it visible both to other group members and to outsiders.

If instruction in smoking was not part of Cinderella's preparation for the ball, neither was her fairy godmother's transformative work met with quite the same response as the one that Tori received in the washroom. Whereas Cinderella spends the entire evening at the ball so completely unrecognizable as herself that even her family cannot guess at her identity, Tori's transformation is not so thorough. "It's the geeky girl," the two other girls say, almost the minute they enter the washroom. While Tori is still identifiably a nerd, this is a contrast which suggests a complicating of the girls' investment in the transformation story. But it also surfaces a structural difference in Cinderella and Tori's positions, demonstrating that "passing" involves the restaging of a fractured history of identifications that constitutes the limits to a given subject's mobility (Ahmed 1999, 93). It suggests that the process of fixation whereby identities are adopted through dress and manner also involves the threatening potential of its own unfixability. The crisis of not belonging for the passing subject then becomes a crisis of knowledge, of knowing there is always a danger of being found out (Ahmed 1999, 100).

As the location in which these activities transpire, the washroom becomes a threshold space, mediating the transition from nerd to popular girl. It is here that the signs and symbols of class, race, sexuality, and gender (the new clothes, makeup, hair, the nerd, the popular girl, the boy and the cigarettes) and that of recognition (the mirror), are brought together to signify the reconfiguration of identity boundaries which are, with the metaphor that Girl 1 supplies, secured with the holding power of hair spray. However, whereas the visual matrix of this video segment may suggest the potential for transformation, the narrative structure, particularly in the first washroom segment, works against the normalizing authority of the transformation genre, creating a turbulence, a site of impossible irresolution. That is, despite the fixity promised by the metaphor of hair spray (or perhaps because of it), the play between identity and difference does not elude the mirror. For as Walkerdine warns, projects for wished-for transformation are "shaky and highly likely to produce forms of anxiety, overt conflict, and other modes of defense" (Walkerdine 1990, 44).

"No one will recognize you," Girl 1 tells Tori early on in their discussion. Later she adds, "You're not going to know who you are." Intended to reassure, the words capture both the promise and terror of transformation. On the one hand, Tori's efforts to position herself as a subject within the discursive and social practices of popularity guarantee that others will be unable to continue to identify her as a nerd. And on the other, as we have already seen, the high price to be paid for inhabiting this desired place is the repudiation of certain identifications, so that even she may no longer recognize herself. Tori's transformation threatens to separate her from her own knowledge of self.

Writing about her own girlhood, Walkerdine offers insights into the workings of this very dynamic by tracing a postwar narrative about girls growing up into upward mobility, found in popular films of the time. These films, she argues, signal a particular trajectory offering transformation through education, leading to respectability, glamor, romance, and marriage. However, in the process, the object of the transformation, the working-class girl, is given nothing to be proud of, even to like about herself. She is shown to move out of the horror that is herself and what is presented as the feared place, to be defended against at all costs, is a return there. The films showed a way out, and imparted self-hatred at the same time (Walkerdine 1997, 95).[13]

Walkerdine suggests that these rags-to-riches film stories constitute a certain truth about class and mobility at a moment when certain paths and fantasies are open to working-class women. Now, half a century later, the girls' story about Tori seems to question both education as a route that will grant them this same possibility for transformation and mobility as well as the high cost of the trade-off that seems an inherent feature of this process. The group articulates this objection as we attempt to negotiate a powerful aspect of Tori's character, an effort we undertook with each of our characters.

1	Marnina:	How about Tori with the popular issue?
2	LeLy:	Oh, the popular? I can't think of any part for her.
3	Mai:	She's weak.
4	Marnina:	Think she's weak?
5	LeLy:	She's not weak, but she always do whatever like—
6	Mai:	the popular people.
7	Marnina:	Is there power in wanting to be popular and working to get there?
8	LeLy:	Okay . . . she change herself, she make her—like she dye her hair or something like that, for example. What is the powerful part? You're giving up your own, the way you are and change to another person?
9	Marnina:	So that's a problem, eh?
10	LeLy:	Kind of. You're like, first of all if you do anything to fit in popular, if you're unpopular; you'd do anything for them.
11	Marnina:	Yeah, that's a problem. [pause] But I'm wondering if there might not be a couple of ways of looking at what a

strong aspect of Tori's character could look like. Like, could we think about what it would mean to want to be popular and to be successful at it and there might be something powerful about that? Or as you were suggesting, maybe to be powerful would mean deciding that being popular isn't worth what you might have to give up to get there—

12 Mai: that's powerful!

13 Marnina: or she might start to question the categories themselves—

14 Mai: I want the second one!

15 LeLy: What's the third one?

16 Marnina: Yeah, well I'm not sure about that one myself, but one of the things we've been asking here is how do these categories happen, right? So what I'm trying to figure out is if we can figure that out maybe there's a way of thinking about nerd and popular categories not as something people actually are—

17 LeLy: Okay, yeah, yeah, I know what you mean. Like you wrote in that letter?

18 Marnina: Yeah, did you get that?

19 LeLy: Marnina, no offense, but like those questions that you ask, I really don't have the answer in my brain. (Trans. 23/05/95)

"Giving up your own" so as to be able to successfully meet the criteria for popularity is deemed so seriously a sign of weakness that Mai and LeLy initially dismiss outright any possibility of attributing anything powerful at all to Tori's character (2, 3). What interests me about this formulation of the popular-power dialectic is how it plays with, perhaps even redefines, the way in which their relationship has signified thus far in the story, suggesting a certain fluidity and lack of fixity in what is experienced as power and powerlessness. Here, rather than designating inscription into popularity and participation in the dominant system of valuation as a route to qualifying Tori as a powerful girl, Mai and LeLy insist that such a position can be attained through the production of competing knowledge of the world, that is by holding onto "her own" (Fiske 1989; Gotfrit 1988). Theirs is a stance that seems to struggle against certain forms of subjection and the privileging of particular regimes of knowledge (Foucault 1982, 782).

This kind of struggle to renegotiate the terms of power-knowledge in the narration of self links the question of the moral content of identity with that of the project of schooling and the rules and ethics of relationships within that community (Fine 1990; Grumet 1997; Luttrell 1997; Nilan 1991; Ryan 1997; West

1995). Among the possibilities for waging this struggle is the reformulation of dominant codes as a means of negotiating political-cultural agency. The practice of critical reappropriation is frequently invoked in discussions of how various sub-altern populations discover a means of actively confronting and resisting margin-alization in the ironic repossession of signs otherwise meant to enforce marginality (Goldberg 1993; Laclau 1977). Goldberg claims, for example that it may be possible for those objectified by these categories to appropriate them, as-suming the categories in assertive self-ascription. This appropriation, which he calls "standing inside the terms,"[14] may give new meaning to and thereby redirect them as forms of political engagement and critique (1993, 174).

However, the girls reject this particular strategy, as a means for holding onto "their own." One day I arrived in our meeting room and found that Fanny had scrawled on the blackboard, "Maria is a nerdy girl!" We had for quite some time been talking about possible names for our group and when I saw her graffiti I half in jest and half seriously suggested we use "The Nerdy Girls" as a name. Mai, with a sideways look, asked uncertainly, "You're joking, right?" I attempted to explain: "It makes fun of the categories popular and nerds, it claims nerdy as something good, instead of something to be gotten rid of." Kenisha, shaking her head, said, "No offense, but your idea sucks!" Maria, a little more diplomatic responded with, "It's not that I don't like it, it's just that, well I don't think anyone else will get it." LeLy completely dismissed the idea: "We're already too nerdy!" And Fanny ac-cused me of practising pop psychology: "You're saying it for self-confidence. I don't think so!" (FN 05/16/95).

They were not, however, without a different kind of strategy for defending against and perhaps defying dominant forms of valuation which marginalized them within the school. Returning to the conceptualization of the individual un-derlying Tori's question without an answer—"Why can everyone always, always judge you by the outside? Is this world a fairness world?"—it is this spatialized sense of self that the girls seem to draw on to interrogate the forms of power-knowledge which categorize individuals, attach identity to them, and assign recognition. More elaborate than the way in which it is used in Tori's question, this formula-tion also makes an appearance in this rather long excerpt of a discussion that took place between Tammy and Trinh while they collaboratively wrote a letter, printed under the title "Teacher Fairness," in the magazine the group produced in the first year of our project. As in Tori's question, here power-knowledge is linked to the critical issues of subjective and intersubjective relations, ethics, and justice.

1 Trinh: We could go like this, write a letter—
2 Tammy: write a letter, put it in the magazine. Say that it's not fair
            how teachers—

3	Trinh:	treat some people better than others.
4	Tammy:	[writing] Say, how come teachers only like students that are smart?
5	Trinh:	Treat everyone fairly.
6	Tammy:	Yeah, treat everyone fairly—
7	Trinh:	everyone is all the same inside. Or no, put, they may look smart from the outside, but inside they really aren't. . . .
8	Mai:	Could you say like, some people are shy? They know the answer but they don't put their hand up?
9	Trinh:	Yeah, some people are shy and don't give the answer, but doesn't mean they're not smart!
10	Mai:	Yeah.
11	Trinh:	Say, they just don't act smart outside.
12	Tammy:	Here, I'll write that one. [to Mai] Beat it! Shoo, shoo! Beat it, shoo, shoo. [to Trinh] So what you want to write?

. . .

13	Tammy:	If teachers don't treat students fairly they shouldn't—
14	Trinh:	be teachers at all!
15	Tammy:	And than what? If you don't respect them, if the teacher no—if the teacher won't respect the students why should the students respect—
16	Trinh:	yeah!
17	Tammy:	No, but that's kind of mean.
18	Trinh:	Ask the teacher, I mean—
19	Tammy:	Marnina? Is it okay? [reads] "If teachers don't respect"— no, you can't use "respect" because we're too young. Like, I want to say something like if they're going to act like this to students they shouldn't be teachers. I don't know how to say it.
20	Marnina:	I think you should say it the way you just did. It's really good.
21	Tammy:	'Kay, tell me the truth.
22	Marnina:	It's really good!
23	Tammy:	Okay, when we tell you something, you have to tell us the truth, okay?
24	Marnina:	Yup.
25	Tammy:	How you feel, really feel. [resumes writing] Some teachers—

. . .

26	Tammy:	At the bottom, say here, "From the people who care."
27	Trinh:	From the people who don't—who are fair.
28	Tammy:	No, from people who cares about—
29	Trinh:	this subject.

30 Tammy: No, people who are scared about this like—from people
                   who have been treated this way. Marnina? Is this okay?
                   [reads] Is that good? (Trans. 05/20/94).

Combining modernist discourses of the self that divide inside from outside
realms with equity discourses that seem to make use of these realms to accommodate difference by announcing sameness, the girls critique the forms of power-
knowledge that marginalize them, even as they postulate another law of truth of
the individual, through which they might recognize themselves and demand to
be recognized by others. While outside is condemned as mere artifice in the
production of self, inside is imagined as a space of wholeness, authenticity, and
potential.[15]

As a strategy for claiming both competing knowledge and alternative identificatory sites of recognition, what is being invested in this conception of body
or space and what does it offer? The answer may in part be found by returning to
that archetypical figure of transformation haunting this story. Read as a narrative
about the struggle for social identity, the story of Cinderella renders a particular
representation of the production of the intersection of subject and subjectivity, its
complexities and relationship to recognition—a central question of Tori's story
and the one that I have been exploring.

In Grimm's version of the story, the prince, upon relocating his mysterious
dancing partner from the previous night's ball, remains undismayed when he finds
Cinderella in rags and filthy from her day's labor because he recognizes her inherent
qualities, quite apart from her outer appearance (Bettelheim 1976, 252). The moral
of the story is, according to Bettelheim, one about true merit being recognized even
when hidden under rags (1976, 239).

For the girls, the inside seems to similarly constitute a sphere where a set of
attributes exists that challenges and extends the organized production process of
subjective value beyond the conditions of intelligibility that are deemed to currently exist within their school. Moreover, it provides the moral grounds for their
critique of how recognition is assigned there. It serves, therefore, as a practical in-
strument with which to assert a claim to the expansion of patterns of recognition
and a means of resisting passive humiliation, helping them to live a positive relation to self. Given the anticipation that a future communication community will
recognize them for their present abilities, they find themselves socially respected
as the person that they cannot, under present circumstances, be recognized for
being (Honneth 1996, 164).

But there is, I think, something more at stake here. In the face of the multiple divisions of power which schooling encodes, constantly inciting difference at the
same time as it perpetually displaces and even denies it (Hey 1997; Walkerdine

1990), the inside may also function as a site of coherence for the girls. For, as we have seen through the discussion of Tori's dilemma, it seems that maintaining positive identifications with configurations of gender, class, race, sexuality, family, and community forms that are sanctioned and valued by the school, as well as those that may not be, often entails a splitting. The anxiety states induced from juggling such contradictory positionings can, as Unwin suggests, be manifest in a variety of ways: from denial of incongruity to a variety of mechanisms for apparently achieving conscious closure and coherence (1984, 225). Perhaps the investment in an inside space is a response to the normative practices of schooling that produce a model of a whole individual with an identity. In that context perhaps an inside presents the possibility of being able to recognize a self at all.

Finally, withdrawing myself from the story, I leave you with the image of a girl, Tori (or is it Mai?), dancing, enclosed within a circle of other dancing, still-thirteen-year-old girls, in a darkened room, with red, green, and yellow streams of light pulsing from the stage in time to the beat of throbbing music; zooming out slowly into longshot, I allow the sound track music to drown my words, because the hit pop song playing is reaching the end, and it also happens to be the theme song the girls have chosen for Tori:

> Don't you stop me now,
> doing what I want to do,
> for you're out of line.
> I can do it alone and I'm feeling fine,
> now I'm here on my own.
> Don't you see my eyes are looking around for something new,
> for you're out of line.
> I can't live another day with you. . . .

(Fade out)

Conclusion

The Good, the Bad,
the Smart, and the Popular:
Living Ambivalence

I've been thinking about the different kinds of shorelines and ways to approach the land.

—Laura Smith, b'tween the earth and my soul (cd)

How does one conclude a discussion in which the limits to understanding have been as central to the analysis as claims to knowledge? Do I now magically reveal the absences and the silences underlying that which has been spoken, assert the authority I have thus far refused to claim, and finally (m)utter summary words? How should I bring this conversation to a close, moving away from the series of stories that have authored me as thoroughly as I them, keeping me company all this time, like a beloved but bad-mannered house guest taking up too much space and staying too long?

Like the way in which I might persuade a recalcitrant visitor to begin preparations for leave taking, one way in which I might mediate my inability to conclude this story is to unfold my map, revisit sites of special interest, trace alternate routes that will make visible important intersecting passageways and perhaps highlight other interesting places to go. The map is, of course, the discourse map of femininity and the intersecting passageways are certain moments that resurface as key elements in the characters' stories, but that have so far been analyzed separately. The sites I am particularly interested in revisiting are the threshold zones of the map where an epistemological splitting is produced. These aporetic moments disclose the doubled ambivalence of the structure of and responses to discourses of femininity. My interest in the irresolvable contradiction of these moments is in their disruptive potential to the hegemony of femininity's authority and in the alternative identificatory possibilities they might engender. For if, as

161

Hall points out, "you cannot, as it were, reverse the discourses of identity simply by turning them upside down" (1991, 57), the question of the ethical-political significance and context of identification becomes, as Fuss (1995) suggests, critical to any project of social transformation. Since such an interest lies at the heart of this work, I want to link the question of irresolvable contradiction to some questions about what the kind of collective imaginative work involved in the video production offers for a feminist agenda of expanding the options in young girls' lives. Specifically, I want to ask how the collective work of imagining might be implicated in the reworking of notions of social difference as a relational form. What, for example, is at stake in a pedagogical practice that attempts to work across the confusions between self and other that takes place in the imaginary dimensions of human experience? What are the possibilities and complications that the confusion of ambivalence might offer for challenging our apparent identity as subjects? And how does the opportunity of doing this kind of work collectively contribute to building the conditions of new knowledge, new practices of identification, and new "scenes of pedagogy" (Todd 1997)?

Recently, authors working within postcolonial, postmodern, and critical race theory have expressed interest in ambivalence itself as a political force of sorts (Ahmed 1999; Ang 1996; Back 1996; Bauman 1991; Bhabha 1990; Garber 1992; Jones 1988; McClintock 1995; Trinh 1991). Bhabha (1990), for example, has coined the term "the third space" to theorize the liminal place of ambivalence. He sees this as the point from where one might go beyond the contained grid of fixed identities and binary oppositions through the production of hybrid cultural forms and meanings: "This third space displaces the histories that constitute it, and sets up new structures of authority, new political initiatives" (1990, 12). Trinh, also suggests that the liminal place of in-betweenness is one that can be mobilized in the interests of an unsettling agenda: "Not quite the Same, not quite the Other, she stands in that undetermined threshold place where she constantly drifts in and out. Undercutting the inside/outside opposition, her intervention is necessarily that of both a deceptive insider and a deceptive outsider. She is this Inappropriate Other/Same who moves about with always at least two/four gestures: that of affirming 'I am like you' while persisting in her difference; and that of reminding 'I am different' while unsettling every definition of otherness arrived at" (1991, 74).

Both quite hopeful about the subversive potential of this liminal space of ambivalence, Bhabha and Trinh's optimism is not necessarily fully shared by others. Ang, for example, suggests there is a romanticizing tendency in this valorization of the ambivalent hybrid, based not only on the assumption that the deconstruction of binary oppositions as such is politically subversive and desirable, but also, an overstating of the power of ambivalence (1996, 45). Anne McClintock (1995) agrees that the lyrical glamor that is cast over ambivalence does not always seem warranted. For McClintock, Bhabha's assertion that the "strategic failure" of colonial appropriation is ensured by its discursive ambivalence is overstated. She suggests that while ambivalence may well be a critical aspect of subversion, it is not in and of itself a sufficient agent for the displacement of authority. Nor is the disruption of social norms always subversive, especially in postmodernist commodity cultures where formal fluidity, fragmentation, and marketing through difference are central elements. Privileged groups can, she argues, on occasion, display their privilege precisely by the extravagant display of their right to ambiguity (1995, 68). Moreover, as Sara Ahmed argues, there may be ways in which relations of power are paradoxically secured, through the very process of destabilization. She asks, "[H]ow do ambiguous bodies get read in a way which further supports the enunciative power of those who are telling the difference?" (1999, 89). Rather than assuming ambivalence as inherently subversive, therefore, there is a need to pay attention to the different ways in which specific forms of ambiguity are deployed (McClintock 1995, 63) and to the possibility of their different effects.

Returning to the stories written and performed by the girls, there is, it seems to me, in each a dramatic tension that is built around a crisis of categories. The girl who "doesn't know how to be good without being bad," and her counterpart, the mixed-race nerd, struggling to "become somebody," both challenge the notion of a noncontradictory subjectivity and an unambivalent acceptance of authoritative discourses of femininity. Where the story of romance intersects with the story of transformation, this challenge produces an interesting negotiation of meaning among competing configurations. For the thresholds that are used to mark the crisis of categories in the stories, at times also threatening or disrupting the conventions of the very genres organizing the telling, are far from random. Rather, they are suggestive of the social contradictions that underlie the discursive formations structuring the lives of girls and perhaps more broadly, those that also underscore Western societies at the beginning of the new century.

MIXED SUBJECTS: DISRUPTIVE FIGURES?

Pam Gilbert and Sandra Taylor, whose work on girls and schooling is among the first to identify contradiction as a structural feature of discourses of femininity (1991, 14), list a series of three sets of contradictions. While, the girls' stories complicate this enumeration significantly, as I will demonstrate shortly, I think it is worth considering them as a point of departure.

The first set of discourses mentioned by Gilbert and Taylor centers on girls' futures, which they characterize as the domesticity/paid work conflict. They suggest that while the majority of girls will undoubtedly be engaged in paid forms of work either throughout or at least at some points in their lives, this conflict signals lingering ideas about the relationship of femininity to the traditional division of labor based on male breadwinners and women's caring responsibilities in the household. The second set of discourses is borrowed from Sue Lees's (1986) work on the importance of reputation in structuring girls' sexuality. The "slags" or "drags" split, Gilbert and Taylor argue, continues to operate as a device regulating girls' sexuality. Finally, the third set of discourses they cite relates to age or maturity and draws on Barbara Hudson's (1984) analysis of the impasse girls face in attempting to position themselves within discourses of both adolescence and femininity.

Of the discourses listed, the girls' stories particularly explore and elaborate on certain contradictory features of those relating to girls' futures and female sexuality and the impossibility of occupying them unambivalently. I want to link these and the related discourses I will use to complicate this list to the questions I raised earlier about the disruptive potential of the "in-between" of discourse, as well as to the consequences for girls' struggle for recognition in having to position themselves within discourses that have these structural characteristics. To do so, I summon from each of the girls' stories a figure that embodies and performs some aspects of the social contradictions referred to above. From Crystal's story I call on the specter of the interracial couple, and from Tori/Kathy's the mixed-race girl herself. Separately, as we have already seen, these figures expose particular elements of the constitutive and formative exclusions productive of certain highly valued forms of the feminine subject. What does their joint presence in the stories offer, I wonder, in the way of insights into the relationship between discursive ambivalence and the "strategic failure" of authoritative discourse?

Enacting and embodying a rupture of fixed categories, both the interracial couple and the mixed-race girl might be considered a "figure that disrupts" (Garber 1992). In Garber's terms such a figure marks the space of anxiety about fixed and changing identities, commutable or absent selves by disarranging, untiding, and subverting binary oppositions. Neither fully good nor bad, English or Vietnamese the figures convey something about the instability and incompleteness of all subject formation. In flagrantly occupying more than one subject position, the figures also represent the ways in which all identifications oscillate between discursive positions. Their hybridity produces a kind of speaking which allows for the possibility of "saying at least, two, three things at a time" (Trinh 1992, 140), something that Trinh argues is vital for dominated and marginalized people. The polyvalent figures operate as dense transfer points for a doubled discussion about, on the one hand, the conflicting expectations and pressures of discourses of femininity. On the other, the layers of meaning produced by the figures may be reconfigured to deliberate different relations to hybridity and ambiguity. That is, it is possible there are disruptions operating with differing psychic, social, and political consequences.

Consider again the respective climactic moments of Crystal and Tori/ Kathy's stories. In the case of the former, this occurs with Crystal's public crossing of the national-racial-sexual border, precipitating what is perceived to be a very visible social transgression. In resisting her family's objections, she announces a "desire in opposition," bringing into consciousness identifications with dominatingly defined good and bad girl positions.

The narrative tension in Tori/Kathy's story also peaks at a moment of forced choice. While Tori is desperate to gain access to the desired place of popularity for the power, privilege and visibility conferred by such a place, to do so entails attempting to pass as English. She must conceal both her Vietnamese mother and her smartness. The prospect of winning such a (mis)recognition rests on a repudiation of the other within.

The negotiation of category thresholds in these climactic moments in the stories turns especially on the relations between romance and individual aspiration, visibility and desire, technologies of the social and cultural-political agency and power. The points at which these cross with the basic structural and institutional formations within Western societies—where romance meets family, where individual aspiration meets class, where visibility meets race, where desire meets gender, where technologies of the social meet school, where cultural-political agency meets sexuality—are the investigative sites I turn to for what they reveal about shifting social contradictions, strategies usable by girls themselves, and the structural ambivalence of femininity itself.

I. INTERSECTIONS. THE BAD GIRL WITHIN: TRANSFORMATIONS BEYOND THE ENDING

For female protagonists of fairy tales and romance stories, happily ever after arrives, more often than not, at the end of an unconflicted and one-way road of successful courtship and marriage. For Crystal and Tori/Kathy the route to happily ever after, as we have already seen, is much less certain. Along the way are bifurcating paths, four-way stops, and numerous traffic jams that must all be negotiated. Returning to the stories again, I want to pull out and cross-reference a few of the complicating strands which are suggestive of a certain ambivalence about this journey.

From Crystal's diary I ask you to reconsider one of the entries which recounts a contest between a series of competing considerations revolving around family, romance, school, and individual aspiration. Alongside it, I draw on a couple of moments from Tori/Kathy's story which pivot on a related chain of discursive fields.

> *We got into a big fight again! My parents say my marks are dropping. Why do I always have to be a straight-A student? Anyways, I'm still getting As with only a few A minuses. I think they might be getting suspicious about Matt. Why can't they give me a break? They're putting their highest hopes on me—now that Cindy is gone. It's so hard trying to be what they want me to be. Why can't I be myself?*

This oppositional organization of options offers Crystal the possibility of assuming either a good girl position by focussing on her parents' priorities of school and grades or a bad girl position if she directs her attention instead towards her boyfriend. Romance and entry into heterosexual relations figure here, as I suggested in chapter 2, as a desire in opposition that in relation to her parents is tied to an individual aspiration separating Crystal from parental dictates. Ironically, of course, the ideology of romance is also, as feminists have argued, precisely what complicates the fulfilment of women's own individual aspirations—at least any that extend beyond domesticity. The ambivalent relation between a good girl femininity, parents, and doing well in school also receives play in Tori/Kathy's story.

1	Maria:	Well, maybe they're smart or whatever. Maybe, because one of the things on the show yesterday was who was popular. Anyways they started getting good grades in school and they weren't popular any more—
2	Mai:	cause she had good grades, right? Like she played sports and stuff like that and she's good at it. And then her parents saying, "Oh, your grades dropping down" and after she didn't play sports that much. So she studies and stuff like that, and she has good grades and people are like this: "Oh, you're a brainer now." Like she's not that popular no more.
3	Samantha:	So if we're going to make her a nerd, she should be a brainer that doesn't like dress good.
4	LeLy:	[inaudible] goody-goody.
5	Fanny:	Not goody-goody!
6	Mai:	Well, yeah, because if you don't talk a lot you have no friends, so if you have no friends you always do your homework.
7	Tammy:	You act like good to the teacher. So you're the goody-goody. (Trans. 12/12/94)

Here the linking of a chain of associated meanings around good girl femininity and grades to the social identities of popular/nerd reveals another internal fissure: too much attention to the relationship management necessary with peers to secure and hold onto a position within popularity threatens academic achievement. And yet, as Tori's story illustrated, the visibility, prestige, and power conferred by popularity combined with gendered and racialized understandings of intelligence are also used and maintained by teachers in their recognitions and designations of smartness.

As in Crystal's story, the oppositional positions emerge through the social technology associated with grades. This convergence produces a tension between relations within and outside the family. In both stories, parents are featured aggressively pushing for their daughters' success in school and against the relationships that could distract them from this goal. It is possible this is an expression of a fantasy about parents taking an active interest in their education, a desire very eloquently articulated especially by Maria in chapter 2, when she says, "Like sometimes I think they feel more happy when I clean the house, like when I do something at home good, like bake a cake, or something like that good, instead of my grades!" (Trans. 05/31/95). Crystal's story suggests that the investment in grades is also closely related to specific class and social circumstances. That is, grades are understood to be about more than a personal achievement important for shaping a promising individual future. Rather, in the context of family migration grades are invested with a very special significance in that they are viewed as stages of enacting an intergenerational responsibility. The exhortation to channel energies towards grades and away from peers and boyfriends—to be a good girl—is one that also emphasizes kinship ties and obligations towards the future prospects of the entire family. "All their hopes are on me," Crystal says.

This sense of a familial stake in the educational achievements of daughters runs directly contrary to much of the discussion current within educational discourses around immigrant families. There families of Asian origin (particularly South Asian and Vietnamese) are singled out for particular mention as problems for their perceived lack of support for and interest in preparing daughters for a future outside of being wives and mothers (Brah 1996; Kenway and Willis 1998). While this is a discourse that can also be found in reference to Portuguese immigrant parents, in that literature, lack of parental concern is seen as an issue for the educational aspirations of both daughters and sons (Nunes 1999).

However, what is perhaps most interesting about this particular intersection of stories is what the girls' investment in grades may gesture towards in terms of their ambivalence about smartness. That is, it suggests that they may be open to the possibility of negotiating new relationships between femininity and smartness.

1 Lan:	So what did I say about her? Oh yeah, and guys don't go near her cause she's so smart and everything. Okay, there's this really cute guy that she has a crush on, right? Okay?
2 Mai:	Why you love Kathy so much?
3 Maria:	Who's Kathy?
4 Lan:	My low life girl.
5 Fanny:	But he doesn't like her—
6 Lan:	no, we don't know if he likes her or not—
7 Fanny:	don't make him like her.
8 Lan:	but he doesn't talk to her a lot, so she figures it's because she's too smart and that's—
9 Kenisha:	she's not—
10 Lan:	. . . why she starts like failing a couple of classes and thing.
11 Kenisha:	alright, okay.
12 Lan:	Cause guys don't like girls who are smarter than them.
13 Mai:	It's true, in magazine, I read it.
14 Fanny:	That's a stupid thing.
15 Kenisha:	Yeah, she's stupid if she did that just for a guy.
16 Fanny:	Yeah, make it end like she knows that the guy doesn't like her so she starts working harder and harder and then she gets better grades back.
17 Mai:	Or—
18 Kenisha:	or she could end with the guy.
19 Fanny:	I know another guy, instead of him another guy, but he's smart—
20 Kenisha:	no, no, no! She could end up with the same guy, when she start putting back school work is first then she might—
21 Lan:	Kathy's I.Q. You know what Kathy's I.Q. is?
22 Marnina:	What?
23 Lan:	200.
24 Kenisha:	Yeah, right! . . .
25 Marnina:	So the brainer gets the guy?
26 Kenisha:	Brainer don't get the guy! In my country the brainer doesn't get the guy!
27 Marnina:	No? What happens?
28 Kenisha:	What you have, they get the guy.
29 Mai:	It does usually happen, the girl that has money gets the guy.
30 LeLy:	Yeah.

31 Kenisha:	The brainer could be, the brainer could have money too. Like my sister she have money and lots of guys like her, cause she goes to high school. In my country why they think we have money because my mom is away and most of my family is away and she sends money.
32 Lan:	I know one! I know one!
33 Marnina:	Go ahead.
34 Lan:	Okay, she ends up with the guy, but he tells her that he likes girls that are smart.
35 Kenisha:	Exactly.
36 Maria:	That's what I was thinking.
37 Marnina:	That's what Kenisha was saying.
38 Lan:	Oh.
39 Kenisha:	Ha, ha, ha! (Trans. 04/05/95)

In this instance, the investment in doing well in school may work against authoritative discourses of femininity which are structured such that girls interested in assuming a position within heterosexuality through securing a male partner in romance are required to subvert their own intelligence. Instead, the dominant and submissive gender relations that underline this valuation are reimagined, allowing the possibility of a positive identification with both the romantic heroine and the girl with the I.Q. of 200. This appears to be a loosening of social forms which, like a Gail Godwin character, allows Kathy to keep "one foot in the door of the Unknown, the other still holding open its place in the book of Old Plots" (Godwin 1978, 45).

Walkerdine, Lucey, and Melody (2000) argue that due to the effects of second-wave feminism, as well as labor market changes that have resulted in a decline in male manual work, the last two decades have seen girls becoming the bearers of what was previously seen to be an exclusively male rationality. They link recent studies showing girls' heightened excellence in academic achievement to the unprecedented possibility of "making the feminine rational and the rational feminine" (2000, 60). However, they also demonstrate that these shifts in social form tend to be a predominately white, middle-class phenomenon. It is white, middle-class girls in particular who become rational subjects, taking up places in the professions once occupied solely by middle-class white men. Thus, it is perhaps not surprising that while the investment in grades may work to unsettle some of the gendered dynamics of displays of smartness, the discussion around Tori's story also hints at an anxiety about school success being able to deliver on its promise of serving as the vehicle of upward mobility. This anxiety accents the contradictory set of social expectations currently circulating around the disparate futures for (white) middle-class and racialized, working-class girls.

Youth researchers note that the 1990s brought both significant disruptions to the circuit of production, reproduction and consumption marking the transition into adulthood (Dwyer and Wyn 1998; Furlong and Cartmel 1997; Griffin 1997; Heilman 1998; Willis 1984; Wyn and White 1997) and a discursive explosion around what constitutes femininity and its ambiguous relationship to feminism (McRobbie 1994). The two are not entirely unrelated. Changes in the economic order, the dismantling of Fordist social structures, rising levels of youth unemployment, credential inflation, and welfare and education spending cuts all coalesce to demand new forms of subjectivity, "subjects who are capable of understanding themselves as autonomous subjects, producers of their present and their future, inventors of the people they are or may become" (Walkerdine, Lucey, and Melody 2001, 2). At the same time, the new vocabularies of femininity found in teen magazines contain more of the self, more autonomy, and encouragement to lavish more attention on the self with the aid of consumer goods (McRobbie 1994, 165). While the invitation to self-invention offered by these new discourses of femininity and demanded by the wider social and structural changes produce new discursive spaces for girls to enter as subjects, these spaces also yield tension and contradiction. Specifically, the loosening of social forms means that youth, particularly the most marginalized, have the difficult task of reconciling the contradiction between the reality of their specific circumstances and the promises of wealth and well-being offered by an increasingly global society. While social rhetoric may espouse a conviction that each individual must render her own life meaningful as an outcome of individual choice, that "anyone who works hard can get ahead" and "women have made great gains towards equality," these girls will be negotiating cultural and political changes and an unpromising economic climate that disturb this debatable relationship between individualism and individual aspiration.

II. INTERSECTIONS. BECOMING SOMEBODY: ROMANCING THE SELF

If once upon a time the end, the proper end, to a girl's story was marriage and failing that, death (Duplessis 1985), the "presiding fiction" (Williams 1991) shaping life stories at the beginning of the century is conceived around a somewhat different quest and series of consequences. That is, with the development of a concept of inwardly derived identity, the defining concern becomes one of an individual negotiation of the shifting conditions of possibility of modern subjectivity—or "becoming somebody." Put another way, while once the singular ensured route to "becoming somebody" for a young woman was through a heterosexual romance leading to marriage, Tori's and Crystal's stories suggest that the gender-making process organizing this becoming in the new century seems, in certain circumstances, to be repositioning its dependence on the repression of a woman's agency, desire, and ambition. "You have to stand up for yourself!" Tori's friends urge her, and "Why can't I be myself?" Crystal asks.

However, as each of the stories underscores, under the conditions of modernity, the struggle to "become somebody" carries with it at least two interrelated contradictions which complicate this emergent formation. Intersecting the contradictions is the question of where the loci of social recognition are achieved. On the one hand, the individual needs to establish a defensible difference between self and the wider social world. On the other hand, to be sustainable, such a difference requires social recognition and must be obtained in a form which also enjoys social approval (Bauman 1991, 201). Built into this formation is the notion of an individuality that depends on forms of sociality while simultaneously disavowing the very dependence out of which it emerges. The scene of self-recognition, therefore, can be produced only within the multiple entanglements of other subjects' histories, experiences, and self-representations; with their texts, conduct, gestures, and objectifications; with their "argument of images" (Battaglia 1995, 2). Thus, a sense of self emerges in the tension between self-assertion and recognition such that "in the very moment of realizing our own independence, we are dependent upon another to recognize it. At the very moment we come to understand the meaning of I, myself, we are forced to see the limitations of that self" (Benjamin 1993, 134). It is where the good/bad girl is constituted in relation to the various pulls of individual and collective selfhood, the sites of apparently autonomous agency (free choice) in contradistinction to a prevailing valuation of collectivity and relationality, that I want to revisit here.

Returning first to Tori's story, I backtrack to the instructional conversation she has with her friends where they advise her on some of the material and social requirements for attaining a position within popularity.

1	Girl 2:	*If you like, get some new clothes.*
2	Tori:	*Yeah, I don't know. I'm so shy to go shopping by myself. I don't know which clothes match me and which not. And my mother always buys my clothes.*
3	Girl 2:	*Well, you have to tell her—*
4	Tori:	*I'm spending their money, so I have to do whatever they say.*
5	Girl 1:	*Yeah, you have to stand up for your rights here.*
6	Tori:	*I don't have that much confidence. You guys are strong. I'm not.*
7	Girl 2:	*How you felt like, you can do it. You know that. You know who you are.*

8	Tori:	But what can a geek do?
9	Girl 1:	You're not a geek! How many times do we have to tell you?
10	Tori:	Yes, I am a geek! Not two people make a difference, when thousands of people call you a geek!
11	Girl 1:	Fine, we're going to change your appearance.
12	Tori:	If you guys change, I'll be a geek still.
13	Girl 1:	No you won't! Meet us after school today and we're going shopping. Tomorrow you'll be a whole new self!

The play here between individuality and relationality produces a self that is at once the mobilizing fiction, the promise and resource by which Tori's transformation becomes both possible and impossible. Her friends' contributions to the discussion produce a reification of an autonomous desiring self whose crisis is the result of an individual shortcoming which is not only Tori's responsibility, but also within her power to fix (1, 5, 7, 9, 11, 13). However, this framework is continually challenged by Tori's own insistence that her problem is the outcome of processes which are largely outside of her own control (2, 4, 8, 10, 12). For her friends, producing a "whole new self" is merely a matter of acquiring a new appearance and the right attitude. The strategy they seem to insist upon suggests a displacement of the scene of recognition to that of the phantasmic image of the popular girl of teen magazines whose practices of consumption can displace immediate social relations and their particular history with the liberatory power of the phantasmic. In contrast, Tori persists instead with a notion of a self whose scene of recognition relies on the citing of a system of categorization defined by social relations of dominance and a dependence on an extended network of others, including parents and peers.

Paradoxically, this is a stance that, in acknowledging the varying contexts and sets of social relations through which the self is contingently produced, seems to elicit an anxious response that reinforces a stable, fixed, and static identity, and a repression of fluidity between identity and difference. "What can a geek do?" Tori plaintively asks, even after her friends have just specified some options. And "I'll be a geek still," she insists, resisting all their suggestions. Perhaps in this instance the anxiety around the kind of self assertion recommended by her friends is related to what Tori must assert herself against in order to successfully assume a position within popularity. Here, as I outlined in chapter 4, the missive "to stand up for your rights" means an individual confrontation with and overcoming of the conditions of regulation structuring her life and the lives of her family and community. The attempt to stand outside these conditions demands not only a repudiation of these elements of herself, but also a risk of exclusion from an identification with a good girl position. Tori's friends are not unaware of this risk, but they invest in the power of representation and the possibility that the social relations of exclusion will be shifted by the phantasmatic as a site of recognition.

Now consider these dynamics through a revisitation of the struggle Maria engages in when trying to both hold onto an oppositional stance on the future Portuguese husband she imagines her father envisions for her and her investment in recognition as a good girl.

1 Marnina:	Is part of what her parents want her to be good about about being a good Portuguese girl?
2 Maria:	Exactly. They want me to marry a Portuguese guy and I don't want to marry a Portuguese guy. Cause please, I don't need that attitude from him like I get from my father.
3 Marnina:	What attitude do you mean?
4 Maria:	Well, he expects me to clean the house, wash the dishes, do my homework, get good grades, get a job, find a husband and everything all at one time. Not all at one time, but what is it called? He doesn't want any-one—he would expect my husband—ahhhh [stops] Okay, I'm trying to say something. I'm trying to put into words here.
5 Marnina:	You're doing a good job—
6 Maria:	it's hard—hard to get, because my father thinks so old fashioned, my mom even says so, okay? My mom tells me, "I'm sorry honey, but your father is really old fashioned, bear with us right now." Cause my mom, okay, okay she's old fashioned too and she does expect me to clean, cook, and have a job and all that stuff but at least she'll let me—I don't know, she knows that like her father was not strict with her. Her father let her do lots of things, right? And she knows that I'm having a hard time when my father doesn't let me go out to a friend's. Like she could go out—she dated when she was fourteen, she—I don't know. She did anyways, but it was with my father. [laughter] "Don't expect that from me," I told her. Anyways, but yeah, like she understands that I like to go out, I like to have my own friends, I like to talk about boys, I like to go to dances, but my father doesn't under-stand that. When I told him I was going to the dance, he made such a big deal, he thought I was ready to leave with a boy or something like that. Now he gets too nuts, I think. He overreacts. . . .

7 Fanny: Oh, my god! Do they want you to be a virgin for the rest of your life?

8 Maria: Yes!

9 Lan: No, they might set her up without her knowing—

10 Maria: They expect me to get married without going out on a date— [laughs]

11 Fanny: oh my god!

12 Maria: how they expect me to do this-

13 Lan: you know how they do this—they set the person up for you, you don't even know him.

14 Maria: I'm not going to marry any person that my dad sets for me, or my mom, excuse me! That is so old fashioned!

15 Fanny: I would go, "Excuse me dad." You know what you say? You say this to your dad, "Excuse me dad, this is the 90s."

16 Maria: You don't talk to my dad like that. Don't even tell him it's the 90s.

17 Fanny: Why?

18 Maria: Cause he gets this lecture about what I did, blahblahblah [inaudible]. You don't talk back to my dad, you can't express your point of view cause he won't listen, nothing like that, cause he'll just lecture you and I don't really want to get any lectures—

19 Fanny: oh god, lock him up—

20 Maria: you know why? Because I'm a good girl! (Trans. 04/11/95)

The specifications for gender and ethnic recognition catch Maria between what appears to be a series of irreconcilable demands confusing the distinctive intentions of individuality and relationality. Formation of group identity is woven through the formation of particular subjects, where hegemonic definitions of the collective body are related to multiple injunctions of individual bodies (Fortier 1999, 43). The complication arises in attempting to meet the injunctions of gendered identity within collective demands of family and community on the one hand and what the girls characterize as the 1990s scene on the other. A social self connected to family and community depends on a repression of autonomous expression by submitting to Maria's father's rules and views on the proper behavior of a good Portuguese girl. On the other hand, maintaining this identification with a good girl femininity interferes with her prospects of establishing a social self within gendered relations of the 1990s and the socially sanctioned sphere of heterosexuality. Capturing the messy imprecisions of femininity, its embattled negotiations over power and agency, and the oscillating series of identifications that ensue, this conundrum goes some distance towards explaining why the answer to the simple entreaty, "Why can't I be myself?" marking the end of Crystal's diary is not so simple at all.

However, if these moments of Tori's and Crystal's stories demonstrate the complications of producing the action between individuality and relationality as incompatible positions, under other circumstances there is an attempt to produce them as complementary, or to appropriate one rhetoric to the cause of the other. Interestingly enough, two of these moments are connected to the group's discussions of how to produce a powerful dimension to the characters of each of their fictional girls.

1	Marnina:	We also want to have girls who are active and powerful right? Is she interested in him and she makes the first move? Can we do that?
2	Mai:	If you want to. Cause, if she's shy—
3	Kenisha:	she's not shy! Is she—
4	LeLy:	what kind of person she have?
5	Kenisha:	She's a strong person. Didn't you guys said that?
6	Marnina:	Yeah, we said she was strong.
7	Kenisha:	She gets to do whatever she wants. Like she goes to him—
8	LeLy:	she have her own opinion—
9	Kenisha:	like at the football game with her friends like she goes up to him. She's always near to him and stuff and then she— she walk up to him and then she said "hi" and then she introduce herself and stuff, and then they start talking, she give him her number and whatever.
10	Fanny:	[sarcastically] Oh my god, she gives him the phone number!
11	Kenisha:	Yeah!
12	Marnina:	Okay good, does everyone agree that makes sense?
13	A few:	Yeah.
14	LeLy:	It's not always the guy that stands up and says "hi" to the girl—
15	Kenisha:	but she's strong so she can do whatever she wants.
16	Fanny:	If you're not a strong person I don't think you'd go up—
17	Kenisha:	go after a guy.
18	Fanny:	If she was like a shy person she wouldn't go up.
19	LeLy:	Let's put it into a sentence. Marnina, help us! Give us a head start.
20	Marnina:	Like Kenisha was saying . . . something like "the next week, we all went out to the movies together." Is that all right, Kish?

21 Kenisha:	Yeah.
22 Fanny:	That's cool, get to go to the movies.
23 Marnina:	So he doesn't notice her, but she likes him so she approaches him.
24 A few:	Yeah.
25 Mai:	That's what he like about her; like she does whatever she wants.
26 LeLy:	Yeah, there.
27 Kenisha:	Everything she wants she go for it.
28 Marnina:	[writing] "The next week we went to the movies together"—
29 Fanny:	"they pushed us together," or something like that.
30 Kenisha:	NO!
31 Mai:	"One of my friends told him I had a crush on him."
32 LeLy:	"My stupid friend," because she feel so embarrassed at that time you know. Like it could be someone from the group, like Tori or something like that.
33 Mai:	Hey, why didn't I think of that? [She plays Tori.]
34 LeLy:	Cause you don't have a brain, remember? (Trans. 06/05/95)

Although the action is neither fully completed nor endorsed by the entire group as believable, it is the prospect of a creative coexistence between autonomy and relatedness that is imagined to animate the powerful self. Perfectly and seamlessly responsible for herself (at least initially), Crystal's flaunting of social convention by her agenetic expression of desire does not, in this instance, jeopardize her realization of a positive gender recognition or social relations with others. On the contrary, it is because Crystal "has her own opinion" and "can do whatever she wants" that she is able not only to initiate a romance, but also to attract the prospective boyfriend: "That's what he like about her, like she does whatever she wants," says Mai. Kenisha (most clearly), LeLy, and Mai (to some extent) are identifying with a subject of desire and agency who is her own source of excitement, rather than one who depends on a man to create it on her behalf (Wyatt 1990). This is a partial resignification of self-other relations within a discursive field of femininity that appears to redraw the boundaries of inclusion and exclusion around the associative fields of goodness, power, and agency.

Meanwhile, in Tori's similar negotiation of power and agency, the reinsertion and centering of family and community considerations circumvents an either-or choice between them and gender recognition. This becomes possible by plotting a slightly different relationary encounter between the signs and codes of individuality and relationality.

1	Marnina:	How about Tori with the popular issue?
2	LeLy:	Oh, the popular? I can't think of any part for her.
3	Mai:	She's weak.
4	Marnina:	Think she's weak?
5	LeLy:	She's not weak, but she always do whatever like—
6	Mai:	the popular people.
7	Marnina:	Is there power in wanting to be popular and working to get there?
8	LeLy:	Okay . . . she change herself, she make her—like she dye her hair or something like that, for example. What is the powerful part? You're giving up your own, the way you are and change to another person?
9	Marnina:	So that's a problem, eh?
10	LeLy:	Kind of. You're like, first of all if you do anything to fit in popular, if you're unpopular, you'd do anything for them.
11	Marnina:	Yeah, that's a problem. [pause] But, I'm wondering if there might not be a couple of ways of looking at what a strong aspect of Tori's character could look like. Like, could we think about what it would mean to want to be popular and to be successful at it and there might be something powerful about that? Or as you were suggesting, maybe to be powerful would mean deciding that being popular isn't worth what you might have to give up to get there—
12	Mai:	that's powerful!
13	Marnina:	or she might start to question the categories themselves—
14	Mai:	I want the second one!
15	LeLy:	What's the third one?
16	Marnina:	Yeah, well I'm not sure about that one myself, but one of the things we've been asking here is how do these categories happen, right? So what I'm trying to figure out is if we can figure that out maybe there's a way of thinking about nerd and popular categories not as something people actually are—
17	LeLy:	okay, yeah, yeah. I know what you mean. Like you wrote in that letter?
18	Marnina:	Yeah, did you get that?
19	LeLy:	Marnina, no offense, but like those questions that you ask? I really don't have the answer in my brain. (Trans. 23/05/95)

The structuration and subversion of selfhood is organized here in an inverted play between the dynamics of relationality and autonomy on the one hand

and the family/community versus peer opposition on the other. In this particular instance, as I suggested in chapter 4, peer and school culture represents dominant social values and norms in contrast to the alternative system of valuation offered by the sphere of family/community. The enabling force for the production of the powerful self is made contingent upon the maintenance of a positive identification with family/community at the expense of peer/school culture. That is, it is this identification that is the inducement for Tori to stand up for herself, in opposition to the dominant norms and values which are experienced as a threat to self. In not submitting to this set of regulative relations, Tori's oppositional stance is also the guarantor of an autonomous expression of selfhood. Autonomy and relationality are therefore conceived of as mutually facilitative mediums of power and agency.

These intersubjective conditions of selfhood highlight the complexities of the struggle for recognition that the good girl encounters. For while the discursive field of femininity yields a bounteous crop of possibilities, it also reaps ambiguity, messiness, instability, and perseverance. Managing the multiplicity that different contexts and media require—the shifting meanings and revolving interdiscursive relations, how to feel and think (especially simultaneously) without destroying herself or others—the good girl is on an inescapable collision course with the contradictory demands of becoming an individual through belonging. The various sites of belonging—the family, community, school, and peer cultures—not only recognize, condone, and condemn differing definitions of and requirements for gendered achievement of individuality and relationality, but their meanings and distinguishing qualities will also vary depending on their intersecting action with other categories of social difference—race, class, and sexuality—and with the particular citable categories within femininity—good, bad, smart, popular, nerd, and so on.

The intersecting moments of the two stories illustrate something about ambivalence as both a structural feature of femininity and as a subjective response to making and maintaining positive identifications with contradictory interpellative positions. This ambivalence is, however, also a feature of the broader shifting conditions of story telling and possibility of subjectivity rendered imaginable by feminism in tandem or tension with postmodern abandonments of Truth and refusals to synthesize difference into a unitary whole. It is, therefore, to a further inquiry into these conditions, the consequences of living with ambivalence, and what it offers to a feminist cultural pedagogy that I now want to turn through a reopening of the question of the subversive potential of ambivalence and a reinvoking of the "disruptive figures" with whom this discussion began.

MIXED SUBJECTS, NEW SUBJECTIVITIES,
AND FEMINIST CULTURAL PEDAGOGIES

The planning and telling of Crystal and Tori/Kathy's stories provided an opportunity for the girls to define and evaluate a series of competing discursive positions available to them as girls. We might say that the exercise was one that gets at the apparatus of the production of subjectivities through examining, as Donna Haraway notes, "the structure of narrative in action, watching how narratives work through many kinds of systems of practice, observing how rhetoric is 'material' and a technology of self making, watching the way the body becomes an inscription device and is made to generate streams of markings that are then worked into both narrative and non-narrative practices, getting at practices of figuration, [and] getting at the way visual and verbal material co-construct subject positions" (1995, 51). However, if, as Charles Taylor (1991, 40) points out, things take on importance against a background of intelligibility then, as Teresa de Lauretis argues, it is a feminist responsibility to create texts using alternative narrative strategies to "shift the terms of representation, [and] to produce the conditions of representability of another—and gendered-social subject" (1987, 109). Such a task is admittedly a complex one, mediated as it is by the pedagogical, social, and ideological conditions and contexts of reading/writing, and the consequences of identificatory responses to social critique and psychic and pedagogical change. Towards bringing this discussion to a provisory closing, (for despite any avoidance of it, there is, doesn't it seem, a certain terrible inevitability to the end?) we might therefore take another look at Crystal and Tori/Kathy's stories. This time not only will our reading focus on their consideration of the apparatuses for the production of various forms of feminine subjectivities and their engagement with the new conditions for the constitution of modern subjectivity, but we will also ask what, if any, feminist strategies they use that shift the terms and conditions of representation and intelligibility? In what, if any, ways is there a reconfiguration of dominant representational practices going on? And what might these strategies offer as insights to a feminist cultural pedagogy?

The fact that the girls' inventions are the embodiment of a certain ambiguity is, as I discussed above, suggestive of ambivalence as a feature of both the discursive structure of femininity and a subjective response to it. But, the interracial couple and the mixed-race girl also facilitate a "re-reading with a kind of acid difference" (Haraway 1995, 51) of the kind advocated by de Lauretis (1987) and Du Plessis (1985). That is, through their performance of social contradiction and the refusal of conventional patterns of narrative closure, they challenge easy notions of binarity, reconfiguring the terms of the story and how it might be told. In doing so they offer us some particular insights into the rearticulation of the process of subjectification to discursive practices, and the politics of exclusion which, as we have already seen, all such subjectification appears to entail.

Such a rearticulation is staged through a double movement of using the plot structure and the driving action to invoke a category and, thereby, provisionally to institute the character's identity and at the same time, through the layers of the story's meaning and indeterminate endings, to reopen the category as a site of ongoing political contest.

Crystal's story, for example, closes with an open-ended question: her irre-solvable problem left hanging between oscillating identifications. The flagrant ex-hibition of ambiguity (the very public exposure of the good girl's desire) suggests that the positivity of desire is productive of new relations and relationships, short circuiting the categorical order of things. In resisting the surveillance which orga-nizes social life ("People stare at us in a strange way . . . but we really don't care," Crystal writes in her diary), the couple disorganizes the process that secures iden-tity through the visual coding of difference. Instead, this double movement of ex-ternalization and incorporation across the racial-sexual border invites an investigation into how the dynamics within and between difference, power, and desire articulate social forms that come to be articulated as identity and other (Todd 1997).

Similarly, the image that brings Tori's story to its end also destabilizes the positions in the discursive field and disrupts categories for identification. De-spite Tori's repudiation of dominant norms and values, she is last seen dancing in a crowded room, encircled by a group of other girls. It is an image which fur-ther muddies the already precarious trajectory of her transformation story, frus-trating conventional narrative closure by alluding to alternative routes to social acceptance, belonging, and possibilities for "becoming somebody."

Tori's mixed-race position brings to a head the crisis of identity which may be concealed by the invisibility of the mark of passing. As we saw in chapter 4, passing, or the act of assuming another identity is not a painless merger. It in-volves considerable risk and loss. Through her refusal to "pass" in order to take up a position within popularity, Tori also refuses the masking of ambiguity that passing entails. She is claiming an identity that is both itself and the other to itself, a position which protests difference as identity.

The ambivalent performance of endings which disrupts the conventional narrative structures of romance, transformation (and ethnographic) genres, should not, therefore, be viewed as a product of incompetent storytellers. Rather, this ambiguity of (self)authorship (Battaglia 1995; Crapanzano 1992; Singley and Sweeney 1993), is, I think, a "writing beyond the ending" (Du Plessis 1985, 4) that seeks to resignify patterns of recognition and render problematic both the

notion of a unitary, unambivalent subjectivity and the modernist rhetoric of individualism. In doing so the stories reveal something of how modern understandings of subjectivity as rooted in the notion of "the self" come to depend on
gender as "one of the conditions of possibility of modern subjectivity. It is intrin-
sic both to (apparently) abstract notions and individual experiences of subjectivity" (Flax 1993, 97). The attention to various technologies of gendering in the
stories and the ways in which, no matter what form femininity eventually takes,
it is shown to be achievable only within and through social relations with others
suggests, as Flax argues further, "the delusionary character of self-determining,
individualistic, and autonomous ideas of subjectivity" (1993, 97).

Such a revelation inverts what Furlong and Cartmel have called the "epistemological fallacy" around which life in late modernity revolves (1997, 109).
Following Elias (1982), they characterise individualism as a public discourse that
obscures underlying social structures, making individuals increasingly account-
able for their own fates. Risk, uncertainty and the "privatisation of ambivalence,"
are the consequences of pressures to adopt individualistic perspectives in a society marked by interdependency (Bauman 1991; Furlong and Cartmel 1997).
The tendency to assume that global-societal problems can be resolved, if at all,
with private means, creates a burden that "calls for a bone structure few individuals can boast" (Bauman 1991, 197). Thus, in occupying the gap between individuality and relationality, self and other, the girl who doesn't know how to
be good without being bad and the nerd who insists on the possibility that she
is already "somebody" pose certain possibilities for thinking further about how
a feminist cultural pedagogy might work with and against this burden and
disavowed dependency.

The anxiety states induced by this burden and the juggling of contradictory
positions may, as we have already seen, manifest in a variety of ways, from denial
of incongruity to a variety of mechanisms for apparently achieving conscious closure and coherence (Unwin 1984, 225). For example, at certain moments in the
characters' stories this is illustrated through the declaration of a certain rationality of choice. A dimension of the "just people" argument is one instance of this.
Used in the context of protesting the categorizations of popularity and its antithesis, "just people" summons a rhetoric of normalcy that both attempts a repair of
the internal fissures of discourses of femininity and asserts a constancy of results
over a random succession of gains and losses. Another instance of this kind of declaration includes the instruction from Tori's friends to "stand up for yourself,"
against the constraints of family dictates and obligations. In assuming that a subject
can choose to stand outside the conditions of her own regulation, this intensely
individualist discourse presents full clarity of the life world and a chance of gains
and freedom from risk of losses as a realistic possibility (Bauman 1991, 225).

In holding the tension between incompatible identificatory positions, contesting an opposition where one side is devalued and the other is idealized, Crystal's and Tori/Kathy's stories struggle with the effects of the many kinds of domination producing the unitary self which, as each character experiences in different ways, can only sustain its unity by splitting off or repressing other parts of its own and others' subjectivity. In playing with how the subject is constituted through an exclusion and differentiation, perhaps a repression, that is subsequently concealed, covered over by the effect of autonomy, the stories reveal how autonomy is the logical consequence of a disavowed dependency (Butler 1993, 157).

While the characters were written as inhabiting zones of ambivalence where the relationship between the *distinctiveness* of different aspects of subjectivity and their *mutuality* is struggled over, the process by which the stories were created offered a similar occasion for the girls themselves to experience how aspects of their own subjectivities interact and intersect with and are mutually determined by, but differentiated from, others (Flax 1993, 109). I am suggesting that the productive work of collective imagining is implicated in the process of reworking notions of social difference as a relational form. If normative social and discursive practices of society are challenged by the existence of excluded sites and the possibilities for what they may bear in the way of other selves—selves that are not synonymous with the subject of discourse—then the work of the imaginary seems a means of accessing and mining these excluded sites and other selves for what they might offer in the way of expansions of human capacity and social forms. It may do so because the imagination grants a certain license from the constraints of the social, the dictates of censorship, and other normative operations of consciousness. In the realm of the imaginary it may be possible to explore fantasies and fears, enact relations that would otherwise be restricted if not taboo, or temporarily dissolve boundaries, facilitating a loss of distinctiveness of the border between self and other. What I am suggesting is that this kind of work may open up the possibility of accessing various forms of internal otherness or in Butler's (1993) terms the "constitutive outside" that is repudiated in the formation of the subject. In turn, these suppressed or abject sites may make possible the imagining of new modes of life, provoking a disruption of conventional thought and action, inciting desire for and engendering strange possibilities extending the range of identities girls and others might negotiate. Exploring issues through fantasy is an invaluable resource for the imaginative construction of subject positionings outside of traditional gendered relations because of the enabling of a temporary experience of undifferentiation and fusion.

We might ask, therefore, what is at stake in a pedagogical practice that attempts to work across the confusions between self and other that take place in the imaginary dimensions of human experience? What are the possibilities and complications this kind of confusion might offer for challenging our apparent identity as individualized subjects? And how does the opportunity of doing this kind of work collectively contribute to building the conditions of new knowledge and new practices of identification?

In analyzing the group interactions, the characters' stories, and the narratives written and enacted in the actual video, the girls are revealed as writers in the process of exploration, struggling over meaning both within the text and as it is socially constituted. The reality that seems to have most thoroughly occupied the girls' attention, driving their interest in the characters' stories, was the meanings and contradictions of social difference. Written like situated accounts of difference, the stories and their writers insist on making sense of how that situatedness is produced and the emergent consequences. They work with and against the differential operations producing both the intelligible girl subject and the excluded sites haunting this subject's boundaries, constantly threatening to disrupt its certainty and security. The process of creating the characters and their dilemmas was an opportunity that the girls used to collectively identify the contradictions in their own lives. Writing enabled them to briefly hold those contradictions together, to examine them, to experiment with engaging them differently in the world and having the world respond. In short, writing enabled the girls to perform an imaginative transformation of reality and an active reworking of experience.

The emphasis on psychic processes and articulatory practices that can accommodate more fluid and multiple forms of subjectivities through an incorporation of difference rather than exclusion seems significantly complicated by taking into account the relationship to otherness that is particular to those most marginalized by structural and cultural processes. Those people who, because of their racialized, gendered, and classed positions, live in relation to systems of commensurability that cannot ever be theirs, who do not fit the system of commensurability, but who are nonetheless made to live inside it. It is urgent therefore to ask what the incorporation of otherness means for these girls when ambivalence is the force that shapes their relationship to so much of what is other to them—the dominant society's thought, values, expression, and practices. Knowing more about this dynamic is crucial to making the case for the political work of the imaginative's activity.

Valerie Walkerdine's (1997) explorations of the ways in which the self-productions of marginalized people may be imbued with the fantasies found within the dominant culture is helpful to reconsider here. Walkerdine's argument is a strong rejection of both the perspective found in much of media studies that presents a public passively duped by popular culture as well as the resistant readings celebrated by some proponents of cultural studies. Instead she argues convincingly for a conceptualization of the space of fantasy as a place for hope and for escape from oppression. She posits that certain forms of engagement with the popular on the part of the marginalized should be seen as a strategy of survival.

There is a way in which the kind of writing the girls engaged in through the creation of the video characters might also be seen as a strategy of survival. Donna Haraway (1995), for example, speaks of what she calls "cyborg writing" as being about the power to survive. Such a writing she suggests is about seizing the tools to mark the world that marked those who have been marginalized as other. For Haraway this releasing of the play of writing is therefore deadly serious. It seems to me that in attempting to understand the terms of their own difference through the writing of the stories, the girls are also working towards a reconfiguring of the terms of recognition. This contest is, I think, crucially facilitated by the boundary flexibility rendered possible by imaginative work, but perhaps not merely through the incorporation of the other. Rather, through contact with the imaginary object, the writers may temporarily assume a position that is not their own and it is possible that this momentary fusion might allow for a certain playing with the very terms of commensurability. It does so by allowing for a taking up and experimentally trying on any vantage point and perhaps even several simultaneously. I am suggesting that idealized images can function in the realm of fantasy to allow for the projection of different concepts of the self. But that does not necessarily mean these images will automatically be taken up. Fantasy spaces are more than the mise-en-scène of desire. Lingering there long enough, however, provides an opportunity to juxtapose the various possibilities and to examine the contradictions within and between them. Emerging out of the sheer confusion or accidental sequence of decisions and actions may be new ways of viewing old situations and hence new possibilities for action.

What I am suggesting, therefore, is that writing, reading, and other imaginative practices are not singular activities. If in engaging in imaginative work the relationship between "me" and "not me" is muddied, this process is further complicated be engaging in this kind of work collectively. In doing so members of the group encounter not only their own projections of different concepts of self onto the idealized images being constructed but also those of their peers. Thus, we are continually having to shift our positions vis-à-vis both each other and the image under debate. This collective process is one that engenders a many-sided engagement supplying participants with a multidiscursive, multiconflictual context and multilayered material with which to both construct a sense of and protest where they are in the world. The group provides practical support, critical challenges, laughter, fierce competition, the expression of fear, and painful vulnerability as they participate in the construction of a space in which, as girls, they might negotiate the new and old meanings they produce. And while I am not suggesting that there are ever any guarantees of a positive outcome, it is also a place where the conflicts and anxieties that may work to inhibit change may also be processed collectively.

The story I want to tell, therefore, about the political work of the imagination's activity is not a story of a single struggle to move from a limited to a more and more expansive view. Instead, it is a story of multiple moves, half-steps that take off in various directions at once. It is a story of accidents, revisions, and synthesis that may eventually produce transforming ideas—ideas that may work towards creating Fanon's "world of reciprocal recognitions," a world in which, as Jessica Benjamin envisions, the goal is "not to undo our ties to others but rather to disentangle them; to make of them not shackles but circuits of recognition" (1988, 221).

Reprise

Mai called the other day (though I remind myself to be careful not to address her by that name). It has been several months since the last time we were in touch. "Not done yet?" she asks. "I'm working on the conclusion," I say. It is possible I am only imagining the incredulousness in her voice. The longevity of this writing process has, by now, become something of a sensitive issue with me. "Everything is way different now," she says and then pauses. "Hey, don't you think that would be a good way to end your book, to say, 'This is what's happening now,' like how everybody has changed so much? We could get the group together again! We'd do it, you know, if it'll help you." I am laughing—laughing at the thought of myself accumulating more transcripts and enjoying the lovely reversal she has just performed of feminist assumptions about recipients and providers of assistance and support in a research project. "I would love to see everyone together again," I reply. "It is a good idea."

"Then instead of putting 'THE END,'" she proceeds, "you could put 'to be continued.'"

"Yeah," I say. "I could do that."

"[O]r the end she reaches leads actually to another end, another opening" (Trinh 1989, 149).

Notes

CHAPTER 1

I use notational devices to mark different sources of ethnographic material. FN indicates fieldnotes and TRANS indicates transcript material which are recordings of the focus group discussions with the girls who participated in the video project. The date follows the FN or TRANS designation. The lines of the transcripts are numbered and the parenthetical references in the texts are to the line numbers. Nonstandard English used by the girls is transcribed as spoken. A transcript line that ends with "—" and is followed by a sentence beginning without a capital in the first word, indicates an interruption to the first speaker by the second.

1. For a very interesting discussion on new forms of classed femininity emerging out of processes of globalization see Walkerdine, Lucey, and Melody 2001.

2. For example, the issue of girls' lack of self-esteem has recently surfaced as one such social concern. In some of the outburst of popular literature on the topic, there is a sense of moral panic in the tone of the argument. See for example Pipher 1994, Sadker and Sadker 1994, and Orenstein 1994.

3. Of the many vocabularies for understanding culture and power currently circulating, I have used two. The first, "discourse," is associated with Foucault and the second, "hegemony," with Gramsci. The former vocabulary is particularly useful for bringing together issues of meaning and practice in examining the construction of power; the latter calls attention to divergent political stakes in processes of social transformation. Used together, they make it possible to ask how people shape the very ideas and institutions that make it possible for them to act as subjects.

4. Although the video consisted of five characters only three of their stories are presented and analyzed in this book.

5. This formulation of the issue has been most significantly developed within certain philosophic and psychoanalytic traditions. Diana Fuss, for example, identifies Hegel and French Hegelianism as having a long history exploring the issue of alterity and its relationship to different attempts to address the question, "[H]ow is it that only through the other I can be myself, only in the place of the other I can arrive at a sense of self?" (1995, 3-4). This work has also been influential within some psychoanalytic discussions, for example, Jacques Lacan's

well-known concept of the mirror phase ("The Mirror-Stage as Formative of the Function of the I as Revealed in Psychoanalytic Experience" *Ecrits*, trans. Alan Sheridan. New York: W.W. Norton, 1977).

6. See the section on "Lordship and Bondage" in G. W. F. Hegel's 1977 *The Phenomenology of Mind*.

7. Axel Honneth presents a similar case for the interrelationship between recognition and identity. Combining the philosophy of the young Hegel with the social psychology of Mead, he argues that the "struggle for recognition" is a condition that gives rise to the possibility of subjectivity. Like Frantz Fanon (1967), who argues for an ethics of mutual identification, "a world of reciprocal recognitions," Honneth sees the promise for an ethical form of life with a moral potential to lie within the dependence on mutual recognition. He says, "[O]ne can develop a practical relation to self only when one has learned to view oneself, from the normative perspective of one's partner in interaction, as their social addressee. This imperative, which is anchored in the social life process, provides the normative pressure that compels individuals to remove constraints on the meaning of mutual recognition, since it is only by doing so that they are able to express socially the continually expanding claims of subjectivity" (1996, 92).

8. While I am focussing on the ambivalent structure of discourses of femininity in the late twentieth century, many commentators writing about women as a group and on female identity in earlier time periods have also noted some kind of dual relationship to definitions offered by various dominant forces. See for example, Rachel Blau Du Plessis's (1985) discussion of the work of Simone de Beauvoir, John Berger, and Gerda Learner. Jane Miller (1991) also presents an interesting discussion of the ambivalence and doubleness associated with women's experience dating back to the nineteenth and early twentieth centuries.

9. I am using the term "negative capability" as Jackson (1998, 14) suggests to mean the capability of "being in uncertainties, mysteries, doubts, without any irritable reaching after fact and reason."

10. See for examples, Davies 1989 and 1993, Essed 1991, Fine and Macpherson 1992, Frazer 1992, and Hey 1997.

11. See Ellsworth and Miller 1996 for an interesting discussion of Patricia William's reading/writing pedagogy.

CHAPTER 2

1. "Fundamental group" is a term Said draws on from Gramsci. For Gramsci fundamental group is an economic class, but as Cocks (1989, 41) points out, other groups are dominant along different axes of power than the one emerging out of productive relations.

2. See for example, Bloom 1998, Britzman 1995, Butler 1993, Fordham 1996, Game 1991, Gordon 1995, Kondo 1990, Marcus 1994, Simon and Dippo 1986, Strathern 1990, Tedlock 1991, and Tsing 1993.

3. See for example Harding 1987, McRobbie 1982, Oakley 1981, Smith 1988, Stacey 1991, and Stanley and Wise 1990.

4. Rather than a conception of power as property, something someone has and can pass on, Gore argues, following Foucault, that power should be analyzed as something that circulates, that people are always in the position of simultaneously undergoing and exercising.

5. See Sultana 1992 for an interesting discussion of how the results of a research project with emancipatory intentions may be used by others in an extremely oppressive fashion.

6. Stacey 1988 suggests that by characterizing itself as authentic, reciprocal and intersubjective feminist ethnography risks even greater violation of the researched than the more distanced objectivity of conventional research methods. The highly personalized relationship between ethnographer and research subjects disguises actual differences in power, knowledge, and structural mobility and places research subjects at grave risk of manipulation and betrayal by the researcher.

7. See, for example, Harding 1986, Hartsock 1983, and Hill-Collins 1990.

8. On a related point Barbara Tedlock (1991) points out that the work of what she calls "native ethnographers" has in some ways complicated the traditional distinctions between self and other invoked in much of this debate.

9. See Alcoff 1995 for a very interesting discussion on the social and political contexts in which speaking for others is problematic, as well as those in which there is a moral and political imperative of doing so.

10. The practical and political problems of securing a room of one's own appears to be quite a common occurrence for those working with girls in schools and youth groups. See, for example, Savier's 1981 discussion of this issue.

11. David Massengill, "Don Quixote's Lullaby" (for Abbie Hoffman), 1992.

12. This is a point made by Haraway 1995.

13. See, for example, Davidson 1996, Davies 1993, Eckert 1989, Eder 1995, Heller 1999, Levinson Foley, and Holland 1996, Proweller 1998, Raissiguier 1994, Valli 1986, and Willis 1977.

14. See, for example, Hey 1997, Inness 1998a and 1998b, Johnson 1993, McRobbie and Nava 1984, McRobbie 1991, Ras and Lunenberg 1993, and Walkerdine 1990 and 1997.

15. See, for example, Clifford and Marcus 1986, Denzin 1997, Marcus 1998, Rosaldo 1989, Trinh 1989 and 1992 and Van Maanen 1988.

16. See, for example, Abu-Lughod 1993, Behar 1993, Britzman 1991, Clough 1992, and Crapanzano 1992.

17. See, for example, Butler 1993, Davies 1994, Ferguson 1993, Frankenburg 1993, Mama 1995, and Weir 1996.

CHAPTER 3

1. The girls also used the name "Tori" for one of their characters, suggesting the possibility of both a certain identification with the actor and an interesting thematic linkage between stories, which I explore in chapter 5.

2. Thanks to Janice Hladki for this insight.

3. This sense of an evacuation of self, concomitant with the taking up of femininity is, interestingly enough, also conveyed in the very name the girls assigned to their character, "Crystal." Thanks to Anita Harris for this insight.

4. Thanks to Roger Simon for this insight.

5. These different discourses are often called on and understood as evidence that black girls have higher self-esteem than other groups of girls. For examples of this argument see Erkut and Marx 1995, Haw 1991, Mirza 1992, and Waters 1996.

6. Bronwyn Davies 1989 describes boundary crossing as an adult researcher working with preschool children. She writes of a very interesting encounter during which she was granted child status and thus gained access to the world of children's play in ways that adults do not usually have.

7. In fact shortly after this episode Lan no longer participated regularly in the group. And while it is entirely possible that these were completely unrelated events, there is, of course, no way of knowing.

8. For some examples of feminist researchers who do take up this kind of question see Fortier 1996 and Wasserfall 1993.

CHAPTER 4

1. As an example of a linguistic transformation, Cameron 1995 discusses in some detail George Bernard Shaw's *Pygamalian*, which later underwent it's own transformation to become the motion picture *My Fair Lady*.

2. See Davidson 1996, Kenway and Blackmore 1995, Safia Mirza 1986, and Steedman 1985.

3. See Brah and Minhas 1985, Gosh 1987, Lee 1996, and Rattansi 1992.

4. See Grant and Sleeter 1996, Hudson 1984, Rezai-Rashti 1995, Steedman 1985, Tsolidis 1990, and Walkerdine 1990.

5. As fairy tales are one of the means by which conceptions of the modern self are circulated, it would be an interesting exercise to trace Taylor's conceptualization of the development of this notion of self with the historical development of the various and perhaps changing meanings and interpretations attached to the story of Cinderella and its central theme of recognition. See Zipes 1993 for a similar kind of analysis of the fairy tale "Little Red Riding Hood."

6. In Patricia Hill Collins's 1990 discussion of literary treatments of relationships between black mothers and daughters she suggests that while mothers may assist daughters, these relationships are characterized by an emphasis on the individual's responsibility for self-definitions and self-valuations.

7. See Valerie Walkerdine 1990 for a discussion on regulation in middle- and working-class child rearing practices.

8. See also Dodson 1998 for a discussion on the reliance on girls' domestic labor in underprivileged families.

9. Thanks to Janice Hladki for this insight.

10. This is in contrast to the findings of playground studies. See, for example, Borman 1979 and Thorne 1995.

11. See for example Gotfrit's 1988 account where the public space of the dance floor is specifically contrasted with the women's washroom as a marginal space.

12. This aspect of women's use of the space of the washroom is explored in the National Film Board of Canada's *The Powder Room*.

13. More contemporary transformation stories circulating in the popular media seem to offer a more ambivalent position on the transformational process. For example, John Hughs's film *Pretty in Pink*, produced in the mid-1980s, finds the heroine highly ambivalent about leaving her working-class roots. Although the plot does get resolved romantically, the tensions around the acceptance of the transformational story seem to remain, as here it is the hero who disavows his own circle of rich and popular friends, recognizing their vapidness.

14. Ernesto Laclau (1977) terms this strategy "disarticulation-rearticulation."

15. This mobilization of inside-outside spheres is reminiscent of the ways in which the girls also used it in Crystal's story to articulate a certain disjuncture between internal emotional states and external performances of femininity. Here, I think its use is suggestive of a certain perceived disjuncture between the official school policy of equity and the actual social relations of the school where the girls express an extreme sense of misrecognition and marginalization despite official policy.

References

Abel, Elizabeth. 1990. Race, class, and psychoanalysis? Opening questions. In *Conflicts in Feminism*, ed. Marianne Hirsch and Evelyn Fox Keller. New York: Routledge.

Abu-Lughod, Lila. 1991. Writing against culture. In *Recapturing Anthropology*, ed. Richard Fox. Sante Fe: School of American Research Press.

———. 1993. *Writing Women's Worlds: Bedouin Stories*. Berkeley: University of California Press.

Adams, Mary Louise. 1994. Almost anything can happen: A search for sexual discourse in the urban spaces of 1940s Toronto. In *Studies in Moral Regulation*, ed. Mariana Valverde. Toronto: Centre of Criminology, University of Toronto.

Afshar, Haleh, and Mary Maynard, eds. 1994. *The Dynamics of "Race" and Gender: Some Feminist Interventions*. London: Taylor and Francis.

Ahmed, Sara. 1999. "She'll wake up one of these days and find she's turned into a nigger": Passing through hybridity. *Theory, Culture and Society* 16 (2): 87–106.

Alcoff, Linda. 1995. The problem of speaking for others. In *Who Can Speak? Authority and Critical Identity*, ed. Judith Roof and Robyn Wiegman. Urbana: University of Illinois Press.

American Association of University Women Education Foundation (AAUW). 1992. *How Schools Shortchange Girls*. Wellesley, Mass: AAUW.

Ang, Ien. 1996. The curse of the smile: Ambivalence and the "Asian" Woman in Australian Multiculturalism. *Feminist Review* 52: 36–49.

Anyon, Jean. 1982. Intersections of gender and class: Accommodation and resistance by working-class and affluent females to contradictory sex-role ideologies. In *Gender, Class and Education*, ed. Len Barton and Stephen Walker. London: Falmer Press.

Ardener, Shirley. 1978. The nature of women in society. Introduction to *Defining Females*, ed. Shirley Ardener. New York: Wiley.

Ardener, Shirley, ed. 1978. *Defining Females*. New York: Wiley.

Asher, Steven, and John Gottman, eds. 1981. *The Development of Children's Friendships*. New York: Cambridge University Press.

Atkinson, Paul. 1990. *The Ethnographic Imagination: Textual Constructions of Reality*. London: Routledge.

Back, Les. 1993. Race, identity and nation within an adolescent community in South London. *New Community* 19 (2): 217–233.

——. 1996. *New Ethnicities and Urban Culture: Racisms and Multiculture in Young Lives.* London: University College London Press.

Bannerji, Himani. 1991. But who speaks for us? Experience and agency in conventional feminist paradigms. In *Unsettling Relations: The University as a Site of Feminist Struggles,* ed. Himani Bannerji et al. Toronto: Women's Press.

Bartkey, Sandra Lee. 1990. *Femininity and Domination: Studies in the Phenomenology of Oppression.* New York: Routledge.

Barton, Len, and Stephen Walker, eds. 1982. *Gender, Class and Education.* London: Falmer Press.

——. 1984. *Social Crisis and Educational Research.* London: Croom Helm.

Bassin, Donna, Margaret Honey, and Meryle Kaplan, eds. 1993. *Representations of Motherhood.* New Haven: Yale University Press.

Battaglia, Debbora. 1995a. Problematizing the self: A thematic introduction. In *Rhetorics of Self-Making,* ed. Debbora Battaglia. Berkeley: University of California Press.

——., ed. 1995b. *Rhetorics of Self-Making.* Berkeley: University of California Press.

Bauman, Zygmunt. 1991. *Modernity and Ambivalence.* Cambridge: Polity Press.

——. 1993. *Postmodern Ethics.* Oxford: Blackwell.

Behar, Ruth. 1993. *Translated Woman: Crossing the Border with Esperanza's Story.* Boston: Beacon Press.

Behar, Ruth, and Deborah A. Gordon, eds. 1995. *Women Writing Culture.* Berkeley: University of California Press.

Benjamin, Jessica. 1988. *The Bonds of Love: Psychoanalysis, Feminism and the Problem of Domination.* New York: Pantheon Books.

——. 1993. The omnipotent mother: A psychoanalytic study of fantasy and reality. In *Representations of Motherhood,* ed. Donna Bassin, Margaret Honey, and Meryle Kaplan. New Haven: Yale University Press.

——. 1995. *Like Subjects. Love Objects: Essays on Recognition and Sexual Difference.* New Haven: Yale Univesity Press.

Best, Amy. 2000. *Prom Night: Youth, Schools and Popular Culture.* New York: Routledge.

Bettelheim, Bruno. 1976. *The Uses of Enchantment: The Meaning and Importance of Fairy Tales.* New York: Alfred A. Knopf.

Bhaba, Homi. 1983. The other question: Stereogtype, discrimination and the discourse of colonialism. *Screen 24* (November/December): 18–36.

——. 1986. Signs taken for wonders: Questions of ambivalence and authority under a tree outside Delhi, May 1817. In *"Race," Writing and Difference,* ed. Henry Louis Gates. Chicago: University of Chicago Press.

——. 1990. The third space: Interview with Homi Bhabha. In *Identity, Community, Culture, Difference,* ed. Jonathan Rutherford. London: Lawrence & Wishart.

Bhavnani, Kum-Kum. 1994. Tracing the contours: Feminist research and feminist objectivity. In *The Dynamics of "Race" and Gender: Some Feminist Interventions,* ed. Haleh Afshar and Mary Maynard. London: Taylor and Francis.

Blair, Maud, Janet Holland, and Sue Sheldon, eds. 1995. *Identity and Diversity: Gender and the Experience of Education.* Clevedon, England: The Open University Press.

Bloom, Leslie Rebecca. 1998. *Under the Sign of Hope: Feminist Methodology and Narrative Interpretation.* Albany: State University of New York Press.

Borman, Kathryn. 1979. Children's interaction in playgrounds. *Theory into Practice* 18: 251–257.

Bottomly, Gillian. 1979. *After the Odyssey: A Study of Greek Australians*. Brisbane: University of Queensland Press.

Bourne, Paula, Philinda Masters, Nuzhat Amin, Marnina Gonick, and Lisa Gribowski, eds. 1994. *Feminism and Education: A Canadian Perspective*. Vol. 2. Toronto: Center for Women's Studies in Education, OISE.

Brah, Avtar. 1996. *Cartographies of Diaspora: Contesting Identities*. New York: Routledge.

Brah, Avtar, and Rehana Minhas. 1985. Structural racism or cultural difference: Schooling for Asian girls. In *Just a Bunch of Girls*, ed. Gaby Weiner. London: Open University Press.

Britzman, Deborah. 1991. *Practice Makes Practice: A Critical Study of Learning to Teach*. Albany: State University of New York Press.

——. 1995. The question of belief: Writing poststructural ethnography. *Qualitative Studies in Education*, 8 (3): 229–238.

——. 1998. *Lost subjects: Contested Objects: Toward a Psychoanalytic Inquiry of Learning*. Albany: State University of New York Press.

Brodkey, Linda. 1987. *Academic Writing as Social Practice*. Philadelphia: Temple University Press.

Budgeon, Shelley. 1998. "I'll tell you what I really, really want": Girl power and self-identity in Britain. In *Millennium Girls: Today's Girls Around the World*, ed. Sherrie Inness. New York: Rowman & Littlefield.

Burgin, Victor, James Donald, and Cora Kaplan, eds. 1986. *Formations of Fantasy*. London: Methuen.

Butler, Judith. 1990. *Gender Trouble: Feminism and the Subversion of Identity*. New York: Routledge.

——. 1992. Contingent foundations: Feminism and the question of "Postmodernism." In *Feminists Theorize the Political*, ed. Judith Butler and Joan Scott. New York: Routledge.

——. 1993. *Bodies That Matter: On the Discursive Limits of "Sex."* New York: Routledge.

Butler, Judith, and Joan Scott, eds. 1992. *Feminists Theorize the Political*. New York: Routledge.

Cameron, Deborah. 1995. *Verbal Hygiene*. New York: Routledge.

——, ed. 1992. *Researching Language: Issues of Power and Method*. New York: Routledge.

Canaan, Joyce. 1987. A comparitive analysis of American suburban middle class, middle school, and high school teenage culture. In *Interpretive Ethnography of Education: At Home and Abroad*, ed. George Spindler and Louise Spindler. Hillsdale, N.J.: Lawrence Erlbaum Associates.

——. 1994. Passing notes and telling jokes: Gendered strategies among american middle school teenagers. In *Sexual Cultures and the Construction of Adolescent Identities*, ed. Janice Irvine. Philadelphia: Temple University Press.

Chapkis, Wendy. 1986. *Beauty Secrets: Women and the Politics of Appearance*. London: Women's Press.

Christian-Smith, Linda. 1990. *Becoming A Woman Through Romance*. New York: Routledge.

——. 1993a. Sweet dreams: Gender and desire in teen romance novels. In *Texts of Desire: Essays on Fiction, Femininity and Schooling*, ed. Linda Christian-Smith. London: Falmer Press.

——, ed. 1993b. *Texts of Desire: Essays on Fiction, Femininity and Schooling.* London: Falmer Press.

Chua, Beng Huat. 1992. Shopping for women's fashion in Singapore. In *Lifestyle Shopping: The Subject of Consumption*, ed. Rob Shields. New York: Routledge.

Clifford, James. 1983. On Ethnographic Authority. *Representations* 1 (2): 118–146.

——. 1986. Partial truths. Introduction in *Writing Culture: The poetics and politics of ethnography*, ed. James Clifford and George Marcus. Berkeley: University of California Press.

——. 1988. *The Predicament of Culture: Twentieth Century Ethnography, Literature and Art.* Cambridge, Mass.: Harvard University Press.

Clifford, James, and George E. Marcus, eds. 1986. *Writing Culture: The Poetics and Politics of Ethnography.* Berkeley: University of California Press.

Clough, Patricia. 1992. *The End(s) of Ethnography: From Realism to Social Criticism.* New York: Peter Lang.

Cocks, Joan. 1989. *The Oppositional Imagination: Feminism, Critique and Political Theory.* New York: Routledge.

Cohan, Steven, and Linda Shires. 1988. *Telling Stories: A Theoretical Analysis of Narrative Fiction.* London: Routledge.

Cohen, Michele. 1996. Is there a space for the achieving girl? In *Equity in the Classroom: Towards Effective Pedagogy for Girls and Boys*, ed. Patricia Murphy and Caroline Gripps. London: Falmer Press.

Cohen, Philip. 1992. It's racism what dunnit: Hidden narratives in theories of racism. In *"Race," Culture and Difference*, ed. James Donald and Ali Rattansi. London: Sage/Open University Press.

Collins, Patricia Hill. 1991. *Black Feminist Thought: Knowledge, Consciousness and the Politics of Empowerment.* New York: Harper Collins.

Comaroff, John, and Jean Comaroff. 1992. *Ethnography and the Historical Imagination.* Boulder: Westview Press.

Connell, Robert W. 1987. *Gender and Power: Society, the Person and Sexual Politics.* Oxford: Polity Press.

Connell, Robert W., Dean J. Ashenden, Sandra Kessler, and Gary W. Dowsett. 1982. *Making the Difference: Schools, Families and Social Division.* Sydney: George Allen and Unwin.

Corrigan, Philip. 1987. In/forming schooling. In *Critical Pedagogy and Cultural Power*, ed. D. W. Livingstone. Boston: Bergin and Garvey.

——. 1988. The making of the boy: Meditations on what grammer school did with, to, and for my body. *Journal of Education* 170 (3): 142–161.

Crapanzano, Vincent. 1986. Hermes' dilemma: The masking of subversion in ethnographic description. In *Writing Culture: The Poetics and Politics of Ethnography*, ed. James Clifford and George Marcus. Berkeley: University of California Press.

——. 1992. *Hermes' Dilemma and Hamlet's Desire: On the Epistemology of Interpretation.* Cambridge: Harvard University Press.

Danesi, Marcel. 1994. *The Signs and Meanings of Adolescence.* Toronto: University of Toronto Press.

Davidson, Ann Locke. 1996. *Making and Molding Identity in Schools: Student Narratives of Race, Gender, and Academic Engagement.* New York: State University of New York Press.

Davies, Bronwyn. 1989. *Frogs and Snails and Feminist Tales: Preschool Children and Gender.* Sydney: Unwin and Allen.

———. 1992. Women's subjectivity and feminist stories. In *Invesigating Subjectivity: Research on Lived Experience,* ed. Carolyn Ellis and Michael G. Flahaty. Newbury Park, Calif.: Sage.

———. 1993. *Shards of Glass: Children Reading and Writing Beyond Gendered Identities.* Cresskill, N.J.: Hampton Press.

Davies, Bronwyn, Suzy Dormer, Sue Gannon, Cath Laws, Sharon Rocco, Hillevi Lenz Taguchi, and Helen McCann. 2001. Becoming schoolgirls: The ambivalent project of subjectification. *Gender and Education* 13: 167–182.

Davies, Carole Boyce. 1994. *Black Women, Writing and Identity: Migrations of the Subject.* London: Routledge.

Dei, George J. Sefa, and Irma Marcia James. 1998. "Becoming Black": African-Canadian youth and the politics of negotiating racial and racialised identities. *Race, Ethnicity and Education* 1: 91–108.

Delamont, Sara. 1980. *Sex Roles and the School.* London: Methuen.

de Lauretis, Teresa. 1984. *Alice Doesn't.* Bloomington: Indiana University Press.

———. 1987. *Technologies of Gender: Essays on Theory, Film, and Fiction.* Bloomington: Indiana University Press.

———, ed. 1986. *Feminist Studies/Critical Studies.* Bloomington: University of Indiana Press.

Denzin, Norman. 1997. *Interpretive Ethnography: Ethnographic Practices for the 21st Century.* Thousand Oaks, Calif.: Sage.

Denzin, Norman, and Yvonne Lincoln, eds. 1994. *Handbook of Qualitative Research.* Thousand Oaks, Calif: Sage.

Dodson, Lisa. 1998. *Don't Call Us Out of Name: The Untold Lives of Women and Girls in Poor America.* Boston: Beacon Press.

Donald, James, and Ali Rattansi, eds. 1992. *"Race," Culture and Difference.* London: Sage/Open University Press.

Driedger, Leo, ed. 1987. *Ethnic Canada: Identities and Inequalities.* Toronto: Copp Clark Pittman.

Duplessis, Rachel Blau. 1985. *Writing Beyond the Ending: Narrative Strategies of 20th Century Women Writers.* Bloomington: Indiana University Press.

Dwyer, Peter, and Johanna Wyn. 1998. A new agenda: Changing life-patterns of the post-1970 generation. Paper presented at the 1998 International Sociology Association Conference, Montreal, Quebec.

Eckert, Penelope. 1989. *From Jocks to Burnouts: Social Identities in the High School.* New York: Teacher's College Press.

———. 1993. Cooperative competition in adolescent "girl talk." In *Gender and Conversational Interaction,* ed. Deborah Tannen. New York: Oxford University Press.

Eder, Donna. 1985. The cycle of popularity: Interpersonal relations among female adolescents. *Sociology of Education* 58: 154–65.

———. 1995. *School Talk: Gender and Adolescent Culture.* New Brunswick, N.J.: Rutgers University Press.

Elias, Norbert. 1982. *State Formation and Civilization: The Civilizing Process.* Vol. 2. Oxford: Blackwell.

Ellis, Carolyn, and Michael G. Flahaty, eds. 1992. *Investigating Subjectivity: Research on Lived Experience.* Newbury Park, Calif.: Sage.

Ellsworth, Elizabeth, and Janet Miller. 1996. Working difference in education. *Curriculum Inquiry* 26 (3):245–263.

Erkut, Sumru, and Fern Marx. 1995. *Raising Competent Girls: An Exploratory Study of Diversity in Girls' Views on Liking One's Self*. Wellesley, Mass.: Wellesley Center for Research on Women.

Espiritu, Yen Le. 1992. *Asian American Panethnicity: Bridging Institutions and Identities*. Philadelphia: Temple University Press.

Essed, Philomena. 1991. *Understanding Everyday Racism*. Newbury Park, Calif.: Sage.

Fanon, Frantz. 1967. *Black Skin, White Masks*. Trans. Charles Lam Markmann, New York: Grove.

Ferguson, Kathy E. 1993. *The Man Question: Visions of Subjectivity in Feminist Theory*. Berkeley: University of California Press.

Fine, Michelle. 1988. Sexuality, schooling, and adolescent females: The missing discourse of desire. *Harvard Educational Review* 58 (1):29–53.

———. 1990. The "public" in public schools: The social constriction/construction of a moral community. *Journal of Social Issues* 46 (1):107–119.

———. 1991. *Framing Dropouts: Notes on the Politics of an Urban High School*. Albany: State University of New York Press.

———. 1994. Working the hyphens: Reinventing self and other in qualitative research. In *Handbook of Qualitative Research*, ed. Norman Denzin and Yvonne Lincoln. Thousand Oaks, Calif.: Sage.

Fine, Michelle, and Pat Macpherson. 1992. Over dinner: Feminism and adolescent female bodies. In *Disruptive Voices: The Possibilities of Feminist Research*. Ann Arbor: University of Michigan Press.

Fine, Michelle, Lois Weis, Linda C. Powell, and L. Mun Wong, eds. 1997. *Off White: Readings on Race, Power and Society*. New York: Routledge.

Fisk, John. 1989. *Reading the Popular*. Boston: Unwin Hyman.

Flax, Jane. 1990. *Thinking Fragments: Psychoanalysis, Feminism, and Postmodernism in the Contemporary West*. Berkeley: University of California Press.

———. 1992. The end of innocence. In *Feminists Theorize the Political*, ed. Judith Butler and Joan Scott. New York: Routledge.

———. 1993. *Disputed Subjects: Essays on Psychoanalysis, Politics and Philosophy*. New York: Routledge.

Fordham, Signithia. 1993. "Those loud black girls": (Black) women, silence, and gender "passing" in the academy. *Anthropology and Education Quarterly* 24 (1):3–32.

———. 1996. *Blacked Out: Dilemmas of Race, Identity, and Success at Capital High*. Chicago: University of Chicago Press.

Fornas, Johan, and Guran Bolin, eds. 1995. *Youth Culture in Late Modernity*. Thousand Oaks, Calif.: Sage.

Fortier, Anne-Marie. 1996. Troubles in the field: The use of personal experiences as sources of knowledge. *Critique of Anthropology* 16 (3):303–323.

———. 1999. Re-membering places and the performance of belonging's. *Theory, Culture and Society* 16 (2):41–64.

Foster, Victoria. 1996. Space invaders: Desire and threat in the schooling of girls. *Discourse: Studies in the Cultural Politics of Education* 17 (1):43–63.

Foucault, Michel. 1972. Two lectures. In *Power/Knowledge: Selected Interviews and Other Writings, 1972–1977*, ed. C. Gordon. New York: Pantheon.

——. 1979. *Discipline and Punish: The Birth of the Prison*. Middlesex: Peregrine Books.

——. 1980a. *Power/Knowledge: Selected Interviews and Other Writings, 1972–77*. Ed. Colin Gordon. Brighton: Harvester Press

——. 1980b. *The History of Sexuality*. Vol 3. New York: Vintage Books.

——. 1982. The subject and power. *Critical Inquiry* 8 (summer): 777–794.

——. 1984. On the genealogy of ethics: An overview of work in progress. In *The Foucault Reader*, ed. Paul Rabinow. New York: Pantheon Books.

Fox, Richard, ed. 1991. *Recapturing Anthropology*. Sante Fe: School of American Research Press.

Frankenberg, Ruth. 1993. *The Social Construction of Whiteness: White Women, Race Matters*. Minneapolis: University of Minnesota Press.

Franklin, Sarah, Celia Lury, and Jackie Stacey, eds. 1991. *Off-Centre: Feminism and Cultural Studies*. London: Harper-Collins Academic.

Frazer, Elizabeth. 1992. Talking about gender, race and class. In *Researching Language: Issues of Power and Method*, ed. Deborah Cameron et al. New York: Routledge.

French, Jane, and Peter French. 1993. Gender imbalances in the primary classroom: An interactional account. In *Gender and Ethnicity in Schools: Ethnographic Accounts*, ed. Peter Woods and Martyn Hammersley. New York: Routledge.

Freud, Sigmund. 1921/1991. Group psychology and the analysis of the ego, in *Civilization, Society and Religion*, Vol. 12, Selected Works, Harmondsworth: Penguin.

Furlong, Andy, and Fred Cartmel. 1997. *Young People and Social Change: Individualization and Risk in Late Modernity*. Buckingham: Open University Press.

Fuss, Diana. 1995. *Identification Papers*. New York: Routledge.

Game, Ann. 1991. *Undoing the Social: Towards a Deconstructive Sociology*. Toronto: University of Toronto Press.

Ganetz, Hillevi. 1995. The shop, the home and femininity as a masquerade. In *Youth Culture in Late Modernity*, ed. Johan Fornas and Guran Bolin. Thousand Oaks, Calif.: Sage.

Garber, Majorie. 1992. *Vested Interests: Cross Dressing and Cultural Anxiety*. New York: Routledge.

Gaskell, Jane, and Arlene McLaren, eds. 1987. *Women and Education: A Canadian Perspective*. Calgary: Detselig Enterprises.

Gates, Henry Louis, ed. 1986. *"Race," Writing and Difference*. Chicago: University of Chicago Press.

Geertz, Clifford. 1989. *Works and Lives: The Anthropologist as Author*. Stanford, Calif.: Stanford University Press.

Gilbert, Pam. 1992. The story so far: Gender, literacy and social regulation. *Gender and Education* 4 (3): 185–199.

Gilbert, Pam, and Sandra Taylor. 1991. *Refashioning the Feminine: Girls, Popular Culture and Schooling*. Sydney: Allen and Unwin.

Gilligan, Carol. 1982. *In A Different Voice*. Cambridge: Harvard University Press.

Gilman, Charlotte Perkins. 1892. *The Yellow Wall Paper*, ed. and with an introduction by Thomas L. Erskine and Connie L. Richards. New Brunswick, N.J.: Rutgers University Press, 1993.

Gilroy, Paul. 1987. *There Ain't No Black in the Union Jack*. London: Hutchinson.

Giroux, Henry. 1984. Ideology, agency and the process of schooling. In *Social Crisis and Educational Research*, ed. Len Barton and Sandra Walker. London: Croom Helm.

———, ed. 1991. *Postmodernism, Feminism and Cultural Politics: Redrawing Educational Boundaries*. New York: State University of New York Press.

Giroux, Henry A., and Peter McLaren. 1992. Writing from the margins: Geographies of identity, pedagogy, and power. *Journal of Education* 174 (1):7-30.

Gitlin, Andrew, ed. 1994. *Power and Method: Political Activism and Educational Research*. New York: Routledge.

Gluck, Sherna Berger, and Daphne Patai, eds. 1991. *Women's Words: The Feminist Practice of Oral History*. New York: Routledge.

Godwin, Gail. 1974. *The Odd Woman*. New York: Warner.

———. 1978. *Violet Clay*. New York: Alfred A. Knopf.

Goldberg, David. 1993. *Racist Culture: Philosophy and the Politics of Meaning*. Oxford: Blackwell.

Goldstein, Rebecca. 1983. *The Mind-Body Problem*. New York: Random House.

Gonick, Marnina. 1997. Reading selves, re-fashioning identity: Teen magazines and their readers. *Curriculum Studies* 5 (1):69-85.

Gordon, Deborah. 1995. Culture writing women: Inscribing feminist anthropology. Conclusion in *Women Writing Culture*, ed. Ruth Behar and Deborah Gordon. Los Angeles: University of California Press.

Gordon, Tuula. 1996. Citizenship, difference and marginality in schools: Spatial and embodied aspects of gender construction. In *Equity in the Classroom: Towards Effective Pedagogy for Girls and Boys*, ed. Patricia Murphy and Caroline Gipps. London: Falmer Press.

Gore, Jennifer. 1992. What we can do for you! What can "we" do for you?: Struggling over empowerment in critical and feminist pedagogy. In *Feminisms and Critical Pedagogy*, ed. Carmen Luke and Jennifer Gore. New York: Routledge.

Gosh, Ratna. 1987. Education, gender and the immigrant experience. In *Ethnic Canada: Identities and Inequalities*, ed. Leo Driedger. Toronto: Copp Clark Pittman.

Gotfrit, Leslie. 1988. Women dancing back: Disruption and the politics of pleasure. *Journal of Education* 170 (3):122-141.

Graebner, William. 1990. *Coming of Age in Buffalo: Youth and Authority in the Post-War Era*. Philadelphia: Temple University Press.

Grant, Carl, and Christine Sleeter. 1996. *After the School Bell Rings*. London: Falmer Press.

Grant, Linda. 1992. Race and the schooling of young girls. In *Education and Gender Equality*, ed. Julia Wrigley. London: Falmer Press.

Griffin, Christine. 1982. Cultures of femininity: Romance revisited. *SP* 69, Centre for Contemporary Cultural Studies, Birmingham University.

———. 1993. *Representations of Youth: The Study of Youth and Adolescence in Britain and America*. Cambridge: Polity Press.

———. 1997. Troubled teens: Managing disorders of transition and consumption. *Feminist Review* 55:4-21.

Grossberg, Lawrence. 1993. Cultural studies and/in new worlds. In *Race, Identity and Representation in Education*, ed. Cameron McCarthy and Warren Crichlow. New York: Routledge.

Grossberg, Lawrence, Cary Nelson, and Paula Treichler, eds. 1992. *Cultural Studies*. London: Routledge.

Grosz, Elizabeth. 1990. Inscriptions and body-maps: Representations and the corporeal. In *Feminine, Masculine and Representation*, ed. Terry Threadgold and Anne Cranny-Francis. Sydney: Allen and Unwin.

Grumet, Madeleine R. 1997. Restaging the Civil Ceremonies of Schooling. *Review of Education/Pedagogy/Cultural Studies* 19 (1):39-54.

Gutman, Amy, ed. 1994. *Multiculturalism*. Princeton, N.J.: Princeton University Press.

Hall, Stuart. 1991. Old and new identities, old and new ethnicities. In *Culture, Globalization and the World System: Contemporary Conditions for the Representation of Identity*, ed. Anthony King. Binghamton, N.Y.: Dept of Art and Art History, State University of New York Binghamton.

——. 1996. Who needs "identity?" Introduction to *Questions of Cultural Identity*, ed. Stuart Hall and Paul du Gay. Thousand Oaks, Calif.: Sage.

Hall, Stuart, and Tony Jefferson, eds. 1975. *Resistance Through Rituals*. London: Hutcheon.

Hall, Stuart, and Paul du Gay, eds. 1996. *Questions of Cultural Identity*. Thousand Oaks, Calif.: Sage.

Haraway, Donna. 1988. Situated Knowledges: The science question in feminism and the privilege of partial perspective. *Feminist Studies* 14 (3):575-599.

——. 1995. Writing, literacy and technology: Toward a cyborg writing. In *Women Writing Culture*, ed. Gary Olson and Elizabeth Hirsh. New York: State University of New York Press.

Harbord, Janet. 1996. Between identification and desire: Rereading Rebecca. *Feminist Review* 53 (summer): 95-107.

Harding, Sandra. 1986. *The Science Question in Feminism*. Ithaca, N.Y.: Cornell University Press.

——. 1987. Is there a feminist method? Introduction to *Feminism and Methodology*. Bloomington: Indiana University Press.

Hargreaves, Andy, and Peter Woods, eds. 1984. *Classrooms and Staffrooms: The Sociology of Teachers and Teaching*. London: Milton Keynes/Open University Press.

Harper, Helen. 1995. *Danger at the borders: The response of high school girls to feminist writing practices*. Doctoral dissertation, University of Toronto.

Hartsock, Nancy. 1983. *Money, Sex and Power*. Boston: Northeastern University Press.

Haug, Frigga et al. 1987. *Female Sexualization: A Collective Work of Memory*. London: Verso.

Haw, Kaye. 1991. Interactions of gender and race—A problem for teachers? A review of the emerging literature. *Educational Review* 33 (1): 12-21.

Hebdige, Dick. 1979. *Subculture: The Meaning of Style*. London: Methuen.

Hegel, G. W. F. 1977. *The Phenomenology of Mind*. Trans. J. B. Baille. New York: Humanities Press.

Heilman, Elizabeth. 1998. The struggle for self: Power and identity in adolescent girls. *Youth and Society* 30 (2): 182-208.

Heller, Monica. 1999. *Linguistic Minorities and Modernity: A Sociolinguistic Ethnography*. London: Longman.

Henriques, Julian, Wendy Hollway, Cathy Unwin, Couze Venn, and Valerie Walkerdine, eds. 1984. *Changing the Subject: Psychology, Social Regulation and Subjectivity*. London: Methuen.

Herrmann, Mareike. 1998. "Feeling better" with bravo: German girls and their popular youth magazine. In *Millennium Girls: Today's Girls Around the World*, ed. Sherrie Inness. New York: Rowman and Littlefield.

Hey, Valerie. 1997. *The Company She Keeps: An Ethnography of Girls' Friendship*. Buckingham: Open University Press.

Hirsch, Marianne, and Evelyn Fox Keller, eds. 1990. *Conflicts in Feminism*. New York: Routledge.

Hirschon, Renee. 1993. Open body/closed space: The transformation of female sexuality. In *Defining Females: The Nature of Women in Society*, ed. Shirley Ardener. Oxford: Berg.

Holland, Janet, Caroline Ramazanoglu, Sue Sharpe, and Rachel Thomson. 1994. Power and desire: The embodiment of female sexuality. *Feminist Review* 46 (spring): 21–38.

Holland, Janet, and Maude Blair, eds. 1995. *Debates and Issues in Feminist Research and Pedagogy*. Philadelphia: Multilingual Matters/Open University Press.

Hollway, Wendy. 1984. Gender difference and the production of subjectivity. In *Changing the Subject: Psychology, Social Regulation and Subjectivity*, ed. Julian Henriques, Wendy Hollway, Cathy Unwin, Couze Venn, and Valerie Walkerdine. London: Methuen.

Honneth, Axel. 1996. *The Struggle for Recognition: The Moral Grammar of Social Conflicts*. Cambridge: MIT Press.

Hoogland, Renee. 1993. Belonging to another person's dream. In *Girls, Girlhood and Girls' Studies in Transition*, ed. Marion de Ras and Mieke Lunenberg. Amsterdam: Het Spinhuis.

hooks, bell. 1981. *Ain't I A Woman: Black Women and Feminism*. Boston: South End Press.

———. 1992. *Black Looks: Race and Representation*. London: Turnaround.

Hudak, Glenn. 1993. Technologies of marginality: Strategies of stardom and displacement in adolescent life. In *Race, Identity and Representation in Education*, ed. Cameron McCarthy and Warren Crichlow. New York: Routledge.

Hudson, Barbara. 1984. Femininity and adolescence. In *Gender and Generation*, ed. Angela McRobbie and Mica Nava. London: Macmillan Press.

Hughes, John. 1986. *Pretty in Pink*. Paramount Studios.

Inness, Sherrie, ed. 1998a. *Delinquents and Debutantes: Twentieth-Century American Girls' Cultures*. New York: New York University Press.

———. 1998b. *Millennium Girls: Today's Girls Around the World*. New York: Rowman and Littlefield.

Irvine, Janice, ed. 1994. *Sexual Cultures and the Construction of Adolescent Identities*. Philadelphia: Temple University Press.

JanMohamed, Abdul R. 1992. Sexuality on/of the racial border: Foucault, Wright, and the articulation of "racialized sexuality." In *Discourses of Sexuality from Aristotle to AIDS*, ed. Donna Stanton. Ann Arbor: University of Michigan Press.

Jackson, Michael. 1998. *Minima Ethnographica: Intersubjectivity and the Anthropological Project*. Chicago: University of Chicago Press.

Johnson, Lesley. 1993. *The Modern Girl: Childhood and Growing Up*. Buckingham: Open University Press.

Jones, Alison. 1993. Becoming a 'girl': Post-structuralist suggestions for educational research. *Gender and Education* 5 (2):157–166.

Jones, Simon. 1988. *Black Culture, White Youth: The Reggae Tradition From JA to UK.* London: Macmillan.

Kaplan, Cora. 1986. The Thorn Birds: Fiction, fantasy and femininity. In *Formations of Fantasy,* ed. Victor Burgin, James Donald, and Cora Kaplan. London: Methuen.

Kaplan, E. Ann. 1987. *Rocking Around the Clock: Music, Television, Postmodernism and Consumer Culture.* New York: Methuen.

Kearney, Mary Celeste. 1998. Producing girls: Rethinking the study of female youth culture. In *Delinquents and Debutantes: Twentieth-Century American Girls' Cultures,* ed. Sherrie Inness. New York: New York University Press.

Kenway, Jane, and Jill Blackmore. 1995. Pleasure and pain: Beyond feminist authoritarianism and therapy in the curriculum. Invited paper presented at the "Is There a Pedagogy for Girls?" Institute of Education/Unesco Colloquium, London.

Kenway, Jane, and Sue Willis. 1998. *Answering Back: Girls, Boys and Feminism in Schools.* New York: Routledge.

——, eds. 1990. *Hearts and Minds: Self-Esteem and the Schooling of Girls.* London: Falmer Press.

Kincaid, Jamaica. 1985. Girl. In *At The Bottom of the River.* New York: Aventura.

King, Anthony, ed. 1991. *Culture, Globalization and The World-System: Contemporary Conditions for the Representation of Identity.* Binghamton, N.Y.: Dept. of Art and Art History, State University of New York Binghamton.

Kinney, David A. 1993. From nerds to normals: The recovery of identity among adolescents from middle school to high school. *Sociology of Education* 66 (January): 21–40.

Kondo, Dorinne. 1986. Dissolution and reconstitution of self: Implications for anthropological epistemology. *Cultural Anthropology* 1: 74–88.

——. 1990. *Crafting Selves: Power, Gender, and Discourses of Identity in a Japanese Workplace.* Chicago: University of Chicago Press.

Lacan, Jacques. 1977. The mirror-stage as formative of the function of the I as revealed in psychoanalytic experience. *Ecrits.,* trans. Alan Sheridan. New York: W.W. Norton.

Laclau, Ernesto. 1977. *Politics and Ideology in Marxist Theory.* London: New Left.

Lamphere, Louise. 1994. Expanding our notion of critical qualitative methodology: Bringing race, class and gender into the discussion (response). In *Power and Method: Political Activism and Educational Research,* ed. Andrew Gitlin. New York: Routledge.

Lather, Patti. 1991. *Getting Smart: Feminist Research and Pedagogy With/in the Postmodern.* New York: Routledge.

——. 1996. Methodology as subversive repetition: Practices toward a feminist double science. Paper presented at the Association of American Researchers in Education, New York.

Leadbeater, Bonnie J. Ross, and Niobe Way, eds. 1996. *Urban Girls: Resisting Stereotypes, Creating Identities.* New York: New York University Press.

Lee, Stacey. 1996. *Unraveling the "Model Minority" Stereotype: Listening to Asian American Youth.* New York: Teachers College Press.

Lees, Sue. 1986. *Losing Out: Sexuality and Adolesent Girls.* London: Hutchinson.

——. 1993. *Sugar and Spice: Sexuality and Adolescent Girls.* London: Penguin Books.

Lesko, Nancy. 1988. The curriculum of the body: Lessons from a Catholic high school. In *Becoming Feminine: The Politics of Popular Culture,* ed. Leslie Roman, Linda Christian-Smith, and Elizabeth Ellsworth. London: Falmer Press.

——. 1996. Denaturalizing adolescence: The politics of contemporary representations. *Youth and Society* 28 (2):139–161.

Levinson, Bradley, Douglas Foley, and Dorothy Holland, eds. 1996. *Cultural Production of the Educated Person: Critical Ethnographies of Schooling and Local Practice.* Albany: State University of New York Press.

Lim, Shirley Geok-Lin, and Amy Ling, eds. 1992. *Reading the Literature of Asian America.* Philadelphia: Temple University Press.

Ling, Amy. 1992. Creating one's self: The Eaton sisters. In *Reading the Literature of Asian America*, ed. Shirley Geok-Lin Lim and Amy Ling. Philadelphia: Temple University Press.

Livingston, David, ed. 1987. *Critical Pedagogy and Cultural Power.* Boston: Bergin and Garvey.

Llyod, Barbara, Kevin Lucas, Janet Holland, Sheena McGrellis, and Sean Arnold. 1998. *Smoking in Adolescence: Images and Identities.* New York: Routledge.

Lorde, Audre. 1984. *Sister Outsider.* New York: Crossing Press.

Lovering, Kathryn Matthews. 1997. Listening to girls' "voice" and silence: The problematics of the menarcheal body. In *Bodily Boundaries, Sexualised Genders and Medical Discourses*, ed. Marion de Ras and Victoria Grace. Palmerston: Dunmore Press.

Luke, Carmen, and Jennifer Gore. 1992. Women in the academy: Strategy, struggle and survival. In *Feminisms and Critical Pedagogy*, ed. Carmen Luke and Jennifer Gore. New York: Routledge.

Luke, Carmen, and Jennifer Gore, eds. 1992. *Feminisms and Critical Pedagogy.* New York: Routledge.

Luthi, Max. 1970. *Once Upon a Time: On the Nature of Fairy Tales.* Bloomington: Indiana University Press.

Luttrell, Wendy. 1993. The teachers, they all had their pets: Concepts of gender, knowledge, and power. *Signs: Journal of Women in Culture and Society* 18 (3):505–546.

——. 1996. "Becoming somebody" in and against school: Towards a psychocultural theory of gender and self-making. In *The Cultural Production of the Educated Person: Critical Ethnographies of Schooling and Local Practice*, ed. Bradley Levinson, Douglas Foley, and Dorothy Holland. Albany: State University of New York Press.

——. 1997. *Schoolsmart and Motherwise: Working-Class Women's Identity and Schooling.* New York: Routledge.

Mac an Ghaill, Mairtin. 1995. (In)visibility: "Race," sexuality and masculinity in the school context. In *Identity and Diversity: Gender and the Experience of Education*, ed. Maud Blair, Janet Holland and Sue Sheldon. Clevedon, England: Open University.

Macpherson, Pat. 1997. The Revolution of Little Girls. In *Off White: Readings on Race, Power and Society*, ed. Michelle Fine, Lois Weiss, Linda Powell, and L. Mun Wong. New York: Routledge.

Macpherson, Pat, and Michelle Fine. 1995. Hungry for an us: Adolescent girls and adult women negotiating territories of race, gender, class and difference. *Feminism and Psychology* 5 (2):181–200.

Mama, Amina. 1995. *Beyond the Masks: Race, Gender and Subjectivity.* London: Routledge.

Manganaro, Marc, ed. 1990. *Modernist Anthropology: From Fieldwork to Text.* Princeton, N.J.: Princeton University Press.

Marcus, George. 1994. What comes (just) after "post"? In *Handbook of Qualitative Research*, ed. Norman Denzin and Yvonne Lincoln. Thousand Oaks, Calif.: Sage.

——. 1998. *Ethnography Through Thick and Thin.* Princeton, N.J.: Princeton University Press.

Martin, Biddy, and Chandra Mohanty. 1986. Feminist politics: What's home got to do with it? In *Feminist Studies/Critical Studies*, ed. Teresa de Lauretis. Bloomington: University of Indiana Press.

Martin, Emily. 1989. *The Woman in the Body: A Cultural Analysis of Reproduction*. Boston: Beacon Press.

Mascia-Lees, Frances Sharpe, and Patricia Sharpe. 1994. The anthropological unconscious. *American Anthropologist* 96 (3):649–660.

McCarthy, Cameron. 1988. Rethinking liberal and radical perspectives on racial inequality in schooling: Making the case for nonsynchrony. *Harvard Educational Review* 58 (3):265–279.

McCarthy, Cameron, and Warren Crichlow, eds. 1993. *Race Identity and Representation in Education*. New York: Routledge.

McCarthy, Cameron, and Greg Dimitriadis. (2000. The work of art in the postcolonial imagination. *Discourse: Studies in the Cultural Politics of Education* 21 (1):59–74.

McCarthy, Margaret. 1998. Transforming visions: A French toast to American girlhood in Luc Bresson's "The Professional." In *Millennium Girls: Today's Girls Around the World*, ed. Sherrie Inness. New York: Rowman and Littlefield.

McCarthy, Thomas. 1992. Doing the right thing in cross-cultural representation. *Ethics* (April): 635–649.

McLaren, Peter. 1991. Schooling the postmodern body: Critical pedagogy and the politics of enfleshment. In *Postmodernism, Feminism and Cultural Politics: Redrawing Educational Boundaries*, ed. Henry Giroux. New York: State University of New York Press.

McClintock, Anne. 1995. *Imperial Leather: Race, Gender and Sexuality in the Colonial Contest*. New York: Routledge.

McRobbie, Angela. 1978. Working class girls and the culture of femininity. In *Women Take Issue: Aspects of Women's Subordination*, ed. Women's Studies Group. London: Hutchinson.

———. 1982a. Jackie: An ideology of adolescent femininity. In *Popular Culture: Past and Present*, ed. Bernard Waites. London: Croom Helm/Open University Press.

———. 1982b. The Politics of Feminist Research: Between Talk, Text and Action. *Feminist Review* 12 (October): 46–57.

———. 1991. *Feminism and Youth Culture: From Jackie to Just Seventeen*. Boston: Unwin Hyman.

———. 1994a. *Postmodernism and Popular Culture*. New York: Routledge.

McRobbie, Angela, and Jenny Garber. 1975. Girls and subcultures. In *Resistance Through Rituals*, ed. Stuart Hall and Tony Jefferson. London: Hutchinson.

McRobbie, Angela, and Trisha McCabe, eds. 1981. *Feminism for Girls: An Adventure Story*. London: Routledge.

McRobbie, Angela, and Mica Nava, eds. 1984. *Gender and Generation*. London: Macmillan.

Mercer, Kobena. 1992. "1968": Periodising postmodern politics and identity. In *Cultural Studies*, ed. Lawrence Grossberg, Cary Nelson, and Paula Treichler. London: Routledge.

Messner, Michael. 1992. *Power at Play: Sports and the Problem of Masculinity*. Boston: Beacon Press.

Michaels, Anne. 1997. *Fugitive Pieces*. Toronto: McClelland and Stewart.

Miller, Alice. 1983. *The Drama of the Gifted Child and the Search for the True Self*. London: Faber & Faber.

Miller, Jane. 1991. *Seductions: Studies in Reading and Culture*. Cambridge: Harvard University Press.

Mirza, Heidi Safia. 1992. *Young, Female and Black*. New York: Routledge.

Moss, Gemma. 1989. *Un/Popular Fictions*. London: Virago Press.

——. 1993. The place for romance in young people's writing. In *Texts of Desire: Essays on Fiction, Femininity and Schooling*, ed. Linda Christian-Smith. London: Falmer Press.

Morrison, Toni. 1973. *Sula*. New York: New American Library.

——. 1992. *Playing in the Dark: Whiteness and the Literary Imagination*. Cambridge: Harvard University Press.

Murphy, Patricia, and Caroline Gipps, eds. 1996. *Equity in the Classroom: Towards Effective Pedagogy for Girls and Boys*. London: Falmer Press.

Myerhoff, Barbara. 1978. *Number Our Days*. New York: Simon and Schuster.

National Film Board of Canada. 1996. *The Powder Room*. Director, Ann Kennard.

Nava, Mica. 1984. Youth service provision, social order, and the question of girls. In *Gender and Generation*, ed. Angela McRobbie and Mica Nava. London: Macmillan.

Ng, Roxana, Pat Staton, and Joyce Scane, eds. 1995. *Anti-Racism, Feminism and Critical Approaches to Education*. Toronto: OISE Press.

Nilan, Pam. 1991. Exclusion, inclusion and moral ordering in two girls' friendship groups. *Gender and Education* 3 (1):163–182.

Nunes, Fernando. 1999. *Portugese-Canadians and Academic Underachievement: A Community Based Participatory Research Project*. Doctoral dissertation, University of Toronto.

Oakley, Anne. 1981. Interviewing women: A contradiction in terms. In *Doing Feminist Research*, ed. Helen Roberts. London: Routledge and Kegan Paul.

Oliver, Kelly. 1993. Introduction: Julia Kristeva's Outlaw Ethics. In *Ethics, Politics and Difference in Julia Kristeva's Writing*, ed. Kelly Oliver. New York: Routledge.

——, ed. 1993. *Ethics, Politics and Difference in Julia Kristeva's Writing*. New York: Routledge.

Olson, Gary A., and Elizabeth Hirsh, eds. 1995. *Women Writing Culture*. New York: State University of New York Press.

Ong, Aihwa. 1995. Women out of China: Travelling tales and travelling theories in post-colonial feminism. In *Women Writing Culture*, ed. Ruth Behar and Deborah Gordon. Berkeley: University of California Press.

Orenstein, Peggy. 1994. *Schoolgirls: Young Women, Self-Esteem and the Confidence Gap*. New York: Doubleday Books.

Orner, Mimi. 1992. Interrupting the calls for student voice in "libratory" education: A feminist poststructuralist perspective. In *Feminisms and Critical Pedagogy*, ed. Carmen Luke and Jennifer Gore. New York: Routledge.

Palladino, Grace. 1996. *Teenagers: An American History*. New York: Basic Books.

Partington, Angela. 1991. Melodrama's gendered audience. In *Off-Centre: Feminism and Cultural Studies*, ed. Sarah Franklin, Celia Lury, and Jackie Stacey. London: Harper-Collins Academic.

Pipher, Mary. 1994. *Reviving Ophelia: Saving the Selves of Adolescent Girls*. New York: Ballentine Books.

Pitt, Alice. 1996. Fantasizing women in the women's studies classroom. *Journal of Curriculum Theorizing* 12:4.

Pratt, Mary Louise. 1986. Fieldwork in common places. In *Writing Culture: The Poetics and Politics of Ethnography*, ed. James Clifford and George Marcus. Berkeley: University of California Press.

Pratt, Minnie Bruce. 1984. Identity: Skin, blood, heart. In *Yours in Struggle: Three Feminist Perspectives on Anti-Semitism and Racism*, ed. Elly Bulkin, Minnie Bruce Pratt, Barbara Smith. Ithaca, N.Y.: Firebrand Books.

Prendergast, Shirley. 1995. With gender on my mind: Menstruation and embodiment at adolesence. In *Debates and Issues in Feminist Research and Pedagogy*, ed. Janet Holland and Maude Blair. Philadelphia: Multilingual Matters/Open University.

Probyn, Elspeth. 1993. *Sexing the Self: Gendered Positions in Cultural Studies*. London: Routledge.

Proweller, Amira. 1998. *Constructing Female Identities: Meaning Making in an Upper Middle Class Youth Culture*. Albany: State University of New York Press.

Rabinow, Paul. 1986. Representations are social facts: Modernity and post-modernity in anthropology. In *Writing Culture: The Poetics and Politics of Ethnography*, ed. James Clifford and George Marcus. Berkeley: University of California Press.

Radway, Janice. 1984. *Reading the Romance: Women, Patriarchy and Popular Literature*. Chapel Hill: University of North Carolina Press.

Raissiguier, Catherine. 1994. *Becoming Women/Becoming Workers: Identity Formation in a French Vocational School*. Albany: State University of New York Press.

Rajchman, John, ed. 1995. *The Identity in Question*. New York: Routledge.

Rampton, Ben. 1995. *Crossing: Language and Ethnicity Among Adolescents*. London: Longman.

Ras, Marion de, and Mieke Lunenberg, eds. 1993. *Girls, Girlhood and Girls' Studies in Transition*. Amsterdam: Het Spinhuis.

Ras, Marion de, and Victoria Grace, eds. 1997. *Bodily Boundaries, Sexualized Genders and Medical Discourses*. Palmerston: Dunmore Press.

Rattansi, Ali. 1992. Changing the subject?: Racism, culture and education. In *"Race," Culture and Difference*, ed. James Donald and Ali Rattansi. London: Sage/Open University Press.

Rezai-Rashti, Goli. 1995. Connecting racism and sexism: The dilemma of working with minority female students. In *Anti-racism, Feminism and Critical Approaches to Education*, ed. Roxana Ng, Pat Staton, and Joyce Scane. Toronto: OISE Press.

Riley, Denise. 1988. *Am I That Name?: Feminism and the Category of 'Women' in History*. Minneapolis, University of Minnesota.

Roberts, Helen, ed. 1981. *Doing Feminist Research*. London: Routledge and Kegan Paul.

Rockhill, Kathleen. 1987. Literacy as threat/desire: Longing to be somebody. In *Women and Education: A Canadian Perspective*, ed. Jane Gaskell and Arlene McLaren. Calgary: Detselig Enterprises.

Roman, Leslie. 1993. Double exposure: The politics of feminist materialist ethnography. *Educational Theory* 43 (3):279–308.

Roman, Leslie, Linda Christian-Smith, and Elizabeth Ellsworth, eds. 1988. *Becoming Feminine*. London: Falmer Press.

Roof, Judith, and Robyn Wiegman, eds. 1995. *Who Can Speak? Authority and Critical Identity*. Urbana: University of Illinois Press.

Rosaldo, Renato. 1989. *Culture and Truth: The Remaking of Social Analysis*. Boston: Beacon Press.

Rossiter, Amy. 1994. Chips, coke and rock-'n'-roll: Children's mediation of an invitation to a first dance party. *Feminist Review* 46 (spring): 1–20.

Rubin, Gayle. 1984. Thinking sex: Notes for a radical theory of the politics of sexuality. In *Pleasure and Danger: Exploring Female Sexuality*, ed. Carol Vance. Boston: Routledge and Kegan Paul.

Rutherford, Jonathan, ed. 1990. *Identity, Community, Culture and Difference.* London: Lawrence and Wishart.

Ryan, James. 1997. Student communities in culturally diverse school settings: Identity, representation and association. *Discourse: Studies in the Cultural Politics of Education* 18 (1):37–53.

Sadker, Marilyn, and David Sadker. 1994. *Failing at Fairness: How America's Schools Cheat Girls.* New York: Scribner.

Said, Edward. 1979. *Orientalism.* New York: Vintage Books.

———. 1993. *Culture and Imperialism.* New York: Alfred Knopf.

Savier, Monika. 1981. Working with girls: Write a song and make a record about it! In *Feminism for Girls: An Adventure Story,* ed. Angela McRobbie and Trisha McCabe. London: Routledge and Kegan Paul.

Scanlon, Jennifer. 1998. Boys-R-Us: Board games and the socialization of young adolescent girls. In *Delinquents and Debutantes: Twentieth-Century American Girls' Cultures,* ed. Sherrie Inness. New York: New York University Press.

Schofield, Janet. 1981. Complementary and conflicting identites: Images of interaction in an interracial school. In *The Development of Children's Friendships,* ed. Steven Asher and John Gottman. New York: Cambridge University Press.

Scott, Joan Wallach. 1992. Experience. In *Feminists Theorize the Political,* Judith Butler and Joan Scott. New York: Routledge.

Shields, Carol. 1993. *The Stone Diaries.* Toronto: Vintage Books.

Shields, Rob, ed. 1992. *Lifestyle Shopping: The Subject of Comsumption.* New York: Routledge.

Shilling, Chris. 1991. Social space, gender inequalities and educational differentiation. *British Journal of Sociology of Education* 12 (1):23–44.

Shor, Ira. 1987. *Critical Teaching and Everyday Life.* Chicago: University of Chicago Press.

Simon, Roger, and Donald Dippo. 1986. On critical ethnographic work. *Anthropology and Education Quarterly* 17: 195–201.

Singley, Carol, and Susan Sweeny, eds. 1993. *Anxious Power: Reading, Writing and Ambivalence in Narrative by Women.* Albany: State University of New York Press.

Skeggs, Beverley. 1997. *Formations of Class and Gender.* London: Sage Publications.

Smith, Dorothy. 1987. *The Everyday World as Problematic: A Feminist Sociology.* Toronto: University of Toronto Press.

———. 1988. Femininity as discourse. In *Becoming Feminine,* ed. Leslie Roman, Linda Christian-Smith, and Elizabeth Ellsworth. London: Falmer Press.

———. 1990. *The Conceptual Practices of Power: A Feminist Sociology of Knowledge.* Toronto: University of Toronto Press.

Spelman, Elizabeth. 1988. *Inessential Woman: Problems of Exclusion in Feminist Thought.* Boston: Beacon Press.

Spence, Jo. 1995. Fairy tales and photography. *Cultural Sniping: The Art of Transgression.* New York: Routledge.

Spindler, George, and Louise Spindler, eds. 1987. *Interpretive Ethnography of Education: At Home and Abroad.* Hillsdale, N.J.: Lawrence Erlbaum.

Spivak, Gayatri. 1987. *In Other Worlds.* London: Methuen.

Sumera, Dennis, and Brent Davis. 1998. Telling tales of surprise. In *Queer Theory in Education,* ed. William Pinar. New Jersey: Lawrence Erlbaum.

Stacey, Judith. 1988. Can there be a feminist ethnography? *Women's Studies International Forum* 11: 163–182.

Stanley, Liz, ed. 1990. *Feminist Praxis*. New York: Routledge.

Stanley, Liz, and Sue Wise. 1990. Method, methodology and epistemology in feminist research process. In *Feminist Praxis*, ed. Liz Stanley. New York: Routledge.

Stanton, Donna, ed. 1992. *Discourses of Sexuality from Aristototle to AIDS*. Ann Arbor: University of Michigan Press.

Stanworth, Michelle. 1984. Girls on the margins: A study of gender divisions in the classroom. In *Classrooms and Staffrooms*, ed. Andy Hargreaves and Peter Woods. London: Milton Keynes/Open University Press.

Steedman, Carolyn. 1982. *The Tidy House*. London: Virago Press.

———. 1985. Listen, how the caged bird sings: Amarjit's song. In *Language, Gender and Childhood*, ed. Carolyn Steedman, Valerie Walkerdine, and Cathy Unwin. London: Routledge and Kegan Paul.

———. 1986. *Landscape for A Good Woman: The Story of Two Lives*. New Brunswick, N.J.: Rutgers University Press.

———. 1995. *Strange Dislocations: Childhood and the Idea of Human Interiority 1780–1930*. Cambridge: Harvard University Press.

Steedman, Carolyn, Valerie Walkerdine, and Cathy Unwin, eds. 1985. *Language, Gender and Childhood*. London: Routledge and Kegan Paul.

Strathern, Marilyn. 1990. Out of context: The Persuasive Fictions of Anthropology. In *Modernist Anthropology: From Fieldwork to Text*, ed. Marc Manganaro. Princeton, N.J.: Princeton University Press.

Sultana, Ronald. 1992. Ethnography and the politics of absence. *Qualitative Studies in Education* 11 (1):21–27.

Tannen, Deborah, ed. 1993. *Gender and Conversational Interaction*. New York: Oxford University Press.

Taylor, Charles. 1989. *Sources of the Self: The Making of Modern Identity*. Cambridge, Mass.: Harvard University Press.

———. 1991. *The Malaise of Modernity*. Concord, Ont.: Anansi Press.

———. 1994. The politics of recognition. In *Multiculturalism*, ed. Amy Gutman. Princeton, N.J.: Princeton University Press.

Taylor, Sandra. 1991. Feminist classroom practice and cultural politics: Some further thoughts about "girl number twenty" and ideology. *Discourse* 11 (2):22–47.

———. 1993. Transforming the texts: Towards a feminist classroom practice. In *Texts of Desire: Essays on Fiction, Feminninity and Schooling*, ed. Linda Christian-Smith. London: Falmer Press.

Tedlock, Barbara. 1991. From participant observation to the observation of participation: The emergence of narrative ethnography. *Journal of Anthropological Research* 47:69–94.

Ternar, Yesim. 1994. *The Book and the Veil: Escape from an Istanbul Harem*. Montreal: Vehicule Press.

Thompson, Sharon. 1984. Search for tomorrow: On feminism and the reconstruction of teen romance. In *Pleasure and Danger: Exploring Female Sexuality*, ed. Carole Vance. Boston: Routledge and Kegan Paul.

———. 1995. *Going All The Way: Teenage Girls' Tales of Sex, Romance and Pregnany*. New York: Hill and Wang.

Thorne, Barrie. 1995. *Gender Play: Girls and Boys in School*. New Brunswick, N.J.: Rutgers University Press.

Threadgold, Terry, and Anne Cranny-Fancis, eds. 1990. *Feminine, Masculine and Representation*. Sydney: Allen and Unwin.

Tinkler, Penny. 1995. *Constructing Girlhood: Popular Magazines for Girls Growing Up in England 1920–1950*. London: Taylor and Francis.

Todd, Sharon. 1997. Looking at pedagogy in 3-D: Rethinking difference, disparity and desire. In *Learning Desire: Perspectives on Pedagogy, Culture and the Unsaid*, ed. Sharon Todd. New York: Routledge.

Tolman, Deborah. 1994. Daring to desire: Culture and the bodies of adolesent girls. In *Sexual Cultures and the Construction of Adolescent Identities*, ed. Janice Irvine. Philadelphia: Temple University Press.

Trinh T. Minh-ha. 1989. *Woman, Native, Other: Writing Postcoloniality and Feminism*. Bloomington: Indiana University Press.

——. 1990. Not you/like you. In *Making Face, Making Soul/Haciendo Caras: Creative and Critical Perspectives by Feminists of Color*, ed. Gloria Anzaldua. San Francisco: Spinsters/Aunt Lute.

——. 1991. *When the Moon Waxes Red*. New York: Routledge.

——. 1992. *Framer Framed*. New York: Routledge.

Tsing, Anna Lowenhaupt. 1993. *In the Realm of the Diamond Queen*. Princeton, N.J.: Princeton University Press.

Tsolidis, Georgina. 1990. Ethnic minority girls and self-esteem. In *Hearts and Minds: Self-Esteem and the Schooling of Girls*, ed. Jane Kenway and Sue Willis. London: Falmer Press.

Unwin, Cathy. 1984. Power relations and the emergence of language. In *Changing the Subject: Psychology, Social Regulation and Subjectivity*, ed. Julian Henriques, Wendy Hollway, Cathy Unwin, Couze Venn, and Valerie Walkerdine. London: Methuen.

Valli, Linda. 1986. *Becoming Clerical Workers*. Boston: Routledge and Kegan Paul.

Valverde, Mariana, ed. 1994. *Studies in Moral Regulation*. Toronto: Centre of Criminology, University of Toronto.

Vance, Carole. 1984a. Pleasure and danger: Toward a politics of sexuality. In *Pleasure and Danger: Exploring Female Sexuality*, ed. Carole Vance. Boston: Routledge and Kegan Paul.

——. 1984b. *Pleasure and Danger: Exploring Female Sexuality*. Boston: Routledge and Kegan Paul.

Van Maanen, John. 1988. *Tales From the Field: On Writing Ethnography*. Chicago: University of Chicago Press.

——. 1995a. An end to innocence: The ethnography of ethnography. In *Representation in Ethnography*, ed. John Van Maanen. Thousand Oaks, Calif.: Sage.

——, ed. 1995b. *Representation in Ethnography*. Thousand Oaks, Calif.: Sage.

Viswasnaran, Kamala. 1994. *Fictions of Feminist Ethnography*. Minneopolis: University of Minnesota Press.

Waits, Bernard. 1982. *Popular Culture: Past and Present*. London: Croom Helm/Open University Press.

Wald, Gayle. 1998. Just a girl? Rock music, feminism, and the cultural construction of female youth. *Signs: Journal of Women in Culture and Society* 23 (3):585–610.

Walker, Alice. 1983. *In Search of Our Mothers' Garden*. New York: Harcourt Brace Jovanovich.

Walkerdine, Valerie. 1990. *School Girl Fictions*. London: Verso.

———. 1993. Girlhood through the looking glass. In *Girls, Girlhood and Girls' Studies in Transition*, ed. Marion de Ras and Mieke Lunenberg. Amsterdam: Het Spinhuis.

———. 1997. *Daddy's Girl: Young Girls and Popular Culture*. Cambridge: Harvard University Press.

Walkerdine, Valerie, Helen Lucey, and June Melody. 2000. Class, attainment and sexuality in late twentieth-century Britain. In *Women and Social Class: International Feminist Perspectives*, ed. C. Zmroczck and P. Mohony. London: UCC Press.

———. 2001. *Growing Up Girl: Psychosocial Explorations of Gender and Class*. Houndmills Hampshire: Palgrave.

Warren, Catherine, and Sharon Frantz-Lutzer. 1994. Moving towards a new text: Research on a kids' computer camp. In *Feminism & Education: A Canadian Perspective*, ed. Paula Bourne, Philinda Masters, Nuzhat Amin, Marnina Gonick and Lisa Gribowski. Vol. 2. Toronto: Centre for Women's Studies in Education, OISE.

Wasserfall, Rahel. 1993. Reflexivity, feminism and difference. *Qualitative Sociology* 16 (1):23–41.

Waters, Mary C. 1996. The intersection of gender, race, and ethnicity in identity development of Caribbean American teens. In *Urban Girls: Resisting Stereotypes, Creating Identities*, ed. Bonnie J. Ross Leadbeater and Niobe Way. New York: New York University Press.

Weedon, Chris. 1987. *Feminist Practice and Poststructuralist Theory*. Oxford: Blackwell.

Weiner, Gaby, ed. 1985. *Just a Bunch of Girls*. London: Open University Press.

Weir, Allison. 1996. *Sacrificial Logics: Feminist Theory and the Critique of Identity*. London: Routledge.

Weis, Lois. 1990. *Working Class Without Work: High School Students in a De-Industrializing Economy*. New York: Routledge.

West, Cornel. 1995. A matter of life and death. In *The Identity in Question*, ed. John Rajchman. New York: Routledge.

Wexler, Philip. 1992. *Becoming Somebody: Toward a Social Psychology of School*. London: Falmer Press.

Williams, Patricia J. 1991. *The Alchemy of Race and Rights: Diary of a Law Professor*. Cambridge: Harvard University Press.

Willinsky, John, and R. Mark Hunniford. 1993. Reading the romance younger: The mirrors and fears of a preparatory literature. In *Texts of Desire: Essays on Fiction, Femininity and Schooling*, ed. Linda K. Christian-Smith. London: Falmer Press.

Willis, Paul. 1977. *Learning to Labour: How Working Class Kids Get Working Class Jobs*. London: Gower.

———. 1984. Youth unemployment: Thinking the unthinkable. *Youth and Policy* 2 (4):17–36.

Wolf, Margery. 1992. *A Thrice Told Tale: Feminism, Postmodernism and Ethnographic Responsibility*. Stanford: Stanford University Press.

Women's Studies Group, eds. 1978. *Women Take Issue: Aspects of Women's Subordination*. London: Hutchinson.

Wong, Sau-ling Cynthia. 1993. *Reading Asian American Literature: From Necessity to Extravagance*. Princeton, N.J.: Princeton University Press.

Woods, Peter, and Martyn Hammersley, eds. 1993. *Gender and Ethnicity in Schools: Ethnographic Accounts*. New York: Routledge.

Wrigley, Julia, ed. 1992. *Education and Gender Equality*. London: Falmer Press.

Wyatt, Jean. 1990. *Reconstructing Desire: The Role of the Unconscious in Women's Reading and Writing.* Chapel Hill: University of North Carolina Press.

Wyn, Johanna, and Rob White. 1997. *Rethinking Youth.* Sydney: Allen and Unwin.

Yezierska, Anzia. 1950. *Red Ribbon on a White Horse.* New York: Persee Books.

Young, Iris Marion. 1980. *Throwing Like a Girl and Other Essays in Feminist Philosophy and Theory.* Bloomington: Indiana University Press.

Zipes, Jack, ed. 1993. *The Trials and Tribulations of Little Red Riding Hood.* New York: Routledge.

Index

215